DATE DUE

THE PLAY
WITHIN
THE PLAY

THE PLAY
WITHIN
THE PLAY

-»»«-

The Inside Story of the UN

BY

HERNANE
TAVARES DE SÁ

NEW YORK: ALFRED · A · KNOPF

1966

Library of Congress Catalog Card Number: 66-12395

THIS IS A BORZOI BOOK
PUBLISHED BY ALFRED A. KNOPF, INC.

FIRST EDITION

This book is dedicated to

M. and I.

CONTENTS

		Page
INTRODUCTION		ix

PART I: The Plot

1	As the Assembly Meets	3
2	The Security Council at the Crossroads	9
3	Article 19 and the 19th	15
4	Finances, Albanian Style	22
5	A Collective Burial	39
6	Is There a Future in Peacekeeping?	45
7	Proliferation Chastens Superpowers	54
8	China Spoils a Mirror	62
9	The 20th Assembly: China and the Pope	70

PART II: The Angels

10	The Tragedy of the Missing "O"	79
11	Archangel Sam	85
12	How International Is an American?	92
13	Lesser Angels Speak German	99

PART III: The Players

| 14 | Togetherness among Diplomats | 105 |
| 15 | Seven Hundred Lovely Parties | 113 |

16 African Myth on First Avenue   121
17 How General a Secretary?   127
18 Hammarskjold and Thant: A Study in
        Contrasts   133
19 The Secretariat's Standards   147
20 The Memo Jungle   157
21 He Has a Problem for Every Solution   167
22 Those UN Russians   181

PART IV: The Stage

23 Sitting Room Only   193
24 The Other UN Capital   199

PART V: The Rehearsals

25 Why the Poor Become Poorer   213
26 When "United" Nations Makes Sense   218
27 Alphabet for Four   225
28 Cloak and Dagger Section   230

PART VI: The World Première

29 Hungary: What Might Have Been   241
30 Congo: The Costly Lesson   267
31 Our Men in Havana   273
32 Failure in Asia: Vietnam   285

PART VII: The Reviews

33 Publicity on the East River   291
34 Do the People Have a Right to Know?   296

EPILOGUE   302

INDEX   *follows page*   310

INTRODUCTION

*Courage? On the level where the only
thing that counts is a man's loyalty
to himself, the word has no meaning.
"Was he brave?"—"No, just logical."*
— DAG HAMMARSKJOLD, *Markings*

For me it was a logical act to write this book. Much of my
professional activities have been in the field of international
affairs. As a professor of journalism at the Catholic University
of Rio de Janeiro and then as editor-in-chief of a weekly news
magazine in my country, I became ever more convinced that to
grasp domestic events fully it was indispensable to follow developments abroad; by frequent trips to the United States and
to Europe I tried to perceive Brazilian affairs from their wider
international context. In 1960 when I accepted Secretary-General Dag Hammarskjold's invitation to head the UN information services, perhaps subconsciously I wanted to write a book
about the years I was to spend at the UN. When I left in 1965
I had consciously decided to write a book about the UN as I
had seen it—a UN that turned out to be, in many of its facets,
quite different from what I had expected. Different, but also
much more challenging, intriguing, and involved than I had
imagined. Therefore, it seemed logical to begin writing immediately after the expiration of my contract, while the impact
and the memories of those eventful years were still vivid.

But the decision, if logical, also required a measure of
courage. Not because what I had to say would conceivably dis-

turb sacred cows that had been contentedly squatting on their
haunches for years. That was unavoidable, but secondary; as
an author and journalist who believes in freedom of thought
and expression I am accustomed to being attacked for presenting facts and expressing views that may not prove popular
in all quarters. It was rather the pervading intricacy of the
subject matter that intimidated me. No contemporary political
institution is more hermetic in its actual functioning or more
elusive in its deeper reactions than the UN. Nor, I suspect, has
there ever existed one where appearances so belie realities. In
a farewell note to my staff I said: "Looking back on these years,
I find that I have attended what is perhaps the world's greatest
university—in that broadest sense of *universitas*. The United
Nations and its Agencies embrace practically the whole gamut
of human endeavor and I can think of no truer privilege than
to have been able to attend its courses for a few years. For this
there is no substitute; I am convinced that whatever one's field
of activity a period at the UN will enable him to better serve
his country and better serve the world community after he
leaves. I know that in my case I have learned a great deal and
I shall strive to put it to good use. For this I am grateful to
the UN. I am also deeply grateful to the UN for the friends I
have gained during these five years. In that the UN also resem-
bles a university; one feels transported back to one's student
days, meeting people who have converged here from every
corner of the world and from every background, and finding
among them some lasting human relationships."

    I dare say the key word in the passage is *student*; five
years would never be enough for absorbing all knowledge about
the UN, nor would fifty years. That is why courage is required
to tell the reader, here and now, that I have no pretension to
being the "owner of the truth," to use a Brazilian expression,
even though UNology is a field where truth-owners abound.
Much of what is written in this book runs counter to current
slogans and hallowed platitudes about the UN. That can't be
helped; at close range UN realities look somewhat different

from what they are purported to be. I have simply described events and issues, and tried to indicate trends that emerged from the forces at play. This book is therefore written in all modesty, and in a style that I hope the reader will agree is neither pontifical nor lyrical. I must also add that I found it very difficult and exacting to write about the UN, that complex and unpredictable institution, which is at one and the same time intimately immersed in world events and yet primly self-contained—truly a "play within the play." Pascal, if he had lived in our times, might well have written the definitive book about the United Nations—and perhaps would have concluded that *l'ONU a des raisons que la raison ne connaît pas*. In any case, let the reader rest assured that this is not a comprehensive book about the UN, much less a definitive one. It leaves many aspects unprobed and many questions unanswered (to probe and answer everything would have required scholarship and wisdom far beyond my own). But if it does prompt the reader to take a fresh and searching look at an institution that calls for understanding rather than for either adoration or abuse, and then to draw his own conclusions, it will have served a useful purpose. And I will feel that I have endeavored to live up to that equation of logic and courage which were described by Hammarskjold, a man I learned to admire.

PART I

THE PLOT

⟫ 1 ⟪

AS THE ASSEMBLY MEETS

As September comes around, the General Assembly normally convenes at United Nations Headquarters for its annual session. The season is about to begin in the world's greatest metropolis, the weather is glorious as Indian summer makes its debut, and what is indisputably the most colorful and lively political show to be held anywhere periodically gets off to a start in a glare of publicity. Several hundred special correspondents swell the ranks of the accredited press corps, and an atmosphere of expectation, mingled with suspense, envelops the East River compound.

Yet some of the more knowledgeable students of international affairs maintain that the General Assembly session is vastly overrated in terms of its political significance. This is quite true in terms of what the "town meeting of the world" pretends to be; but it should rather be judged for what it really is.

When the Assembly pretends to debate and solve the problems of the globe, no one is convinced or even impressed; the agenda, solemnly prepared every year and usually numbering about a hundred items, serves principally as a façade of respectability to justify the considerable expense and effort involved in gathering together at one time so many of those who actually handle the affairs of the world. Yet this annual

feat requires no justification; assembling and mingling the
special delegations to the Assembly from every member state
is in itself a considerable achievement in terms of the logistics
of politics, and one which is welcome to every foreign ministry
capable of functioning at a professional level.

Almost invariably delegations are headed by their foreign
ministers. Although they rarely remain for the duration of the
Assembly, they will be there during the opening phase, which
affords a unique opportunity for a foreign minister to compress
into a week or two in New York, if he so wishes, the equivalent
of months of traveling tens of thousands of air-miles. He can
achieve this by navigating between committee rooms, the floor
of the Assembly, the delegates' lounge—and last but not least
the galaxy of receptions and parties. The longest excursions
will take him no farther than one of Manhattan's better restaurants. At every turn he will be in personal contact with his
colleagues from almost every country around the globe.

Their wives come too, or a great many of them, but it
remains basically a man's show. Everything that is true about
the UN throughout the year acquires sharpness and added
significance when the General Assembly is in session. The
halls and corridors become a combination marketplace and
sidewalk cafe for the world, yet UN headquarters does not
lose altogether its year-round status as an exclusive men's
club.

Matters of moment are discussed and debated, but international trivia also commands attention. And sometimes the
momentous and the trivial get inextricably tangled—as at the
1960 General Assembly when the French language became
the center of a heated if hushed debate which stirred suscepti-
bilities and made delegates lose their tempers. But this happened outside the glare of publicity and very little reached the
world press. Some of this clash occurred not on the floor of
the assembly or in one of the committee rooms, but rather in
the normally sedate offices of the financial officers of the UN
treasury.

Seventeen new countries were admitted to the UN in 1960 and most of them were former French colonies in Africa. Their delegates, entitled like all others to the UN subsidy (the organization pays travel expenses for five delegates from each member state), on arrival went promptly to collect their checks but had innumerable difficulties, because no one in the treasury offices spoke a word of French. Clusters of French-speaking Africans protested volubly to UN officials, who showed annoyance and genuine amazement that any country would send delegates who did not speak English to New York. There are not many French-speaking officials in any UN department, except in the French translation and simultaneous interpretation services. Very few are in the Controller's Office, the treasury and budget department, which has remained as in the first years an Anglo-Saxon preserve. Americans, Britons, and Commonwealth personnel fill almost all the posts and expect everyone to conduct business in English.

The delegates from ex-Arique Equatoriale and Afrique Occidentale Française almost to a man, did not speak English. Many, however, spoke French well and proudly, having been educated at French universities. They were indignant to find how difficult it was to collect their money without speaking English. One day an exasperated French-speaking African let loose a torrent of French to a blandly uncomprehending UN official in the cashier's office, but finally turned to a colleague of his delegation, complaining bitterly: "C'est fantastique. Langue officielle, langue de travail, mais personne ne semble capable de parler français." Whereupon the official beamed, saying: "I understood you perfectly, in fact if you would only speak slowly our personnel would probably understand. In any case, I shall speak slowly to you in English."

This solution was not accepted then or later, and as protests mounted the UN treasury finally began to search for French-speaking personnel. It was one of the first successful skirmishes in the running battle that since 1960 has gained some ground for the French language in the UN.

Western countries assume that the Assembly has become highly emotional and consequently irresponsible since the massive entry of Afro-Asian members. What Westerners mean by this is that most of these countries in proclaiming themselves "nonaligned" are in effect—and sometimes deliberately—giving aid and comfort to the communists. The succession of military coups in Africa in 1965 and 1966 has, however, considerably attenuated this assumption. Even earlier, moreover, irresponsibility and anti-Western bias of the General Assembly was not always borne out by the record. During the stormy 1960 session, for instance, it was the Africans who in the last instance stood firmly behind Dag Hammarskjold and thus squelched Khrushchev's heavy-handed attempt to impose the "troika" formula on the office of the Secretary-General. The African delegates acted not only because they felt that Hammarskjold was on their side, but also because they were looking beyond the man to the office. Of course it was in their own interest as small and helpless countries to resist an impotent "troika" in the place of a dynamic and determined Secretary-General, but still a statesmanlike stand. On another occasion, during the 1961 General Assembly, the Afro-Asians banded together with the Latin Americans and the small European democracies to push through a resolution urgently calling on the big powers to stop nuclear tests. All four big powers voted against it: USA, USSR, Britain, and France. But only sixteen of their allies stood with them. The resolution was passed by seventy-one votes. At the time it looked like an empty gesture, yet, together with the eighteen-nation Disarmament Committee which the Assembly established on December 20, 1961, it had a limited but real bearing on the Russian and American change of heart that led to the signing of the Moscow treaty only two years later. It was a case where world public opinion had made itself felt, and big powers on both sides of the cold war eventually heeded it. And it made it somewhat easier for Presi-

dent Kennedy and Premier Khrushchev to reach an understanding in the aftermath of the Cuban missile crisis, which
led to the 1963 test-ban treaty.

Even with the pendulum of power swinging back to the
Security Council, as it is doing at present, the Assembly will
retain considerable political influence, provided its Afro-Asian
majority continues to show a sense of responsibility as it did
when defeating the "troika" proposal or when nudging the
superpowers into stopping their poisonous nuclear testing. The
"Uniting for Peace" resolution will not be written off the books
in the immediate future, and thus the "residual power" which
the United States claims for the General Assembly will continue to mean something, particularly since the Afro-Asians,
with their many votes, are all for it. A majority of member
states feel that although the Security Council is primarily
responsible for international peace and security, if the Council
fails to act in a crisis then the General Assembly should be
regarded as competent to decide on a peacekeeping operation.
The Soviet Union and France, among others, have never subscribed to this concept of the Assembly's "residual power," first
formally embodied in the "Uniting for Peace" resolution.
Trygve Lie called this resolution "a profoundly important shift
of emergency power from the veto-ridden Security Council to
the veto-less General Assembly—a shift the full potentialities
of which have still to be realized." The resolution allows for
an emergency session of the General Assembly to be called on
24-hour notice by a vote of seven members of the Security
Council, or by a majority of the entire membership, and for
the Assembly to assume responsibility for a peacekeeping
operation.

In the autumn of 1950, in the wake of the Korean War,
when "Uniting for Peace" was proposed and debated in the
Assembly, the Soviet Union was vitriolic in its protests, nor has
it ceased to denounce the resolution over the years as "totally
illegal." In point of fact, the Russians have a case of sorts, and
many independent legal experts nurture serious doubts about

the possibility of reconciling the resolution with the privileges
and the independence that the UN Charter confers upon the
Security Council. Furthermore, in recent years Washington
has come to regard with some misgivings the "Uniting for
Peace" resolution, since the assured majority which the US
enjoyed for so many years in the Assembly is no longer a
"mechanical majority," as the Russians insist on calling it.

≫ 2 ≪

THE SECURITY COUNCIL
AT THE CROSSROADS

The average citizen in the United States, and for that matter in most of the Western world, would define the Security Council of the United Nations, as the place where the Russians have used their veto more than one hundred times to prevent something useful being done to stop a war. He would not hesitate to add, if pressed, that he considers this wrong if not immoral on the part of a big power, and would point out that the United States has never used the veto. He would probably be unaware of the few instances in which Britain, France and China had recourse to it.

This current and popular appraisal of the Security Council is a triumph for the Western press that for twenty years has played up and dramatized every Soviet veto. It falls somewhat short, however, of a genuine understanding of what the Security Council is supposed to do and, above all, of what it is not supposed to do. Article 27, paragraph 3, which establishes the veto privilege for the five permanent members, had as its central political objective to prevent the Council from taking a decision whenever any of the five big powers states its opposition. This veto provision reflects the conviction of those who drafted the Charter that the United Nations would be unable to take an important initiative for the maintenance of peace and security unless there was unanimity among the big powers, and that to attempt to do so would be a futile gesture, endangering the organization.

It is true that the first Secretary-General, Trygve Lie, brought the UN into a major conflict, the Korean War, against the desires of the Soviet Union but in accordance with a Security Council resolution. The Soviet delegate, however, was at the time boycotting the Council, and the resolution was passed in his absence. Everyone has long since agreed that this was a freak episode which will never again recur.

Dag Hammarskjold, who succeeded Trygve Lie, felt that the utmost restraint should be the rule in regard to "problems which are clearly and definitely within the orbit of present day conflicts between power blocs." He felt that the Congo operation fell within his definition; in fact, he wrote that it was "rendered possible by the fact that both blocs have an interest in avoiding such an extension of the area of conflict because of the threatening consequences, were the localization of the conflict to fail." The Soviet Union seemed to agree with him at the beginning, by voting in favor of the first resolutions on the Congo. When the Soviets reversed themselves, it was too late. The Secretary-General was of course the great victim of this reversal, which was compounded by the attitudes of Britain, France, and Belgium. But in a cruelly ironical manner the Congo affair proved beyond dispute that a major political and military effort by the United Nations should never be undertaken against the determined opposition of a big power— let alone several. This was what those who drafted the Charter had in mind in the first place.

ᔒ   ᔒ   ᔒ

There is a famous story about a US senator who, as a member of his country's delegation to the 1948 General Assembly which met in Paris, was standing in the receiving line at a reception given by the American delegation. He had been shaking hands with what seemed to be an unending procession of

ambassadors from countries from all over the world and trying
to say a few appropriate words as he greeted them. The next
man in line looked unmistakably European, but was presented
to the senator as "the representative of UNESCO." The senator
pumped his hand warmly and said: "We all know in America
of your brave little country's fine record during the war."

The story has been recounted with glee over the years,
but nowadays a permanent delegate could be similarly confused. It has become difficult to keep track of who is a member
of the United Nations, who is about to become a member,
which member will become two members because the country
is breaking in two, and which member has declared it is no
longer a member although the Charter makes no provision for
anyone leaving the organization.

There are specific instances of each of these confusing
situations. At any given moment there are several Afro-Asian
lands about to become independent and claim UN membership.
Some join as one country and then break in two: Senegal and
Mali, Malaysia and Singapore. Some join as two countries,
merge into one state, then become two again; such was the
minuet played by Egypt (also known as the United Arab
Republic) and Syria. Indonesia quit the UN but will have no
problem in coming back since the Charter makes no provision
for a member leaving of its own free will (but does provide
for expulsion).

However, these are not real problems but merely comic-
opera episodes. What does represent a growing danger for the
effectiveness—and also the decorum—of the UN is the implac-
ably rising tide of "nations" that insist on joining but possess
few of the basic characteristics of a nation or even a state. In
raising the flags of two of the three new members at the outset
of the 20th General Assembly, U Thant observed with uncon-
scious humor that this had become a tradition. Incidentally, he
could raise only the flags of Singapore and The Gambia; the
third newcomer, the Maldive Islands, had not yet sent a delegation. That archipelago in the Indian Ocean has a population

of only some ninety thousand people, not enough to fill a
good-sized football stadium, and a national income so diminu-
tive that living expenses for its UN delegation represents a
major financial problem.

Nor were the other two new members in an appreciably
better position. Gambia is a sliver of territory inserted much
like a needle into Senegal, which is itself a less impressive
"State" than when it became independent as it was part of the
Mali-Senegalese Federation. Singapore, of course, is not a
country at all but merely a fairly large city surrounding a
busy harbor whose strategic reputation was given a sensational
if farcical twist when the new Prime Minister mentioned that
he would consider leasing the naval base to the Soviets.

United Nations membership has today almost attained
120, and shows every sign of going higher. A few years ago
when it was decided to expand accommodations in the General Assembly Hall, at considerable expense, enough seats
were allotted for delegates from 120 countries. The magic number was arrived at after consulting unologists within and without the organization, and it was in a way a pessimistic conclusion: at the time membership had not yet attained one hundred,
and nobody really believed that the Afro-Asian flood would
sweep in more than twenty new members. Now it is realized
that there will be considerably more; no one really knows how
many. It is not difficult to add up the remaining African territories that presumably will become independent sooner or later,
but there are dozens of archipelagoes dotting the oceans which
have as much claim to full-fledged membership in the United
Nations as the Maldive Islands.

Probably the real danger of an unwieldly UN membership
resides in the trend to balkanization in Africa and Asia. Countries like Sudan, Indonesia, and the Congo have come danger-
ously close to breaking up in recent years. However, the real
nightmare is the splitting up of India into its many component
units. Shortly after the death of Jawaharlal Nehru, a veteran South American delegate was saying in the delegates

lounge: "Even at the height of his power and prestige Bolivar was not capable of holding together the Spanish colonies after independence, and we became some twenty different countries. Now that Nehru is dead, will the same thing happen to India?"

Whether the danger be balkanization or recognition as an independent sovereign state of small clusters of islands, only the Security Council can prevent the United Nations from being swamped by a growing number of operetta member states, since the Council's recommendation for membership is automatically endorsed by the General Assembly. The danger was underlined by France during the embarrassing debate on the admission of the Maldive Islands. The French delegate pointed out that Article 4 of the Charter says UN membership is open to "all other peace-loving states which accept the obligations contained in the present Charter and, in the judgment of the Organization, are able and willing to carry out these obligations." And he discreetly inferred that the Maldive Islands were obviously unable, even if willing, to carry out these obligations. He was supported by the representative of the United States.

෴   ෴   ෴

This curious episode merits being inserted in a survey of the changing nature of the Security Council or, as some students of international affairs prefer to call it, the "return" of the Council to its original purposes and functions. The admission of new members is not one of the Council's central responsibilities, and until a very few years ago it would have been hard to imagine any two of the big powers agreeing on the need for disciplining future admissions, with the tacit acquiescence of the other two. That this could happen means that the Council is at last ready to reaffirm the authority with which the Charter endowed it. It is only a small sign but more significant ones have not been lacking.

The turning point, curiously enough, was the Cuban

missile crisis, the last time when the United States and the
Soviet Union confronted each other bitterly in the Security
Council chamber, reflecting their threatened confrontation on
the high seas. Ever since then the USSR has slowly but unmistakably drawn closer to the US in important Council debates
and decisions. Even the war in Vietnam has not seriously impaired the *rapprochement* between the two, and the decisions
of the Council during the India-Pakistan clash over Kashmir
would have been unthinkable had not the two superpowers
stood firmly side by side.

Of course this budding Soviet-American cooperation in
the Council chamber is not altogether within the spirit of the
Charter. One of the reasons why the Soviets are drawing close
to the Americans is that they are also resolved to keep Peking
out of the Security Council.

Consequently, the Council finds itself now at a curious
crossroads. Both superpowers are intent on restoring its prerogatives, due to their wariness of the General Assembly and
in order to implement the tacit but genuine "entente" they have
reached in the post-missile crisis years.

There will be a Security Council dominated by the great
powers, as the Charter intended, but one of the great powers,
China, will be kept out. If Washington and Moscow, in alliance, cannot prevent the seating of Peking in the near future,
then the Council will again pass into limbo, for an indefinite
period as far as its essential peacekeeping role is concerned.

ARTICLE 19 AND THE 19TH

One of the first suggestions Thant made to his assembled undersecretaries, shortly after he took office, was that a lottery be run to rescue UN finances. This was early in 1962, but the financial tangle that was to develop into the Article 19 crisis was already looming large in the preoccupations of the thirty-eighth floor. As there was no enthusiastic response from his top aides, the Burmese did not insist, although, like most Orientals, he had a much more uninhibited approach to gambling than the Anglo-Saxons and other Westerners who were in the majority among those present.

In May, 1965, the *New York Daily News* put the following question on its ballot at the News Public Opinion Poll, which Manhattan's biggest newspaper (circulation over two million) had organized at the World Fair: "Would you favor a UN lottery with a sales office on UN territory to help defray the costs of the UN to the United States, annually about 170 million dollars?" The answers were two to one in favor of a lottery.

The twin proposals, made three years apart at the thirty-eighth floor level and at the *Daily News* level, indicated how permanent and anguishing the financial crisis had become for the world organization. Yet the total sums discussed in the thousands of articles and hundreds of editorials dealing with the "bankruptcy" of the United Nations seem puny when pitted against the issue at stake, which during the year of 1965 was the very survival of "mankind's best hope," the organization dedicated to maintaining the peace of the world.

Already the year before, as the crisis was burgeoning and the debate began to rage inside the United Nations and in the world press, the phrase had been coined that "never in the course of human conflict have so many spoken so much about so little money." The total deficit of the United Nations was barely the equivalent of what is spent on any given day on armaments by the member states during a ten-hour period. Moreover, the amount involved (at the time approximately 150 million dollars) appeared even more irrelevant when considered in terms of the economic and financial resources of the USSR and France, the two great powers refusing to pay their assessments for peacekeeping operations.

∽   ∽   ∽

From its very beginnings the crisis was falsely labeled as financial: the Article 19 controversy was essentially political, centered on peace-keeping operations involving the commitment of an international army, obviously a subject on which the great powers—not to mention the medium and small ones— were bound to have strong views. And once two great powers like the Soviet Union and France had chosen to take a stand in open opposition to the United States and the majority of the UN membership, it was clear that a solution for the impasse could be found only through a political compromise. Having refused to recognize this in time, Washington was forced to retreat, under the pressure of rather embarrassing circumstances, from the juridically sound but politically unrealistic position it had enjoined on the United States delegation to the UN. A position somewhat reluctantly assumed, for that matter, as there were indications that Ambassador Adlai Stevenson was not particularly happy about the instructions he was re-

ceiving from the Department of State, where Secretary Rusk
was giving blanket approval to the "tough" approach ("those
Russians must pay their bills like everyone else") devised
by two very talented aides, Harlan Cleveland and Richard
Gardner, respectively Assistant and Deputy Assistant Secretary
of State for International Organizations Affairs.

Perhaps the most paradoxical aspect of the so-called financial crisis was that Washington and Moscow were never fundamentally in disagreement, and that, furthermore, as the crisis
worsened their points of view got closer. Both the United
States and the Soviet Union want to curtail the power of the
General Assembly and reinforce the Security Council's authority—a state of affairs that France has been proposing for several years. Gone are the times when the US would joyfully
repair to the General Assembly whenever it felt stymied by
Soviet vetoes in the Security Council.

Early in 1965 the Americans became intent on retreating
from their unwise backing of the Assembly against the Council,
without losing too much face in the process. Even a nation
as uninhibited in the conduct of its foreign policy as the US
has at times to worry about face. The new mood was aptly
described by a junior member of the US delegation, who said
the day following President de Gaulle's press conference on
February 4, 1965: "That is precisely the way everyone is
beginning to feel in Washington; but since it was not said by
one of the gang, but by our problem child at the Elysée, now
everyone in Washington will shake his head and deplore the
blunt language." He was referring to the passage in De
Gaulle's press conference which reads:

We know that, by virtue of that constitution, the
United Nations was composed firstly of a Council charged
with watching over international security and able to mobilize the means desired to make it respected, and secondly
of an Assembly whose debates would result in recommendations, with the right to take action belonging, nevertheless, to the Council alone. Among the eleven members of

the latter were five permanent members, that is, the five victorious powers, each one having the veto power. An Economic and Social Council and a Court of Justice were added to these two great bodies. A Secretary-General was to ensure the practical functioning of the Organization. In addition, the Charter provided that the United Nations should not intervene in the internal affairs of a State.

This Charter was reasonable. It resulted in the normal and continuous meeting and confrontation within the Assembly of almost all the world's nations in a kind of forum from which international public opinion could emerge and which, by virtue of the equality of all its members, conferred upon each of them, especially those which had just acquired sovereignty and independence, a highly esteemed dignity. Within the Council, moreover, five powers whose policies, economy, armed forces and influence gave them worldwide responsibilities, were brought to meet, and if possible to collaborate, in maintaining the peace. These arrangements thus corresponded to what was both possible and prudent; they undoubtedly did not establish a world government and a world parliament, which in this century could exist only in dreams. But, given the realities, and especially the rivalry between Soviet Russia and the United States which was spreading over the whole world among an increasing number of nations, it was a wise idea that the Organization gave itself the conditions for balance and impartiality, rather than aspiring to impose the impossible.

_ᵔ   _ᵔ   _ᵔ

It is now abundantly clear that neither the United States nor the Soviet Union wants to go again through the unnerving experience of that 19th session of the General Assembly which culminated in a cunning parliamentary blocking play planned by a country that is not even a member of the United Nations: the People's Republic of China.

After two postponements, the 1964 session opened in gloom and suspense, with the Article 19 conflict hanging like a sword of Damocles over every delegation's head. The United

States, the USSR, and France were deadlocked in controversy, and Washington had threatened time and again to bring about a showdown to prevent the Soviet delegation from casting a vote. Presumably the US would interrupt the Assembly proceedings on a point of order just as the first roll call was announced for balloting, and invoke Article 19 of the Charter, which says:

> A Member of the United Nations which is in arrears in the payment of its financial contributions to the Organization shall have no vote in the General Assembly if the amount of its arrears equals or exceeds the amount of the contributions due from it for the preceding two full years. The General Assembly may, nevertheless, permit such a Member to vote if it is satisfied that the failure to pay is due to conditions beyond the control of the Member.

Luckily for the United States, France would not officially become the ally of the USSR under the provisions of Article 19 until a few weeks later, on the first of January, 1965, when it completed the equivalent of two full years of arrears because of its refusal to pay for the Congo operation. But the prospect of a showdown between the two superpowers, the United States and the Soviet Union, was more than sufficient to throw the entire UN membership into panic. The Soviets had darkly hinted that they would leave the United Nations if Article 19 were applied against them. They of course never officially said so, but Soviet delegates had been going around for months telling Africans, Asians, and Latin Americans that they would walk out of the General Assembly and not come back if they were beaten in a showdown with the United States. They failed to add that they would be most careful about not leaving the Security Council, which is independent of the General Assembly and where they have the veto power; but it was clear to all informed observers that never again would Moscow walk out of the Council in a huff as it did in early 1950, allowing by default for the Korean War to be fought by the Americans and their allies under the United Nations umbrella.

Under the imminent threat of what came to be known, according to the jargon of the day, as a "confrontation" between the two superpowers, the other delegations thrashed about frantically searching for a compromise formula. Twice the opening of the 19th session was postponed in order to gain time for the emergence of a face-saving formula. When the session finally started on November 10, 1964, an ingenious but fragile stratagem had been concocted. The Assembly would never take a formal vote, but instead would reach decisions solely on a "no objection" basis.

On the opening day a new president was elected, Ambassador Quaison-Sackey of Ghana, without anyone "objecting." In fact, many Latin Americans decided he had been elected "by acclamation." (Latin Americans are not privy to the intricacies of British parliamentary procedure, which are subconsciously embodied in the political education of a Ghanaian President and a Burmese Secretary-General.)

Election of the vice-presidents and the chairmen of the several committees, however, was not risked, since there was some doubt that there would be "no objection" to some of the eager candidates. For the key First political committee, the Latin Americans and the West in general were backing the Colombian ambassador, while the Afro-Asians, including supposedly impartial Assembly President Quaison-Sackey of Ghana, were behind the scenes bolstering the candidate proposed by the communist countries, the permanent representative of Hungary. The bloody streets of Budapest in 1956 seemed to have receded into some sort of pleasant limbo, in the view of most of the *tiers monde*, whose delegates could not understand why many Westerners still regarded communist Hungary with revulsion.

Electing only a president meant, among other things, that the Assembly could be in session only with Quaison-Sackey in the chair, since there were no vice-presidents to fill in for him during any temporary absence.

There were three weeks of grace during the "general

debate," an opening phase of the General Assembly which is really not a debate at all, but consists rather of policy statements by the head of each delegation, usually the foreign minister. Everyone felt that these few weeks could be put to good use to press the negotiations for a solution, since the Kafkaesque situation of a General Assembly that could not follow up its discussions to a logical conclusion by voting a resolution could not long endure.

Negotiations conducted by the Secretary-General and the President of the General Assembly achieved nothing, except to send Thant to the hospital with an ulcer. It was at this point that a veteran European correspondent composed the irreverent little jingle:

> Le Président ne peut pisser
> Le Secretaire est alité
> Personne ne veut payer
> Et tout le monde est emmerdé.

»»» 4 «««

FINANCES, ALBANIAN STYLE

Nothing seemed left but to carry on till adjournment day the thin pretense that the 19th Assembly was functioning by unanimous consent. At least there appeared to be ample consent for adjourning the Assembly until the next autumn, for during the winter months it had become clear to everyone that a big-power compromise was as far away as ever. So it became tacitly understood that on Tuesday, February 16, the Assembly would adjourn until the following September, after agreeing by unanimous consent on a few matters that could no longer be postponed. A budget of sorts was to be approved, so that UN officials would continue to be paid their salaries and thus the machinery of the world organization would not grind to a complete standstill. Several other items were included with the budget in this "package deal" of decisions that just could not be postponed, such as expanding the Pension Fund. It was not clear why the employees of the UN and its agencies could not wait a little, given the circumstances then prevailing. But UN bureaucrats were not to be deviated from the pursuit of their common welfare by such a little thing as a conflict between the big powers leading to a major crisis for their organization. And so a closing session on the "package deal" was mapped out.

But no one had foreseen that the Peking government, which was not even represented at the UN, would be able to dramatically upset the carefully planned adjournment. That nonetheless happened during the February 16 and the February 18 sessions. Time and again the spokesman for Peking, Ambassador Halim Budo of Albania, ambled to the green marble podium to make the apparently reasonable request that the General Assembly reach decisions through voting. By the time he had concluded his performance, the French-speaking Albanian had thoroughly confused Assembly President Quaison-Sackey of Ghana, and thrown the meeting into turmoil and frustration.

No more unlikely conscience for the world body could have been devised than the representative of that obscure Balkan backwater, known mostly because of the anachronism of its Stalinist regime until it gained a minor stature in world events by becoming Peking's European agent. Inside the UN no other member had ever quite achieved Albania's low status; for it probably had fewer friends than even South Africa, being held in contempt by the communist as well as the Western delegations. In a way, of course, there was some ironical logic in an inconsequential member state such as Albania casting itself in the role of the child who remarked that the emperor had no clothes.

The press release issued by the UN information services on the Thursday session renders more effectively than any of the dramatic accounts appearing in the world press what occurred during that extraordinary afternoon in the life of the United Nations. For all its succintness in summing up each statement or speech, this press release ran to 31 pages. Those pages leading up to the Kafkaesque "voting on not voting" are worth transcribing:

> The General Assembly met this afternoon to take up items on the election of one member of the Economic and Social Council, interim financial arrangements and authorizations for 1965, a proposal for United Nations supervision

of elections in the Cook Islands in April, a comprehensive review of the question of United Nations peace-keeping operations, and the status of the agenda of the current session of the Assembly.

At the last meeting of the Assembly, on 16 February, Albania asked that the Assembly resume its normal procedures and that a vote be taken on this proposal. After appeals made by several representatives, the Assembly President adjourned the meeting until today.

This afternoon's meeting was called to order by the President of the Assembly, Alex Quaison-Sackey (Ghana), at 3:33 P.M.

The President said that delegates were all aware of what had happened at the last meeting.

Halim Budo (Albania) asked for the floor on a point of order.

The President said that the representative of Albania could not interrupt him at this stage.

Mr. Budo came up to the rostrum and began to speak. (There was no interpretation.)

The President asked him to accord courtesy to the Presidency. He had not given the representative of Albania the floor, he declared.

Mr. Budo continued to speak.

The President said that he would give the floor to the representative of Albania at the proper time. Now, as President, he had a statement to make. He was following the rules of procedure, he said.

Jamil Baroody (Saudi Arabia) came to the rostrum and spoke to the representative of Albania, who then returned to his seat in the Assembly Hall.

The President said that there was no intention of denying any delegation the right to speak. "After all, we are a democratic body," he stated.

He then went on with his statement.

The President said that the representative of Albania had made certain proposals at the last meeting. Although these proposals were not submitted in writing, they were available in the verbatim records, he added.

The President then stated that he wanted to recapitulate the various decisions taken at previous meetings.

On 27 January, he recalled, he had announced that the general debate had been concluded.

On 8 February, he had made a statement, the President went on, in which he had proposed that the General Assembly recess once it had, on a non-voting basis, agreed upon the machinery for a review of peace-keeping operations and disposed of the items on which a decision was necessary before a recess.

The President recalled that at the same meeting he had stated that his own consultations had borne out the Secretary-General's conclusions, and he had declared that if the General Assembly agreed, decisions on the four questions proposed by the Secretary-General might be taken on 10 February at 3 P.M.

When he had asked whether there was any objection to this procedure, the President said, there had been no objection and he had declared that it was so decided.

Continuing, the President noted that, at the meeting on 10 February, decisions were taken on filling seats in the Economic and Social Council, on filling vacancies on subsidiary bodies, on the report of the Staff Pension Fund, on the continuation of UNRWA, on the United Nations International School, and on the United Nations Conference on Trade and Development.

The only items remaining on the agenda were the ones listed in the *Journal* for 16 February and they were repeated for today's meeting, the President declared.

Regarding the first item, he said, a procedure of consultations had been followed and Albania had participated in it. He was grateful to Albania for this co-operation, he added.

Thus, it was clear, the President went on to say, that the General Assembly had, "by its decisions, by its consent and by the procedure it had consistently followed since," agreed to proceed without a vote, and to recess when it had completed action on the items on which action was needed. He could not help expressing the view, the President declared, that if the representative of Albania had desired a different procedure, the occasion for doing so had been the meeting on 8 February, since, at the previous meeting, the general debate had been declared concluded.

The proposal by Albania must, however, be disposed of now, the President continued. The effect of this proposal would be to reverse the decision to which he had just referred.

The purpose of this decision was to avoid a confrontation, the President added, and to set up machinery for negotiations during the recess which, hopefully, would lead to a solution of all the financial, peace-keeping and voting problems.

Thus, the General Assembly would first have to decide whether it wanted to reconsider its own decision before it could take up the motion of Albania.

Since he was still bound by the non-vote decision, the President declared, he had to follow the procedure heretofore followed. Under these circumstances, the President stated, he would declare that there was a consensus against reconsidering that decision.

It was so decided, the President declared.

"Mr. Budo (Albania) said he first wished to protest for having been interrupted by the President while making a point of order.

Mr. Budo then expressed "deep regret" at the way the President had adjourned the previous meeting when the Assembly was seized of the Albanian motion. The President, he said, should have, in accordance with Rule 35 of the Rules of Procedure, submitted this motion to the vote of the Assembly. The President had also ignored his last point of order at the previous meeting, he added.

Mr. Budo declared that he was coming back to his motion and formally requesting that the General Assembly start immediately on its normal work, in accordance with the Charter, and proceed to the election of its officers and the approval of its agenda, as laid down by Rules 21, 31, 38, 40, 67, 85 and 105 of the Rules of Procedure.

The Albanian motion, he said, should be given absolute priority and submitted to a roll-call vote.

Mr. Budo said that the sense of his proposal was very simple.

Mr. Budo said that the consensus procedure had come to an end with the completion of the general debate in the

Assembly, and he could not agree with the view of the President that a new consensus procedure had since been approved.

In support of his argument, Mr. Budo quoted from a statement by the President on 18 January that the General Assembly should start work as soon as possible with the normal procedure. He also quoted from a statement by the President on 27 January to the effect that before reconvening on 1 February delegations should consult on the candidatures for offices. He went on to quote from a statement by the President on 1 February that the General Assembly should now decide on its procedure and prepare proposals for future work.

Mr. Budo went on to say that at last Tuesday's meeting the representatives who took the floor had not alluded to the consensus procedure. They had confirmed, he said, that Albania had the right to present its motion. If the President disagreed, he added, his ruling could be challenged under rule 73 of the rules of procedure.

In conclusion, the representative of Albania declared that his concern was the safeguarding of the Charter, the United Nations and the principle of the equality of all Member States.

The President stated that, with regard to the complaint of the representative of Albania concerning the adjournment of the meeting of 16 February, he must apologize to that representative as he did not see the representative of Albania raise his hand.

The President went on to say that he had declared that there was a consensus against reconsidering the decision already taken. Might he take it, he asked, that the representative of Albania was appealing against his ruling?

On a point of order, Mr. Baroody (Saudi Arabia) said he had asked to speak not in order to support one side or the other.

The President had been perfectly right in enumerating what had happened, he said. The small countries sometimes considered that peace demanded conformity from them. However, there was no longer any fear of confrontation, as the session had ended, to all intents and purposes.

There was no confrontation. There was, he said, "full agreement among the contestants."

He had come to the Assembly Hall last night, he went on to say, "because I missed the constructive work of the Assembly."

At this point, Tesfaye Gebre-Egzy (Ethiopia) asked for the floor on a point of order.

Mr. Baroody asked if there could be a point of order on a point of order.

The President asked if delegations would observe decorum. He said there had been a challenge to his ruling, but he would allow the representative of Saudi Arabia to continue if he kept it short.

Mr. Baroody said that delegations had been "muzzled long enough." They did not want to be "a rubber stamp."

For all intents and purposes, this session was over. For the sake of peace, many delegations had agreed to conform to the procedure followed. But last night, in this Hall, they had heard from the Vice President of the United States that this Organization would not founder, that it would go on. He regarded that speech as the best he had heard since 1 December. It was "an encouraging sign." Nobody wanted to see the United Nations destroyed. There should be harmony and concord here. Delegations should not doubt each other's motives. They should not doubt the motives of the representative of Albania, he said.

The representative of Saudi Arabia said that he was going to make a proposal, and no one should think he had been talking to the representative of Albania. He did not have a plan, but he had certain suggestions to make. After the mechanics of challenging the President's ruling, he believed there would be "pandemonium" here. He could not divulge what was going to happen, but something was going to happen, he said.

The small Powers had no assurance, Mr. Baroody went on, that in September the problems would have been solved. They were afraid that in the meantime "a deal" might be made at their expense, he said.

The representative of Saudi Arabia criticized what the Press was saying about the representative of Albania. Too many papers, he said, were calling Albania "the stooge of

another country." Tomorrow they would be making the
same charge against other small nations.

Mr. Gebre-Egzy (Ethiopia) again asked for the floor
on a point of order.

Mr. Baroody asked the representative of Ethiopia "not
to bother me any more." He asked him not to "make a
scene unnecessarily."

The representative of Saudi Arabia then said that, if
the two contestant Powers would agree today to make an
exception only to dispose of the remainder of the business
in the normal way—"by vote, not consultation"—he would
seek to prevail on the representative of Albania not to challenge the President's ruling. Thus, he said, "we will avoid
pandemonium." Both Powers would have made a concession and shown, he said, that they were not "stubborn."

The President said that he was sure that the representative of Albania would heed the appeal of the representative of Saudi Arabia.

Mr. Budo (Albania) thanked the representative of
Saudi Arabia for the kind words he had addressed to
Albania. The people of the world, he said, knew well how
Albania had struggled against all imperialist attacks. Those
who spread rumours knew well how the plots contrived
against Albania had ended.

Albania, he went on, was led today by the same
leaders who had made it a sovereign State and turned it
from a backward agricultural State to a modern State.

Mr. Budo stated that he disagreed with the President's
summation of what had happened on 8 February and that
was why he was challenging the President's ruling. He
asked for a roll-call vote.

The President declared that the representative of
Albania had appealed against his ruling and a procedural
vote could not be avoided.

"Since it was solely on the question of whether the
General Assembly should continue its work without voting,
the vote could proceed on the basis of full reservation as to
all legal issues and without prejudice to the respective
positions of Members, the President said.

Rule 73 would therefore apply, the President said.

Rule 73 reads as follows:

"During the discussion of any matter, a representative may rise to a point of order, and the point of order shall be immediately decided by the President in accordance with the rules of procedure. A representative may appeal against the ruling of the President. The appeal shall be immediately put to the vote and the President's ruling shall stand unless overruled by a majority of the Members present and voting. A representative rising to a point of order may not speak on the substance of the matter under discussion."

Those supporting the appeal against the ruling would vote "yes", and those opposing it would say "no", the President stated.

Adlai E. Stevenson (United States) asked for the floor on a point of order. He came to the rostrum.

Mr. Budo (Albania), from his seat in the Assembly Hall, also raised a point of order and said that, under the rules, there should be an immediate vote.

The President said he believed the representative of Albania was right. The Assembly would now proceed to the vote.

Mr. Stevenson (United States) said that, in accordance with rule 90, he was making a point of order in connection with the voting, "and I should like to be heard."

He said that since 1 December the General Assembly had agreed without objection to act according to a procedure, the purpose of which was to avoid a confrontation on a basic principle, and thus allow time for an agreement to be eventually reached.

Mr. Budo (Albania) continued to ask for the floor on a point of order.

Mr. Stevenson (United States) asked that order be maintained in the Hall. He then went on with his statement.

Mr. Stevenson went on to say that one Member had challenged the procedure agreed upon by all Members in the best interests of the Organization.

The General Assembly, therefore, was faced with a situation where a procedural vote was regarded by many Members as necessary to confirm the clear desire of the overwhelming majority of the General Assembly, said the representative of the United States.

Inasmuch as the procedural vote dealt only with the issue of whether the General Assembly should or should not continue to proceed on a non-voting basis and would not prejudice the question of the applicability of Article 19, the United States would raise no objection to the procedural vote on the challenge of the President's ruling, Mr. Stevenson declared.

The President said that the challenge to his ruling would now be put to the vote.

Those voting "yes" would be supporting the challenge to his ruling.

Those voting "no" would be supporting the ruling, he stated.

The roll was then called.

The challenge to the President's ruling was defeated by a vote of 2 in favour to 97 against, with 13 abstentions.

The roll call was as follows:

In favour: Albania, Mauritania.

Against: Afghanistan, Argentina, Australia, Austria, Belgium, Bolivia, Brazil, Bulgaria, Burma, Byelorussia, Cameroon, Canada, Central African Republic, Ceylon, Chad, Chile, China, Colombia, Congo (Democratic Republic of), Costa Rica, Cyprus, Czechoslovakia, Dahomey, Denmark, Dominican Republic, Ecuador, El Salvador, Ethiopia, Finland, Gabon, Ghana, Greece, Guatemala, Haiti, Honduras, Hungary, Iceland, India, Iran, Iraq, Ireland, Israel, Italy, Ivory Coast, Jamaica, Japan, Jordan, Kenya, Kuwait, Laos, Lebanon, Liberia, Libya, Luxembourg, Madagascar, Malawi, Malaysia, Malta, Mexico, Mongolia, Morocco, Nepal, Netherlands, New Zealand, Nicaragua, Niger, Nigeria, Norway, Pakistan, Panama, Paraguay, Peru, Phillipines, Poland, Rwanda, Sierra Leone, Somalia, South Africa, Spain, Sudan, Sweden, Syria, Thailand, Togo, Trinidad and Tobago, Tunisia, Turkey, Uganda, Ukraine, USSR, United Kingdom, United States, Upper Volta, Uruguay, Venezuela, Yugoslavia, Zambia.

Abstaining: Algeria, Burundi, Congo (Brazzaville),

Cuba, France, Guinea, Mali, Portugal, Romania, Senegal, United Arab Republic, United Republic of Tanzania, Yemen.

Absent: Indonesia.

The representatives of Cambodia and Saudi Arabia stated that they would not participate in the vote.

Mr. Budo (Albania) said he wanted to express his regrets at, and protest against, the way an effort had been made to violate the rights of a sovereign State. It was not only the rights of his country which had been trampled on, he declared.

The attack on the rights of Member States and their dignity would seriously damage the United Nations, he stated. These were dangerous steps taken by those who wanted to use the United Nations for their hegemony, Mr. Budo declared.

What had happened today would disillusion the peoples of the world, he said.

Mr. Budo went on to say that the General Assembly today had brought the rules of procedure again into play, since all Members had voted, even those who had been denied the vote by others.

This, he observed, had shown that this procedure had been a subterfuge to make the United Nations unable to function.

The "bluff" of the United States had been called today, he declared. There was no threat of confrontation; there had been only a pretext, he added.

His country was motivated only by the desire to see the United Nations function properly and to save the Organization before it was too late.

Numerous delegates had congratulated him, he said, and his delegation had done its duty. It would continue to attempt to save the United Nations, he declared, but the situation was grave and efforts would have to be redoubled.

The peoples of the world would condemn those who were responsible for the present situation, he declared.

He represented only a small Power, he continued, but he did not fear to face "the giants" since his country was not alone. His advantage was that right was on his side, he added.

He was proud of the cause he had defended, since it was the cause of all peoples who were struggling against imperialism, Mr. Budo said in conclusion.

Mr. Gebre-Egzy (Ethiopia), in explanation of his vote, stated that his vote should be understood to mean that he agreed with the procedure. His vote, he added, should be looked at in the light of what was said at the previous meeting.

He also explained that when he sought to raise a point of order during the statement by the representative of Saudi Arabia, it was because rule 73 stated that an appeal against the ruling of the President shall be immediately put to the vote.

Ahmed Baba Miske (Mauritania) expressed his regret that the President had not made it possible for more representatives to put their views before the Assembly prior to the vote.

He also expressed astonishment at the fact that the United States and the USSR had yet to reach agreement on the question of voting rights. Was it, he asked, because these two great Powers were eager to prevent China from joining the United Nations, or to stress the fact that the two were the only "masters of the world"? Mr. Miske declared that he rejected such a "colonialist" attitude, whether it implied a two-super-Power rule or a five-big-Power rule as advocated by President de Gaulle.

Mr. Miske also expressed his disagreement with the Soviet thesis that contributions assessed by the General Assembly should actually have been approved by the Security Council. He also disagreed with the United States attitude on the applicability of Article 19. Large voluntary contributions on the part of the United States, he said, should not provide the United States with a means of pressure on the Organization. He further expressed disagreement with the "paternalistic" stand of France towards the United Nations membership.

Concluding, Mr. Miske formally proposed that the General Assembly by a roll-call vote: reaffirm its attachment to the principle of the equality of Member States;

condemn all attempts at "blackmail" on the part of the great
Powers; and adopt the African-Asian plan for the settlement of the problem facing the present session of the General Assembly.

Sori Coulibaly (Mali) said he had abstained because
his delegation considered that the General Assembly had
been indirectly requested to express itself on the motion of
Albania.

His delegation had expressed its regret over the para-
lysation of the General Assembly and its readiness to support the President to normalize it.

But the way in which the vote had been held had not
been in line with the rules of procedure.

His delegation believed, he stated, that the General
Assembly should have pronounced itself on the Albanian
motion. The linking of the motion with the consensus did
not seem correct, he said.

He would have voted in favor of the Albanian motion,
had it been put to the vote, Mr. Coulibaly declared.

The presidential conclusion had been accepted in an
abnormal situation, he observed.

The rules of procedure had been "manipulated," and
this was a dangerous precedent, Mr. Coulibaly declared.

His delegation was convinced that the General Assembly should be able to work normally at the time when an
imperialist war was going on in Viet-Nam, Mr. Coulibaly
declared.

José Sette Camara (Brazil) expressed the regret of
his delegation regarding the procedure followed, and regis-
tered his formal reservations thereto.

The procedure followed, he said, conformed neither
with the spirit nor the letter of the Charter.

The vote of his delegation, he said, should be interpreted exclusively in the light of those considerations.

Achkar Marof (Guinea) said he had had the impression, in the course of the earlier discussion, that there was
an attempt to place the blame for the present difficulties of
the General Asselbly on Albania. The two alternatives
created by the Albanian motion would have been to apply
either rules 81 or 83 of the rules of procedure.

Mr. Achkar declared that if the Albanian motion had

been put to the vote, he would have voted for it. His delegation had abstained in the earlier procedural vote in order
to facilitate the task of the President and to allow for time
to reach an agreement on the problem before the General
Assembly.

Lord Caradon (United Kingdom) said that the circumstances of the vote just taken were exceptional. More
than that, they were unique. His delegation had no doubt
that the action taken this afternoon was "right and proper
and necessary."

It was necessary, he said, to support the President in
the discharge of his responsibilities. Moreover, the action
taken reflected the overwhelming wish of the Members, he
stated.

The representative of Mauritania, Lord Caradon continued, had spoken disparagingly of his country and had
talked as if he spoke for the majority. But, in fact, the
representative of Mauritania had been shown to be in "a
minority of two," he said.

Lord Caradon went on to say that his delegation had
also taken its stand today because there was an opportunity
now, after weeks and months of patient negotiation, to go
forward. Everybody was interested in solving the problems
of peace keeping and finance, and if that could be done,
this session would prove to be a success and not a failure.

His delegation had been against a confrontation and
also against a postponement unless there were to be negotiations on peace keeping, he said. Now there was an opportunity for those negotiations.

"We do not want a cold war victory but a United
Nations success," he said, and expressed the hope that the
Assembly would have that today.

John W. S. Malecela (United Republic of Tanzania)
said he wanted to protest against certain procedures. This
did not mean that he did not support the President, he
added, but a number of things had "gone wrong." Members
had been subjected to indignity, he said.

Regarding the question of consensus, he said that this
did not mean an agreement but a matter of convenience,
so that the General Assembly could work.

Albania, he observed, had sought the resumption of

normal work. Today's vote, he went on, had been a very
dangerous procedure, and it would go down in history as a
"shocking warning."

He expressed the hope that "such things" would not
be repeated, and that, in future, small countries would not
be subjected to such indignity.

This was why his delegation had abstained, he concluded.

The President said he would be entitled to answer to
the attack made on him. But this, he said, was an extraordinary session, and he would behave in an extraordinary
way, namely, not to reply to the attack.

ے   ے   ے

The entire text of the UN press release reveals that the
February 18 session of the General Assembly, which lasted
five hours and eighteen minutes and was of crucial importance
for the United Nations, was virtually monopolized by a handful
of countries, mostly African, who represent very little on the
world scene.

The rest of the globe hardly got a word in edgewise.
Statements from the Western Hemisphere took up twenty lines:
seven by Brazil, seven by Canada, and six by Colombia. All
from Western Europe took up only 10 lines, those in the press
release given to Lord Caradon of the United Kingdom. Even
the Communist countries, except for Albania, were laconic:
four lines for Poland and three lines for Hungary. There was
a short, acrimonious exchange between Ambassador Stevenson
and Ambassador Fedorenko, but after all it was reasonable
that the two superpowers would have something to say in a
culminating debate on the issue by which they had paralyzed
the United Nations.

Seven full pages of the press release summarized pro-
nouncements by the representatives of Saudi Arabia, Ethiopia,
Mauritania, Mali, Guinea, Tanzania, Senegal, Sierra Leone,
Cyprus, Kenya, Morocco, Burundi, Congo—a group of coun-

tries representing rather low stages of civilization, and most of them organized as feudal or tribal societies. (Some of these member states still engage such practices as slave trade and cannibalism.)

What the proverbial visitor from Mars would have concluded, had he been sitting in the press gallery during that crucial debate, was that to carry weight in the United Nations and be heard in this world forum it is preferable to have a black skin and indispensable to be a thoroughly underdeveloped nation. Well versed in mathematics, the Martian would have been further puzzled that a debate on the finances of the world organization had been dominated by a group of countries that in their aggregate pay 0.74 percent of the United Nations budget, as per the official scale of assessments:

Albania	0.04%
Burundi	0.04%
Congo	0.07%
Cyprus	0.04%
Ethiopia	0.05%
Guinea	0.04%
Kenya	0.04%
Mali	0.04%
Mauritania	0.04%
Morocco	0.14%
Saudi Arabia	0.07%
Senegal	0.05%
Sierra Leone	0.04%
Tanzania	0.04%

Of course it was not the first time an important debate in the UN had been dominated by countries without political maturity, economic significance, or civilized background. The trend began at the 1960 session of the General Assembly and gathered momentum at every subsequent session. But this time it made many people wonder not only about the futility of this kind of debate, but about the wisdom of holding any kind of debate in a world forum dominated by scores of unimportant and irresponsible countries.

One who seemed well satisfied with the debate was Ambassador Budo. Already the next day, a Friday, and through most of the following week he haunted the UN television services, asking to be shown the entire footage that had been taken on the Tuesday and Thursday sessions. He was particularly interested in the close-ups of delegates, noting carefully individual reactions and gestures, which a television camera often shows with pitiless candor. He became quite friendly with French-speaking staff members and delighted in pointing out to them that there were many more delegates reacting in his favor, and even applauding him, than the press reports indicated.

Other delegates did not feel quite so jaunty and smug about the proceedings. On that Thursday in February, after the General Assembly had been adjourned until the following September, at well past eight in the evening a small group of delegates still lingered by the top of the escalator leading down to the main entrance (the session had ended at 7:51 P.M.), talking in subdued tones. As they finally dispersed, one of them, the ambassador of a Western European country, said sadly: "What is disturbing about this 19th session is that it has been showing to the world at large that the General Assembly of the United Nations may be quite unnecessary."

A correspondent hovering nearby overheard the remark and passed it on as "the epitaph of the year."

>>> 5 <<<

A COLLECTIVE BURIAL

The word epitaph carried with it a disquieting logic; as the
events described fell into their proper perspective with the
passing of time, it became increasingly evident that the very
existence of a General Assembly of the United Nations was
bound to be challenged. For the agenda of this 19th session,
laboriously drawn up and consisting of some hundred items
covering practically every topical (and quite a few non-topical)
areas of international tension or dispute, had never come under
debate. The world was not demonstrably the worse for it.
(In another field, the 19th assembly did formalize the UN
Conference on Trade and Development as a continuing organization, potentially helpful to underdeveloped countries.)

Later on the pointlessness of having a General Assembly
would begin to be seriously examined. But for the time being
professional diplomats had their attention riveted on Washington. It seemed to most of them that the Thursday session
marked the beginning of a retreat by the Americans that
would eventually lead to surrendering the legal and political
position meticulously erected over so many months, accompanied by lavish publicity and much pressure on all their friends
and allies to stand with them and to prevent voting by countries guilty of refusing to pay for peace-keeping operations.

And yet the Albanian threat had been considered serious

enough for the US delegate, Ambassador Adlai Stevenson, to
join Ambassador Fedorenko of the USSR and the overwhelming
majority of fellow delegates in voting it down. But in so doing
he had not merely joined in the Alice-in-Wonderland vote on
an earlier decision that nobody would vote until the controversy
was settled; he had also weakened irremediably the position
of the US delegation on the entire issue. Of course Stevenson
did not take such a grave decision on his own; although it
seemed to be his personal conviction that this course of action
represented the lesser evil under the circumstances, he obtained
the consent of the White House and the State Department
before casting the vote of the US delegation. It was not easy
to obtain this consent, as was candidly admitted by the spokesman of the US delegation at a press briefing on the following
day, Friday, February 19. Asked by a correspondent when the
US delegation had made the decision, he replied that it had
been at about one P.M. on the previous day—only a couple of
hours before the session began.

Nor was this surprising. There had been a number of
official pronouncements indicating that the US was prepared
to carry the Article 19 issue to a showdown. On October 5,
1964, Under Secretary of State George Ball had said, "We
have taken a very firm position . . . we are going to insist
on the full carrying-out of provisions." Three days later the
administration had served formal notice that it would insist
that the General Assembly, on its opening day, November 10,
squarely face the decision of whether or not to invoke Article 19.
And on November 6 news was leaked from Washington that
the United States would withhold its usual pledge to under-
write 40 percent of the funds for the UN Special Fund and
Expanded Program of Technical Assistance. The Americans
were pointedly showing that two could play at the game of not
paying for UN expenses. A feeling of dismay descended upon
Turtle Bay (as Headquarters is still known to old-timers).

Finally, as late as January 14, 1965, Ambassador Stevenson told a subdued meeting of the Latin American group that

a showdown on Article 19 could not be avoided when the General Assembly reconvened a few days later; he predicted that the US would find a majority of the delegations ready to support the US position (actually a simple majority would not have been sufficient; in the opinion of most delegates a decision could be won by the US and its allies only if they could count on two-thirds of the delegations, an unlikely possibility).

No wonder that under such circumstances the article "The Retreat From the UN Showdown," by Arthur Krock, in *The New York Times* of Sunday, February 21, was held to reflect the prevailing mood of despondency and resentment of American public opinion. Wrote Krock:

"Brag is a good dog, but Holdfast is a better," runs the old English proverb. But in the flight from Article 19 of the United Nations Charter, which the United States Government masterminded on the last day of the sterile session of the U.N. General Assembly that began on Nov. 10, 1964, only the second estimate in the proverb was confirmed by the event.

The Johnson Administration abandoned its often reiterated "firm stand" that nations which have refused to pay their U.N. assessments for "special peace-keeping activities" be barred from voting on any proposition before the Assembly. But the Governments of France and the U.S.S.R. held fast to the position that they would neither pay their arrears nor promise to make any part of them under the threat that Article 19 would be invoked against them. This provides that members thus defaulting "shall have no vote in the General Assembly."

"To avoid both the crises which would have been created by invoking Article 19—the repudiation of the Charter if the Assembly refused to enforce it against this clear violation, or the emasculation of the U.N. as a representative world body that enforcement would effect—the United States delegate, Adlai E. Stevenson, was obliged to read something into the Article which isn't there. His sudden discovery was that the words "no vote" referred only to votes on "substantive" matter, whereas the motion of the

Albanian delegate that the Assembly resume roll calls on pending issues concerned only a "procedural" matter. Therefore, said Stevenson, the "no vote" mandate of Article 19 did not ban the defaulters from participating in the roll call by which the Albanian motion was rejected.

This casuistry suited every Government but that of Communist China, which is not a member of the U.N. but had inspired its member satellite, Albania, to try to force a showdown on Article 19. Nothing could have been more pleasing to the defaulters, particularly France and the U.S.S.R., than Stevenson's parliamentary chicane. It exposed the Johnson Administration fleeing at high speed from the showdown it inwardly shrinks from but for months has been outwardly "demanding." It postponed the issue until next September by the recess of the Assembly, leaving this much more time for face-saving all around. And the artifice also preserved the façade and whatever else remains of the U.N. Charter after violations of its letter and spirit by several member Governments and by the Assembly majority as a whole. . . . When Albania sought to test this prediction there was indeed an Assembly vote. But it wasn't the showdown Stevenson had prophesied; instead it was a maneuver, devised by the United States Government, to evade the prophecy. Moreover, it granted to the defaulters the vote this Government had sworn they would not be permitted to cast on any proposition laid before the Assembly. So ended the bluff by Brag that was called Holdfast.

Outside the United States, however, there was a feeling of satisfaction amounting almost to euphoria. It was not only the Soviet bloc and France who had reason to be pleased with what had happened on February 18. Many of the most sincere friends of the United States could not help expressing their contentment at seeing the world's most powerful nation abandon its lofty but unrealistic attitude. On that same Thursday that had seen the General Assembly adjourn in an atmosphere of frustration and ridicule, a newly arrived Western diplomat, who was a veteran in his country's foreign service and had been a delegate to many NATO meetings, said in a group that had stayed on in the South Lounge until late in the evening: "Today's performance seems to me to presage a quiet burial of America's holier-than-thou approach to foreign policy, so beloved of men like Wilson and Foster Dulles. An approach that has created for us at NATO a number of unnecessary problems over the years, I might say from personal experience.

"The burial services will be held in the Calvinist rites," added a young secretary of the same delegation, who was also in the group.

The burial took place in effect six months later almost to the day. On August 16, 1965, only a few weeks before the next Assembly session, the new US delegate former-Supreme Court Justice Arthur J. Goldberg stated before the Committee of 33 that the United States would bow to the wish of the majority and permit the General Assembly to revert to normal functioning without a "confrontation" with the Soviet Union over the application of Article 19. In surrendering the American position which had kept the Assembly paralyzed for almost a year—and was at the root of the five-year-old "UN financial crisis"—Ambassador Goldberg made two significant points. First he explained that the reversal in the US position was due to the realization that the General Assembly wanted to proceed as if Article 19 had never been in the Charter.

> Without prejudice to the position that art. 19 is applicable, the United States recognizes, as it must, that the General Assembly is not prepared to apply article 19 in the present situation and that the consensus of the membership is that the Assembly should proceed normally. We will not seek to frustrate that consensus, since it is not in the world interest to have the work of the General Assembly immobilized in these troubled days.

For the first time the US government recognized publicly that it could no longer marshal the necessary votes in the Assembly. It was an extraordinary development, all the more so since the issue was one in which Washington could claim the support of the Charter and of a pronouncement by the

World Court. (A year before a majority of the Assembly had backed the US delegation in accepting the advisory opinion from The Hague, which held that UN members were collectively responsible for financing peacekeeping operations.)

Actually the change in the American attitude toward the United Nations was much more radical, since in the same statement Ambassador Goldberg went on to say that the United States reserved the right to follow the example of the other delinquents and refuse to pay assessments for UN operations not acceptable to the US government. "There can be no double standard among members of the organization," he said.

It was not only a retreat from the legal position adopted by the US, but also seemed like an abandonment of the principle of "collective financial responsibility," a recognition that an interpretation of an article of the Charter would not ultimately be accepted by the membership even if upheld by the World Court in advisory opinion. It was more in the nature of a reversal of policy by Washington than merely a retreat from an untenable position. In effect the United States was adopting the stand of the USSR, France, and the other "delinquents" by saying that, like them, it could pick and choose those UN peacekeeping operations for which it would share expenses.

It was duly noted that an ex-Supreme Court Justice of the United States officially announced this abandonment of the moralistic and legalistic approach to foreign policy problems that had been the hallmark of America. But the reaction in the world's chancelleries was one of relief mingled with respect. For once the world's most powerful country was willing to play the international game according to the rules accepted by everyone else—and play it on an issue of genuine significance.

⋙ 6 ⋘

IS THERE A FUTURE
IN PEACEKEEPING?

There are two schools of thought on the future of peacekeeping operations, which in a very real sense involves the future of the United Nations. The first school maintains that dispute will continue about this crucial political responsibility of the world organization, unless and until it becomes specifically incorporated into the Charter. Many member states are now on record as favoring this approach, which was first formally presented at the general debate of the 19th Session of the General Assembly in November, 1964. The head of the Brazilian delegation gave the opening address, as by established tradition Brazil always opens the general debate. The Brazilian Foreign Minister made a far-reaching proposal: since a peacekeeping operation was not foreseen in writing the Charter, a new chapter authorizing and regulating such operations should be introduced between Chapter VI, which deals with the pacific settlement of disputes, and Chapter VII, which authorizes the employ of force by the member states. This new chapter, he suggested, would provide for a "gradual crescendo" in the arsenal of UN actions.

In the months following this proposal, a consensus has developed among member states that the new concept should be incorporated into the Charter, since peacekeeping operations

accumulated from UN experience are altogether different from
the enforcement measures provided in Chapter VII.

This would of course require revision of the Charter, a
long and tedious process at best. In this specific case it would
probably be blocked by the Soviet Union, because the Russians
would be reluctant to legalize a type of UN activity which has
thwarted their foreign policy objectives on more than one occasion over the last few years. However, since a peacekeeping
operation could not be planned without a minimum of consent
among the big powers, it is quite possible that the USSR would
go along with an informal inclusion of peacekeeping operations
among the functions of the United Nations. The motivation
for Soviet Union consent—and for that matter consent by any
big power—was best expressed in 1964 when the Pakistani
delegate advanced a definition of peacekeeping operations: "it
connotes an operation of an executive nature which interposes
a UN presence in a situation likely to lead to a breach of the
peace." Experience has proved that by engaging in a peacekeeping operation the UN invariably interposes its presence
in a conflict that already involves or ultimately may involve
two or more great powers; and that in the last analysis this
interposition is always welcomed with visible relief, even
though the powers may go to great lengths of propaganda
and diatribe not to admit it publicly.

Central to the Article 19 crisis was the role of the Security
Council in launching and governing peacekeeping operations,
as against that arrogated to itself by the General Assembly.
The irony of the controversy was that fundamentally the United
States and the USSR were not in disagreement. Both super-
powers wanted to curtail the power of an increasingly unruly
General Assembly and reinforce that of the Security Council,
where each possesses a veto. This of course had been France's
contention since the beginning, as succinctly expressed by De
Gaulle in his press conference of February 4, 1965.

∽   ∽   ∽

Restoring pre-eminence to the Security Council would require the General Assembly to surrender the powers arrogated
to itself during the Korean War and embodied in the "Uniting
for Peace" resolution rammed through in 1950 by the Western
countries under American leadership. This controversial resolution allows the General Assembly to assume peacekeeping
powers reserved to the Security Council under the Charter,
although the Charter is far from crystal-clear in the matter.
There are growing indications that Washington, alarmed by
the irresponsibility of the General Assembly since 1960, is
willing to shelve for all practical purposes the "Uniting for
Peace" resolution.

Power is indeed reverting to the Security Council, but
not altogether. The Americans will probably continue to insist
that the General Assembly keep for itself some "residual
authority" and the Russians may give a little in this regard, as
indicated by Ambassador Fedorenko in his statement of April
22, 1965: "If the Security Council is unable to adopt a decision
on any given concrete question related to the maintenance of
peace, then, of course, nothing can prevent the General Assembly from considering the whole question anew in order to adopt
new recommendations based on the terms of reference of the
General Assembly."

There is hopeful feeling in the UN that the two superpowers are slowly coming around to considering the powers
of the Security Council and the Assembly mutually comple-
mentary rather than competitive in matters of peacekeeping
operations. However, too much hope should not be roused.
Experience has shown that each peacekeeping operation is
highly individual, and that while the big powers have been
involved in every instance, their interest was manifested in
widely different ways. It would be rash to assert that UN peacekeeping operations have either a bright future or no future
whatsoever. All will depend on the individual case.

Cyprus and Yemen offer good proof. In Cyprus and in

Yemen the two superpowers were interested but not vitally involved. The UN succeeded in Cyprus and failed in Yemen, which seems to indicate that when there is a measure of abstention by the two superpowers, medium and small powers can determine the issue. When Cyprus exploded, Greece and Turkey, under persistent prodding from their allies, decided that rather than have a showdown it was better to bring in the UN. In Yemen, the Egyptians and the Saudi Arabians consented to a UN observer mission and even agreed to share its costs. Normally this would have evolved into a peacekeeping operation, but the UN observers were withdrawn after a number of months because Nasser mistakenly believed at one point that he could win a military decision in Yemen, and preferred to have no UN witnesses.

Of course both in Cyprus and in Yemen the financial crisis arising from the Suez and the Congo was neatly avoided by financing both operations primarily by the powers concerned and on a voluntary basis. In this sense Cyprus and Yemen laid the groundwork for the basic solution to future financing of peacekeeping operations by the UN. There is a great show of resistance to this "voluntary basis" approach in the West, particularly in the United States, because it runs counter to the concept of "collective financial responsibility" by all UN member states. This concept, which was at the root of the Article 19 controversy, sounds convincing, but even the countries upholding the United States position had serious reservations about the political wisdom of a moralistic approach. While the debate raged on financing peacekeeping operations, a Latin American delegate expressed the doubts of many of his colleagues by saying to a group in the delegates lounge one afternoon:

"The Americans keep talking about collective financial responsibility of our whole membersihp and its sounds proper and virtuous. And that is precisely why I don't like it. One should never try to inject virtue into international life."

"What would you inject instead?" asked a young member of the United Kingdom delegation.

"A sense of reality, precisely as you British have been doing for centuries. No country in the world likes to pay for a peacekeeping operation it doesn't approve of, but it may be forced to do so, if it is a small and weak power. But making a big power pay for the Congo or Suez or any other peace-keeping operation it doesn't particularly like is completely out of the quetsion, as we all know by now."

"But neither the Soviets nor the French vetoed the Congo or the Suez operation as they could have done," interposed a Scandinavian delegate. "Why shouldn't they pay if they con-sented?"

"You are confusing consent with tolerance," retorted the Latin American. "I have a son who stays out late almost every evening. I don't like it, but I don't try to stop him because he's nineteen years old and he keeps telling me he shouldn't be treated like a child any more. He's right in that. But ever so often he tries to borrow my car and every time I refuse. I tolerate his staying out late, but I won't go as far as actively subsidizing it by providing transportation."

ഗ   ഗ   ഗ

The so-called financial crisis of the United Nations turns out to be a travesty in semantics as it reaches its epilogue. There is every indication that voluntary contributions will wipe out the cash deficit of the organization. The ten million dollars given by the United Kingdom in July, 1965, set the ball roll-ing, together with smaller gifts from the Scandinavian coun-tries and Canada.

Serious students of UN affairs were not surprised at the ingenious solution. They had known all along that the crisis— for it was a real crisis—was political not financial. It stood to reason that the survival of the world organization was a neces-sity for every member state, even though the Western powers, the Communist countries, and the *tiers monde* had quite dif-ferent reasons for wanting a UN. The United Nations would never be allowed to flounder because of money, particularly for want of a sum which, as Lord Carnarvon pointed out from the rostrum of the General Assembly, would not cover the price of one single submarine.

The political scars of that major political crisis were another matter. By losing the diplomatic battle it so rashly engaged, the United States killed once and for all its cherished concept of financial collective responsibility. In so doing it had probably unwittingly rendered a real service to the United Nations. A stark fact of international life had been made clear to all by blundering American diplomacy: no great power would ever pay a penny for a peacekeeping operation of which it disapproved. The Soviets converted the fact to their own currency by saying for the record "not a single kopek." Medium and small powers are already demanding the same privilege of refusing to pay for a peacekeeping operation they don't like.

The results for the UN will be painful but salutary. From now on the regular budget will be the only financial commitment of the organization covered by assessing all member states. It will be essentially a housekeeping budget, thrashed out by the Advisory Committee on Budgetary and Administrative Questions, where all groups of states and all points of view are represented, and then approved by the General Assembly as a pure formality.

Any other activities of the world organization, including peacekeeping operations, will be financed by the whole membership only by their unanimous and active support. And even in those rare cases it will never be by assessing the member states, but rather by having the Secretary-General solicit voluntary contributions. In fact, voluntary contributions will become a way of life with the UN (as it has in effect already been to an unsuspected degree for some years); the puritanical and slightly hypocritical concept of "collective financial responsibility," so dear to the Anglo-Saxon heart, shall be laid to rest once and for all. That will be the first political scar left by the Article 19 battle.

Another scar will be the World Court's immense loss in

prestige and authority. It deserves this in any case, since it has been in the postwar years a pompous institution commanding an undeserved respect from the world community. In point of fact, the fifteen judges sitting at The Hague have never made a contribution to world peace, or even to the settlement of a significant international dispute, that would justify the munificent salaries they are paid. A reassessment of the World Court is overdue; its sorry performance in the Article 19 controversy, where it gave an opinion of highly dubious juridical value with the justices splitting along nationalistic and ideological lines, may healthfully result in reorganization of the world's highest tribunal or push it into limbo once and for all.

The third political scar results from the clash between the great powers versus the medium and small ones. In spite of the romantic notion that the little fellows always command attention, in this case they never did, nor did they deserve it. For months on end the most respected representatives of small and medium powers at the UN bent every effort to reconcile points of view among the big powers. They were invariably ignored by the Soviet Union, France, and the United States. A compromise solution was eventually worked out among these three, and outside help came ironically from another big power, the United Kingdom.

The Article 19 controversy drove home with merciless clarity the fact that whenever an important issue is at stake it is decided exclusively among the great powers. Specifically, the Article 19 episode burst the bubble of Afro-Asian influence on world affairs. In this instance the Latin Americans had sufficient common sense for not trying to solve anything for the big powers. But a dozen representatives of Afro-Asian countries, including medieval kingdoms such as Afghanistan and Ethiopia, and tight dictatorships like Ghana and the United Arab Republic, negotiated for months on end, trying to bring about an agreement between Moscow, Paris, and Washington. By mid-1965 it had become clear to anyone experienced in UN affairs how much importance Moscow, Paris, or Washington attached to the opinions of Kabul, Addis Ababa, Accra, or Cairo. Again, this was a salutary outgrowth of the crisis. For too long the world had been given the impression that a hundred-odd countries of little consequence who orate endlessly at the UN carry some weight in world affairs.

The solution of the crisis showed that the big power that suffered a diplomatic defeat, the United States, in reality gained considerable political advantage, since the strengthening of the Security Council at the expense of the General Assembly benefits the US as it does any of the veto-wielding powers. Toward the end of 1964 Washington clearly desired this. The majority of the medium and small powers that had sided with the United States were left with nothing to show except the loss in importance and prestige of the General Assembly, their own cherished forum.

Ambassador Fedorenko of the Soviet Union put it bluntly at the end of one of the stormy Assembly sessions in February, 1965. The representative of a small power had delivered a particularly biting attack on the USSR. Asked by a fellow delegate if he was going to answer, an angry Fedorenko shook his head and answered simply: "We will just show them what power means."

ぬ   ぬ   ぬ

In retrospect, the Article 19 crisis, if it did shake the UN to its foundations as was often said, in the end rendered an inestimable service to the world organization by introducing a measure of realism and a sense of proportion into its approach to the crucial tasks embodied in a peacekeeping operation. There are those who think that the UN has become powerless in this field. On the contrary: the future will show that the world body will be called upon to engage in many more peacekeeping operations and thus perform a vitally needed function. But it will do so under three inflexible injunctions.

First, decision will rest with the big powers, and the other hundred-odd countries will merely play a peripheral role of persuasion and mild pressure. This is a deplorable state of affairs, but it mirrors faithfully the world in which we live.

Second, no country will ever again be charged for a peacekeeping operation of which it does not approve. It will not even have to say that it will not pay. But peacekeeping operations will take place just the same, costs being defrayed by those countries who satisfy an interest by sharing the bill.

Third, the General Assembly will never again be taken as seriously as it used to be. It will become mostly the "useful forum" of which De Gaulle speaks. And the Security Council will again come into its own. This was an overdue development, since the only real power the UN possesses is vested in the Council.

๛   ๛   ๛

All this will not necessarily mean a total eclipse of medium and small power influence. During 1965 all the big powers ratified an amendment to the Charter bringing the membership of the Council from eleven to fifteen. This is a very genuine concession they have made to the rest of the world, and is more meaningful than pretending that the General Assembly counts in the realities of power. From the first of January, 1966, there were ten nonpermanent members of the Security Council, instead of six. The great powers will hold unflinchingly to their veto power, but they are at least willing to listen to the rest of the world, not only in a "useful" forum like the General Assembly, but also where action can be generated to block and circumscribe a dangerous conflict anywhere on the globe.

»»» 7 «««

PROLIFERATION CHASTENS
SUPERPOWERS

The cloak-and-dagger aura of nuclear weapons was dramatized during the late forties by several espionage episodes. Among them was the trial of nuclear physicist Klaus Fuchs, who confessed in detail how he had passed on to the Soviets atomic secrets to which he was privy. It was said at the time that the development of nuclear weapons in the USSR had been accelerated considerably on account of Fuchs's scientific contributions.

While atomic espionage still claims headlines episodically, in recent years it has lost deep political significance. Nowadays, not only scientists but also statesmen and diplomats are aware that although the powers belonging to the "nuclear club" continue as security-conscious as ever, there are few, if any, secrets left whose knowledge by the potential enemy would measurably upset the balance of atomic power—or the "balance of terror" as it used to be called.

There is no longer anything fundamentally mysterious or even recondite about setting up an atomic explosion. The first conference on the peaceful uses of atomic energy, held under UN sponsorship in Geneva in 1955, demonstrated to some two thousand nuclear scientists who attended that the United States and the Soviet Union had, independently of each other, reached surprisingly equivalent levels in the development of nuclear technology. Since then the United Nations has held two other conferences on the same theme, and an ample program for developing peaceful uses of atomic energy has set in motion an even more rapid and comprehensive dissemination of nuclear technology among dozens of nations capable of absorbing it.

There are today close to fifty power reactors in operation around the globe which could serve as the starting-point for the manufacture of nuclear weapons. True, the UN through its International Atomic Energy Agency has mounted an intricate inspection system to prevent this occurrence. But political events may supersede any agreement a country has signed with the IAEA. During the hostilities between India and Pakistan in September, 1965, eighty-six members of the Indian parliament demanded that their government engage in the manufacture of atomic bombs. In Pakistan this was taken seriously enough to be used as an argument for trying to win by conventional warfare before the possession of nuclear weapons by India would make it possible for the stronger of the two adversaries to dictate terms to the weaker.

India is only one of twenty-four countries that today possesses not only the technology, but also the industrial infrastructure and the body of trained scientists, needed to embark on the production of nuclear weapons. The other twenty-three are Argentina, Australia, Austria, Belgium, Brazil, Canada, Czechoslovakia, Denmark, Finland, Germany (FRG), East Germany (GDR), Holland, Hungary, Indonesia, Israel, Italy, Japan, Mexico, Poland, Sweden, Switzerland, Egypt (United Arab Republic), Yugoslavia.

What is equally sobering is that any of these twenty-four could afford to join the heretofore exclusive "nuclear club," because membership no longer places an intolerable burden on the national budget. Ten nuclear weapons a year can be manufactured with an initial investment of seventy to eighty million dollars. Operating costs following this initial investment would be of the order of twenty to twenty-five million dollars a year.

Any of those countries could afford expenditures of this magnitude.[1]

The sophistication of delivery systems for these nuclear bombs would depend on the adversary. Intercontinental ballistic missiles would seldom be needed. The national airline, especially if it includes jet aircraft in its fleet, which each of these countries does, would usually be adequate for the delivery of an atomic bomb against a potential enemy.

We have entered the age of the "Nth country" in deadly earnest. (In the literature on disarmament it is customary to use the letter "N" to designate the indeterminate number of countries capable of gaining nuclear weapons in the future.) Several more countries will undoubtedly be added in the years ahead.

The danger of nuclear proliferation presents two distinct political threats. The first is the relationship between Nth countries and the five big powers now in the "nuclear club": United States, Soviet Union, United Kingdom, France, China. An Nth country, once having acquired atomic bombs, would be capable of forcing one superpower into attacking the other. The premise to this nightmarish line of reasoning is that a surprise attack by a Nth country upon one of the superpowers might trigger a nuclear retaliation by that superpower, who would be unaware of the true origin of the surprise attack, against the presumed attacker, its potential and principal adversary. The rationale for the surprise attack by the Nth power would be that it would survive undamaged the nuclear exchange between the United States and the Soviet Union and be then in a position to dominate the world. This is sometimes called "catalytic nuclear war." Fortunately its danger has been exaggerated, and it is taken more seriously by the general public, informed by works of science fiction, than by the experts. By 1970, and possibly

---

[1] Carnegie Endowment for International Peace: *Issues Before the 20th General Assembly* (1965), p. 24; and Institute of Strategic Studies, London: *The Spread of Nuclear Weapons* (1962), pp. 21-2.

before, both the superpowers will be equipped with "invulnerable retaliatory forces," which means that neither the Americans nor the Russians will feel immediately committed to launch full strategic nuclear forces in response to nuclear attack. In fact, since their "second strike capability" would not be significantly impaired there is reason to believe that either the United States or the Soviet Union would have a sufficient incentive to "ride out" an attack and determine its origin before retaliating. As Henry Kissinger points out in *The Necessity for Choice:*

> The hope of inheriting the world after the major powers have destroyed each other seems too vague. The probability that the country launching the blow would be discovered and subjected to overwhelming retaliation seems too high; the gains to be achieved too problematical; the risks out of proportion to any objective—particularly if one considers that even if successful in starting an all-out exchange, the country launching the war might become the victim of heavy fall-out.

Actually the truly ominous aspect of nuclear proliferation stems from the relations of Nth countries to each other. In the first place, during the period in which it is known that a given country is engaged in manufacturing atomic bombs the government of a political rival may find itself under tremendous pressure from its military leaders to launch a pre-emptive attack with conventional weapons. While the Pakistan-India case has acquired ominous overtones because of the hostilities over Kashmir, this hypothesis is even more plausible in the case of either Israel or Egypt. If either were to embark on the development of a nuclear capability—and it seems by no means impossible—either the UAR or the Israeli government, as the case may be, will be told by its most responsible military advisors that to fail to engage in conventional warfare will mean running the risk of nuclear blackmail within a year or two.

There is another equally disturbing possibility, described by Leonard Beaton and John Maddox in *The Spread of Nuclear*

Weapons as "the inevitability of imbalance . . . between rivals as the spread goes on." If two rival countries develop an atomic arsenal at approximately the same time, the first to achieve its goal will be tempted to capitalize on its transitory superiority by dictating a political settlement or, failing that, by launching a surprise attack with its newly acquired atomic bombs. Its military leaders would argue that failure to grasp the opportunity of a temporary superiority would run the risk of an expensive and indefinite atomic race. Also it would have to face, with insufficient means, the same problems that confront the two superpowers: rapidly changing technology and the imperative need to maintain an absurdly expensive warning system over all its territory.

On the other hand, some of the more penetrating studies of the dangers of nuclear dissemination draw distinctions among Nth countries. The possession of nuclear weapons by countries of political maturity and economic and social stability would be quite different from the introduction of atomic bombs into critical areas such as the Middle East, the Indian sub-continent, or Southeast Asia. In fact, these political analysts like to underline the "educational" impact inherent in the acquisition of atomic weapons, which would encourage deliberate and cautious moves in the field of foreign relations rather than a tendency to adventurousness.

∽ ∽ ∽

Almost ten years ago the United Nations for the first time took cognizance of the looming problem of nuclear proliferation. At the 13th Session of the General Assembly in 1958, Ireland asked for inclusion in the agenda of an item entitled "Prevention of the Wider Dissemination of Nuclear Weapons." Nothing happened, but the Irish delegation again took initiative the following year, and the Assembly adopted a resolution asking the Ten-Nation Disarmament Committee to study the question. The Committee failed to respond, and the 15th General Assem-

bly in 1960 called upon the nuclear powers to prohibit dissemination of nuclear weapons to countries not possessing them.
And the 16th Assembly adopted the "Irish Resolution," which
called on all states to endeavor to reach an agreement on nuclear
weapons. Under such an international agreement the nuclear
powers "would agree not to relinquish control of nuclear weapons or to transmit information necessary for the manufacture
of nuclear weapons to states not possessing such information,
and states without nuclear weapons would agree to refrain from
manufacturing or otherwise acquiring control of such weapons."

The task facing the UN is seriously complicated by the
growing influence of incentives to enter the "nuclear club," as
described in a study by the Carnegie Endowment for International Peace:

The incentives motivating nations to acquire nuclear
weapons fall into three broad categories: military, political, and psychological. The most obvious of these is the
military advantage over its foes that accrues to a state
possessing nuclear weapons. Another is the military incentive for the acquisition of nuclear weapons that arises in
alliances which include a major nuclear power and a number of non-nuclear powers. A non-nuclear member of the
alliance may believe that the acquisition of nuclear weapons
will amplify its military power. It has been argued that
an ally having a very small nuclear force could—with effectiveness varying according to the vulnerability of the
opposing strategic nuclear forces of the major powers—
pursue its interests assured that if it were in fact attacked,
its nuclear force would be sufficient to release the larger
nuclear force of its major ally. The assumed ability to
invoke the force of one of the nuclear superpowers through
the use of a small nuclear force gives many states an incentive for adding nuclear weapons to their arsenal.

The second class of incentives is political in nature.
To a considerable extent, the possession of an autonomous
nuclear capacity is considered a status symbol. This mark
of great-power status is of particular importance to states
attempting to regain the lost grandeur of the past, for

example, France and the People's Republic of China. The increase of influence on allies is an additional political incentive expected from the possession of nuclear weapons. France's drive for nuclear weapons is often attributed to its desire to exert influence on the United States. A further political incentive is the autonomy within alliances which nuclear weapons confers. The inability of France and the United Kingdom to operate independently of their major nuclear ally, the United States, was demonstrated at Suez. Similarly, the dependence of the People's Republic of China on the Soviet Union was demonstrated in the Taiwan Straits in 1958.

The last category of incentives is psychological. Nuclear weapons may be sought as a means of reconciling an army to the loss of an empire. This is certainly one factor in the continued French pursuit of nuclear weapons. Another possible psychological phenomenon is the drive to "task-completion." Once a country has started on a nuclear program, it may find increasing difficulty in stopping short of the construction of nuclear weapons.

Nuclear weapons may be acquired by a state through independent and unaided development or through the transferral of either the weapons or the necessary information for their production. Many believe that the second of these ways will be the more common in the long run. Those who foresee the greatest danger in the first path propose various renunciation schemes that attempt to control nuclear proliferation by binding the non-nuclear powers, through treaty commitment, not to undertake the development of nuclear weapons. Those who consider the second path the more dangerous propose various non-dissemination schemes covering one or more of the following: nuclear weapons, weapons information, fissionable material, strategic weapons delivery systems, and important components of the over-all nuclear weapons system.

Joint renunciation by potential Nth countries of the right to develop nuclear weapons seems to offer a promising escape from the dangers of nuclear proliferation, but it raises some serious problems. Since the greatest probability of the use of nuclear weapons arises from the relationship of Nth countries to each other, even a very small number of nuclear weapons hidden by a Nth country could have a profound effect on the balance of power between Nth countries. The national existence of Malaysia, for example, could be threatened by even a few nuclear weapons in the hands of Indonesia. It is, therefore, unlikely that countries would be willing to renounce the development of a nuclear capacity without firm assurances that clandestine operations were not in existence elsewhere. This would require an extremely rigorous and complex inspection system capable of detecting any diversion of atomic materials to weapons construction. But if a sufficiently thorough inspection scheme could be developed, the problem of devising adequate sanctions would remain. The size of the smaller Nth countries prevents them, even as a group, from threatening effective sanctions against the larger Nth countries for violation of the renunciation ban. Hence such sanctions could only be provided by the major countries. It is by no means clear, however, that it would be in the interest of the great powers to invoke sanctions indiscriminately against violators without regard for other political concerns.

The second method of halting nuclear proliferation, a non-dissemination agreement by the major powers, also raises some very serious problems. First, such an agreement would fail to halt the independent development of nuclear weapons. Unaccompanied by any provision to close the Pandora's box of instability provided by locally produced nuclear weapons, a non-dissemination scheme could, at best, only slow down proliferation. Second, inspection would become more and more difficult as the number of nuclear powers increased.

With these difficulties looming, the need to halt proliferation is recognized as increasingly urgent. The non-nuclear countries feel strongly that the big five have a binding obligation to restrict these instruments of mass murder; that only when their nuclear arsenals are scaled down will they be in a position to call on the rest of the world to exercise self-restraint in this apocalyptic field.

»» 8 *«««*

CHINA SPOILS A MIRROR

U Thant frequently repeats that the United Nations mirrors
the contemporary world scene; if one does not like the image
in the mirror one should blame the world, not the UN. Besides
expressing this pious postulate in public, he has delivered it
to diplomats and cabinet ministers in private exchanges at UN
Headquarters or during his trips.

The present Secretary-General has been using this simile
ever since he took office, and there is no reason to believe that
he will not continue to do so as long as he is the official spokesman for the United Nations. By now there are those who are
impatient with Thant, like one correspondent who remarked
not long ago:

> The first time I heard the SG give us the mirror
> treatment I liked it fine. It made me feel a little sorry for
> the UN, always getting the blame for the mess the world
> has got itself into. But I have been hearing it too often,
> and now it's not only the SG but almost any of his aides
> who will give me the little story about the damn mirror
> whenever I try to get a bit of news out of them. I feel like
> telling them not to pass the buck to the world at large.

Neither Thant nor his parrot-like aides deserve to be
blamed, for they did not think up the "mirror of the world"

explanation; it harks back to the very early years of the UN
and its paternity has not been clearly established. Hammarskjold had recourse to it, although not as often as Thant. The
reason could be that the sophisticated Swede did not for a
moment believe in such a simplified explanation, while the
literal-minded Burmese seems to take as much pleasure in this
facile reasoning as the worthy NGOs (colloquial for members
of non-governmental organizations) to whom he has proposed
it on many an occasion. Indeed Thant gives the impression
that he believes in the truth of the statement, perhaps the only
reproach that can justly be aimed at him. For he also believes
and has often said that China should be represented at the
United Nations. Since the Peking government, which rules over
700 million Chinese (one quarter of all mankind) and the
entire territory of China except for the island of Formosa, has
been kept out of the world body for seventeen years, it is unconvincing to insist that the UN mirrors the world as it is.
Indeed it is easy to argue that only during the first four years
of its existence could the world organization lay any claim to
being a mirror, for only from 1945 to 1949 was China represented at the UN through a government, that of Chiang Kai-
shek, which in effect then ruled the country.

ᔑ   ᔑ   ᔑ

Keeping China out of the UN has been either a great
American victory or a great American mistake, depending on
who voices the opinion. But almost everyone seems to agree
that, whether or not it was wise to ostracize Peking for seventeen years, the credit for this political and diplomatic achievement belongs solely to the United States.

It is not commonly realized that the American position
was not always so unyielding. At the earliest stages of the
communist take-over in China there was a considerable chance
that the Peking government would replace the Taipeh government in representing China at the UN. The first Secretary-

General of the United Nations personally conducted a persistent diplomatic offensive for the acceptance of Peking; he was about to succeed when a different kind of offensive was launched in Korea.

Early in 1950, only a few months after the communists had completed the conquest of China and chased Chiang Kai-shek to Formosa, Trygve Lie began to press for acceptance of the new government at the UN. His main argument was that the world body should have a member state represented by the government in effective control of the territory and not by a government in exile, and that the political and ideological position of the new Chinese state was no concern of the world organization, which already counted several communist states among its members in good standing. Lie was advocating the "mirror of the world" approach.

As he explains in his book *In the Cause of Peace*, Lie was alarmed when the USSR boycotted the United Nations because Taipeh's representatives were not replaced by Peking's after the communists had expelled the nationalists from China. He felt that Peking had a clear case, and that the Soviet boycott, although he did not condone it, was a grave menace to the survival of the world organization. On January 13, 1950, Ambassador Jacob Malik, the Soviet representative, walked out of the Security Council after failing to secure the necessary votes for seating Peking. Then, remarks Lie, "over the next few weeks the Russians actually marched out of no fewer than twenty-one United Nations councils and committees, duplicating the spectacle of the Security Council."

Lie argued his line of reasoning not only at the UN but also in lectures to American audiences, for which he was severely criticized in the US press. In a lecture delivered in Washington on May 20, 1950, the Secretary-General said: "The 475 million people of China are collectively original members of the UN by the terms of the Charter itself. They have a right to be represented by whatever government has the power to 'employ the resources and direct the people of the

State in fulfillment of the obligations of membership' in the
United Nations. I repeat—whatever government is thus qualified regardless of its ideology."

At the time there were two schools of thought in the
councils of US government; Lie believed there was a reasonable
chance of getting Peking in and Moscow back since Washington's opposition was not adamant. Ambassador Ernest A.
Gross, speaking in the Security Council for the United States, said
that his government would "accept the decision of the Security
Council in this matter when made by an affirmative vote of
seven members." Of course, the conviction prevailed in Washington that seven votes could not be mustered, since only five
of the eleven members of the Security Council had at the time
recognized Peking: Great Britain, India, Norway, Yugoslavia,
and the Soviet Union. But the Secretary-General thought dif-
ferently. He approached the other members of the Council,
having first sent them a memorandum prepared by his legal
counselors within the Secretariat, in which he pointed out that
in terms of international law Peking had a stronger case than
Taipeh for claiming to represent China.

Ironically, there were growing indications that Lie was
about to succeed, when the onset of the Korean War wiped
out Peking's chances.

By the middle of 1950 there was evidence that France
might range herself with Britain and Russia on the question of
acknowledging the rights to the UN of China's communist
government. If that were to happen, the general feeling was
that the seventh vote would not be too difficult to come by; it
could be provided by either Egypt or Ecuador, who were serving on the Council at the time. Of course "China" was represented in the Security Council by Chiang Kai-shek's envoy,
Dr. Tsiang, who would have voted against admission even if
the United States were to abstain. In that event, however, the
Secretary-General was convinced the veto privilege of a permanent member would not apply. "My legal advisers had concluded that the veto did not apply here, as the question of who

should represent China was of a 'procedural nature,' being, in the final instance, a matter of credentials."

But then in the last week of June, 1950, the communist North Koreans embarked on their invasion of the anti-communist south; the United States, and then the United Nations, came to the support of South Korea. On its side, North Korea obtained support from China, a support that was to become a massive military commitment when the forces under General MacArthur approached the Yalu River and the Chinese frontier (Peking continued to speak of "volunteers" even while it was pouring over the border regular army units in army division and subsequently corps strength).

As the United Nations ranged itself with the United States in the defense of South Korea, with more than half of the member states making an active contribution (and with fifteen of these sending troops), the climate in regard to Peking changed almost overnight at Turtle Bay. There was no question of accepting North Korea's ally in the councils of the UN while the Korean War raged.

After the end of the war, however, support for Peking began to develop again at a surprising pace, as evidenced by the voting on the question of "credentials of the representatives of China" from one General Assembly session to the other. Nevertheless, until the middle 1960s there was never any serious possibility of Peking being accepted into the UN because United States opposition had become adamant, and evenly highly emotional, in the wake of the Korean conflict. No Washington administration could afford to affront American public opinion by countenancing the seating of "Red China," an appellation adopted by most of the American press (which seldom referred to "Red Russia" or "Red Poland").

The bloody Korean campaign had ended in a frustrating stalemate; for the first time in its history, the United States had failed to win a war. With an almost hopeless situation saved and with victory within its grasp, the army commanded by MacArthur had finally been fought to a standstill by Peking's

flood of "volunteers." No wonder that across the breadth of the
United States, through the fifties and well into the sixties, any
suggestion of seating Peking would raise the indignant protest:
"Red China cannot shoot its way into the UN!" The slogan
came to be used by the U.S. mission itself; Ambassador Henry
Cabot Lodge was one American chief delegate who, although
himself quite aware of the many ramifications of the Chinese
question, was not averse to ending a debate with the popular
slogan that would command approving headlines in his country's press the following morning.

Oddly enough, during these years when the United States
was holding off Peking's admission against a rising tide of
member states who wished that the "mirror" would indeed
reflect the realities of power in the world, the Russians turned
out to be the most effective allies of the Americans. The curious
episodes, although inscribed in the UN annals, have rarely been
discussed publicly, since it was not in the interest of Washington to call attention to the unexpected but welcome assistance it was receiving from the Kremlin. Attention was even
less in the interest of Moscow, since Soviet diplomacy had
reached a new height of disingenuousness, and was in effect
behaving with a hypocrisy that since the days of Vishinsky
had been fashionable to ascribe to the Americans. Yet, a careful
ex-post-facto appraisal of the trend of thinking and voting in
the United Nations during the post-Korea years indicates that
Washington would have had a much more difficult task in
keeping Peking out were it not for the help obligingly supplied
by the Soviet delegation. Not only obliging, it showed a
machiavellian subtlety and an unexpected Anglo-Saxon mastery
of parliamentary tactics.

A growing number of nations, diverse geographically and
politically, were each year more convinced that to accept Peking
would do no harm to the UN and could conceivably be of
measurable help in tackling the main problems confronting the
organization—disarmament and the control and proliferation
of nuclear weapons. But every time enough pro-Chinese com-

munist votes could be mustered, the Russians would present resolutions couched in such extreme and tactless language as to alienate otherwise open-minded countries and prejudice Peking's very real chances. Whatever sins of hypocrisy in UN debates had been accumulated by Britain and the US, the twin Anglo-Saxon powers, these were easily surpassed by the USSR and India (who also insisted on presenting a resolution for the seating of Peking every year). The two vociferously chanted praise for a regime that spelled uneasiness for Moscow, even before the schism became apparent, and fright for New Delhi, even before Chinese divisions perched on the Hymalayas showed how easily they could descend upon Mother India.

✍   ✍   ✍

In the peregrination to the capitals of the major powers early in 1950 the Secretary-General came close to obtaining the seven votes needed for the acceptance of Peking's credentials by the Security Council. He believed he had convinced the British to vote "affirmatively" instead of abstaining. And on his second visit to Paris he received a clear indication from Foreign Minister Maurice Schumann that France was considering reversal of her position in the months ahead, perhaps not later than the summer of that year. Writes Trygve Lie in *In the Cause of Peace*, referring to the interview with Schumann on May 20: "Not once in all my conversations on the subject had I heard a statesman of the Western democracies express himself more clearly as to just who governed China and—consequently—who should represent that country in the United Nations." Moreover, during the course of his European journey the Secretary-General was told that Egypt was about to recognize the Peking government. This would have meant the needed seventh vote.

What would have happened if the Secretary-General had won the race against time? Says Lie in his book: "I have also wondered whether there might have been any Korean War at all, had the Peking government been permitted to represent the United Nations in the spring of 1950." Another authoritative voice is that of Sir Gladwyn Jebb, who served as interim UN Secretary-General during the formative months of the organization. Speaking at Baltimore on January 13, 1954, Sir Gladwyn said: "It could even be argued with some force that, had the government of Peking been represented in the United Nations at the beginning of the spring of 1950, the North Korean aggression might never have occurred at all."

➻ 9 ❮❮

THE 20TH ASSEMBLY:
CHINA AND THE POPE

The 20th General Assembly of the United Nations met in the autumn of 1965, which an earlier Assembly had designated as the Year of International Co-operation (ICY). The most visible tribute the Twentieth paid to ICY was to split itself by a 47-to-47 vote on seating China. During those four months the one and only call to international cooperation that had any impact on world opinion was made by Pope Paul VI, who represents a spiritual power, the Catholic Church, as well as the Vatican State, a non-member state. The Pope, incidentally, included in his emotional appeal to cooperation and brotherhood an unmistakably clear suggestion that the communist representatives of the People's Republic of China be at long last given a seat in the world body.

The China debate was undoubtedly the high mark of the Twentieth; it was conducted, from beginning to end, in an Alice-in-Wonderland atmosphere spiced with subtle touches of Oriental inscrutability. The exercise in absurdity was admirably rounded out by ranking government leaders of the People's Republic of China. During those weeks when about half the UN members were rallying to their cause, the communist Chinese not only failed to express any desire to take their "lawful seat," but also repeatedly denounced the United Nations, through their controlled press and news agency, as "a tool of American imperialism." The U.S. delegation might well have wished the claim were true in this particular instance: when the vote was taken on the substantive resolution to seat Peking, they could "command" only enough votes for an embarrassing tie.

But since hardly anything at the UN is as it appears, the facts described above have only sinuous and paradoxical connections with "the facts of international life," to which the British delegate referred in justifying his vote in favor of seating China. In reality, Pope Paul VI may not have been anxious to see his suggestion, advanced from the marble rostrum of the General Assembly on October 4, enacted a bare six weeks later. Nor was the Vatican alone in wishing that its expressed opinion not be converted too swiftly into an uncomfortable reality. At least nine of the 47 member states who proclaimed themselves anxious to see the PRC "in" cast affirmative votes only because they knew that even if the "substantive resolution" were to pass the People's Republic of China would not be in. For a vote on a "procedural resolution" taken immediately before had reaffirmed, by 56 to 49, that a two-thirds majority was needed, if the "substantive resolution" were to be converted into a bona fide UN decision.

Incidentally, Burundi, one of the twelve countries listed on UN documents as sponsoring the substantive resolution, provided a badly needed comic episode by abstaining when it came to a vote. This was most extraordinary, and soon afterwards a member of a European delegation was circulating in the corridors the explanation that the Burundi delegate had been persuaded, at the last minute, to accept a fifty thousand dollar "grant" from the Americans.

Also, Peking was less than candid in sulking throughout the proceedings, since the campaign for seating the PRC was led in the Assembly by a confirmed puppet, Albania, together with an aspiring puppet, Cambodia. Neither member of this odd team would have faced the ordeal without a green light from Red Cathay. (The Soviet delegation, while going through the motions of supporting the seating of Red China was almost olympian in its lack of interest and refused to make any serious effort to bolster Peking's chances.)

As to the other Communist countries, only one, Cuba, evinced any possibly genuine desire to see their Chinese comrades in the General Assembly, the Security Council, or any other bodies of the UN. Fidel Castro's reasons are anything but simple to discern, yet they somehow fit rather neatly into the rambling and turgid mental processes of the free-wheeling Caribbean Machiavelli. Peking's presence in UN councils would demand almost daily decisions from the Cuban delegation on whether to back the Chinese or the Russians in the struggle over policy and influence which would doubtless develop between the two big communist powers. But Castro would probably welcome this, since it would offer the Cuban delegation constant opportunities for maneuver and negotiation, thus inflating little Cuba's bargaining power toward its giant Soviet protector and its doctrinaire Chinese wooer. Fidel is sufficiently remote geographically from the USSR and more than close enough to United States shores to allow himself, on the large and publicity-bathed UN stage, the sort of sly, unpredictable tactics that he has pursued in the closed arena of Moscow-Peking power politics.

Poland, Czechoslovakia, Hungary, Rumania, and Bulgaria would find themselves in a perennially uncomfortable position if China were in the UN. Like Cuba, they would have to make almost daily decisions on what position to take between Moscow and Peking. But while Cuba did not mind this, and in fact seemed to relish the prospect, those five Eastern European countries would not welcome having to incur, week in and week out, the displeasure of either Moscow or Peking, or possibly both.

Finally, many of the non-aligned countries that were among the 47 casting a vote for Peking did so in the smug certainty that the preliminary "procedural resolution" had postponed for at least one year, until the 1966 General Assembly, the seating of the PRC. For all of them depend substantially on American foreign aid to buttress their shaky economies. Like the communist countries, albeit for different reasons, they feared the official presence of Peking in the UN, which would force them to incur frequent US displeasure in the course of debates and votes.

Thus a *reductio ad absurdum* was attained. While as many countries voted for Peking as voted against, almost all of those who so did were secretly jubilant at the providential "procedural resolution" which had in effect made the issue academic in 1965. As one British correspondent put it: "Practically all of these chaps were jolly glad at the way the two votes went, whether they said yes, no, or abstained. In my opinion, there are only five countries in the whole blasted United Nations who at the same time want Peking in and have nothing to gain from it. The five little Scandinavian countries. Everybody else is scared stiff of the Americans, or of the Russians, or of the Chinese, and keep on hoping that Peking will be kept out for another sixteen years." Whatever the true motives behind the 1965 voting on the Chinese question, Peking will not be kept out for another sixteen years.

The problem that now really begins to seriously concern diplomats is what to do with Formosa. This is sedulously referred to in UN circles as the "two Chinas problem." What to do with Formosa in the UN is not in itself an insoluble problem. Over the last few years a number of delegations, whose votes could presumably swing the issue, would have been willing to vote for seating Peking provided this did not automatically entail the expulsion of Taipeh. They would be resigned to see Mao's representatives both in the Security Council and the General Assembly but would like to retain membership for Chiang Kai-shek's government.

There is nothing untoward in two UN members from the same nation, since Russia has three: the URSS, the Byelorussian SSR, and the Ukrainian SSR. This point of view, which very much annoys the Russians, was aptly expressed by the

Jamaican delegate who suggested, during the 1965 debate that the precedent established by the Soviet Union could well be applied in favor of Formosa.

This quibbling over absurdities is not as inconsequential as it may seem, since it represents the last and best hope the United States has of keeping Peking out. For those who predict that communist China is drawing inexorably close to full UN membership usually do not give due weight to the problem of what to do with Formosa, compounded by the oft-repeated assertion by Peking that it would not come into the world body if the "Chiang Kai-shek clique" were not expelled at the same time.

∽   ∽   ∽

The one other important debate that took place during the 20th General Assembly, resulting in a resolution to convene a worldwide disarmament conference, was also directly connected with China. On the face of it there seemed to be no need for such a conference. Two bodies connected with the United Nations have been dealing with disarmament: the Commission on Disarmament (on which all UN members sit) and an 18-nation conference on disarmament, which has been meeting in Geneva for months at a time since 1962, and which groups the main NATO and Warsaw Pact nations, as well as eight of the more important countries not belonging to either military bloc. (The 18 are USA, UK, France, Canada, Italy, USSR, Poland, Rumania, Czechoslovakia, Bulgaria, Brazil, Mexico, India, Japan, Ethiopia, Nigeria, UAR, and Sweden. France, however, has refused to sit from the outset, hence for practical purposes it is a 17-nation group.)

But the People's Republic of China was not a member of either body; hence, the passing of that resolution calling for a world disarmament conference. One of the stipulations was that the conference would not be held under UN auspices, which seemed *prima facie* an odd decision to be taken by the

UN General Assembly. But the membership expected that this
would allow the Peking government to take part without losing
face. Or so ran the reasoning of the many delegates who in
the course of the prolonged debate said it was pointless to discuss disarmament without Peking—all the more so since China
is now a nuclear power.

When the United States delegation came over, somewhat
reluctantly, to the view of the majority, the resolution was
passed without dissenting votes. But within 72 hours Peking
made it known that under no circumstances would it attend
such a worldwide meeting—unless by the time the conference
was convened the People's Republic were a full-fledged member
of the United Nations. Incidentally, by taking this stand Mao's
government tacitly admitted how insincere had been its protes-
tations of unwillingness to join the UN. It was a clever counter-
move, but it should not have caused as much consternation
at Turtle Bay as it did. Too many of the delegates had actually
credited the denunciations of the UN by Peking. Diplomats,
even the best of them, tend to see too much importance in
pronouncements by a government, and lose sight of cold realities. That Peking wants very much to sit on the Security Council and other UN bodies belongs in this category.

ᔑ ᔑ ᔑ

Nothing else that took place at the 20th Assembly, except
perhaps the Pope's visit, had as much significance as these two
episodes directly connected with China.

PART II
THE ANGELS

⋙ 10 ⋘

THE TRAGEDY OF THE
MISSING "O"

The publisher of an American liberal magazine once remarked that "most of the problems of the UN could be traced to the tragedy of the missing 'O.' "

The official title, United Nations Organization, calls for three initials, and all three are used virtually everywhere in the world—except in the United States, where the third word, and consequently the third initial, have been dropped. The English, although under the influence of the American abbreviation, often write and speak all three initials. In France the three letters have even given birth to an expression, *les onusiens*, which means those who work for the UN. And the USSR is punctilious about the three initials, except that the Cyrillic alphabet adds an extra "O" and the "N" is written like a "H," but their "OOH" also has an onomatopoeic sound.

Once the "O" was dropped by the Americans, slips of the tongue were to be expected. That they would occur with disturbing frequence and in high places came, however, as a surprise. It has happened in the General Assembly and in committee sessions, in informal gatherings at the delegates' lounge, and at formal receptions at the missions. It has happened to the chief delegate of the United States and to practically every other ambassador at the UN. It has happened to the Secretary-General of the United Nations. Their tongues have slipped and "United States" has been spoken in the place of "United Nations."

The symbolism was too obvious not to be pounced upon and dissected by those who are convinced—or who are intent on convincing others—that the United Nations Organization is merely an appendix of the United States of America.

Quite a few arguments have been marshaled in support of this point of view. For instance, a visit to United Nations Headquarters can be described in terms justifying the slip of the tongue. Slogans about an international, polyglot UN, like the one about it being a place where one meets such interesting foreigners, are easily exploded. Perhaps the foreigners one meets are interesting, but statistically there are not many of them. Of some four thousand persons who work at UN Headquarters, fully two thirds, not being subject to "geographical distribution," are United States citizens. Of the remaining thirteen hundred that are culled from member states, by far the largest contingent, some four hundred consists of Americans who serve as international civil servants. (The American quota is by far the largest for the whole organization, in accordance with the criteria set down by the United Nations.)

The slogan about a multilingual UN can also be exploded. There are five official languages—Chinese, English, French, Spanish, Russian—and of these English and French are "working languages." In the General Assembly and the Economic and Social Council, Spanish also has been accepted as a working language. Delegates from countries speaking one of the official languages are punctilious in the usage of their native language when making a speech. The only exceptions are the delegates of Formosa, known in the UN as the Republic of China, who prefer to speak in English rather than in Chinese. Also, French- and Spanish-speaking delegates always clamor for the prompt distribution of documents in their language.

But in effect the only language that counts at the UN is English. It remains the one and only *lingua franca*. Even the French-speaking African delegates, who in 1960 did so much for a rebirth of French in the UN, have since then found themselves obliged to learn to speak English.

On another front, the daily and meaningful contact with what is happening in the outside world, is through the American press and American television. In an organization where everyone, from ambassadors and under-secretaries down to the lowliest translator, is expected to be aware of what is happening in the outside world, the channels of communication are thus supplied by U.S. information media, which naturally present an American interpretation of world events. Of course the delegates receive newspapers from home (usually late by days or weeks) and several missions receive a daily cabled digest of their own press. But the first and strongest impact is always made at the breakfast table by the New York papers, and specifically by *The New York Times*, known in UN circles as "The Bible."

Even in the food served at UN Headquarters, American influence shines through an unconvincing effort to establish a certain cosmopolitan flavor. The cafeteria is much like any other in the city of New York, and no attempt is made to depart from standard cafeteria fare. In the delegates' dining room, however, there is a pretense at international cuisine; in fact, every day a typical dish of a different country is featured. These national dishes are immensely popular with civic-minded American ladies, who patronize in droves what they consider to be an exotic restaurant. Diplomats from the country honored, on the other hand, are careful never to order the dish thus featured, which they have learned by painful experience to be a tasteless travesty of the national cuisine. A few days after being elected, Thant invited one of his under-secretaries to lunch in the restaurant; on that day a Burmese national dish was by coincidence displayed on the menu. The Secretary-General pulled out his pen, corrected the spelling, and ordered something else.

꿍   꿍   꿍

Many delegates, however, do not take exception to the Manhattan personality of the United Nations. They happen to be enthusiastic New Yorkers, and indeed feel much happier in the United States than in their own country, as becomes blatantly evident when a political upheaval at home threatens them with the dire possibility of having to go back and actually live for a while among their countrymen. This is true almost without exception of the Central Americans; delegates from those countries almost to a man have been educated in U.S. colleges and often have also gone to an American high school; it is quite common for a Central American delegate to have spent more years of his life in the United States than back home. Although their countries are located right next to the U.S., they are singularly reluctant to return even for a short vacation, as if once they set foot on the native soil there would be present danger that they might not be able to return to New York.

Diplomats from those South American countries facing the Caribbean have on the whole the same reactions as their Central American colleagues. Those from the other countries of South America (particularly Argentina, Brazil, Chile) feel much less the need to be in the United States, and in fact many of them openly voice their preference for Europe.

Next to the Latin Americans the Asians are the ones most attached to New York. Not only the Indians, but also the Filipinos, the Ceylonese, and to a lesser degree the Pakistanis. They are not, however, quite as reluctant to go home as the Central Americans, provided they are assured of returning to Manhattan. As to the Africans, although relative newcomers they have already developed a visible preference for New York over the home country.

To understand why it seems that so many of the UN diplomats let their national identity fade, and by a process of mimetism become faithful imitators of a New Yorker in habits and customs, it should be remembered that at least three fourths of them come from countries in such dismal conditions of backwardness that any Western city would look like paradise in terms of comfort, cleanliness, and excitement. To be transferred from their dingy, sleepy capital to the most vital and most diverse of all the great cities of the Western world is an intoxicating experience from which many of them never quite recover.

Their wives usually have a more ambivalent reaction. As a rule they never master English as well as their husbands, and they never quite blend into American life. But since diplomatic salaries are usually munificent for envoys of backward countries, the fairyland world of shopping in New York lies wide open before their fluttering provincial souls. The large Manhattan department stores have long since awakened to these insatiable and affluent customers and have mustered multilingual vendeuses, and developed public relations gimmicks aimed primarily at the wives of UN diplomats. These sales campaigns reach their orgiastic climax in the autumn, when the annual session of the General Assembly brings wives of delegates to Manhattan by the hundreds.

‿ﬃ　‿ﬃ　‿ﬃ

Shopping on Fifth and Madison—night-clubbing in the East Fifties—Broadway and the theater district—concerts and art galleries—elegant restaurants and exclusive clubs—sailing in Long Island and riding in Westchester County.

The glitter and glamor, the pomp and circumstance of New York cast a mundane spell over the delegates from five continents who every September flock to the metropolis with wives, mistresses, courtiers. The General Assembly session is the pretext and the UN impartially spreads its protective umbrella of respectability over underdeveloped Afro-Asians and sophisticated Europeans alike. One hundred foreign ministers, and in their tow, by the thousands, experts and counselors, senators and deputies, cynical disheveled foreign correspondents and cynical pommaded third secretaries. They roll into New

York and the UN for the great annual jamboree dedicated to world peace.

But they would not come so eagerly if they were not encountering the lights of Broadway and the towers of Manhattan. And so New York is host to the world, and every autumn the United Nations Organization finds itself a little more involved, a little more integrated into the United States of America.

ை   ை   ை

Perhaps the sleek young Central American "diplomat" was right. His father owns some of the biggest coffee plantations and the only television station in one of the tiniest Central American republics, so the local dictator had benevolently made the son an ambassador and sent him to represent the country at the 18th General Assembly. The youthful ambassador was at a party given by the chairman of the Latin American group, listening to a small circle of fellow delegates while some excellent after-dinner coffee was being served in the living room.

The talk was about the meeting of the First Committee that same afternoon, where the US delegate had made the usual slip of the tongue, saying "United States" for "United Nations." Another member of the US delegation was in the group, a tall, lanky press attaché. The Latin Americans were kidding him; the conversation was in English; someone mentioned the story of the missing "O." The young Central American had never heard the joke, and it had to be repeated for his benefit, for he was not as bright as he was rich. Finally understanding, he commented, in a proud display of his knowledge of American slang: "For crying out loud: What the hell is there to complain about? The UN should thank its lucky stars it's in Manhattan for keeps."

»» 11 ««

ARCHANGEL SAM

To label publicly the United Nations as a "tool of United States foreign policy" is done only in unfriendly quarters, such as Moscow and Peking. And yet at UN headquarters this thesis is also often discussed in the lounges and corridors, most frequently (oddly enough) by delegates of countries friendly or even allied to the United States. Always in private conversation, and almost invariably qualified by a gesture and the remark "But of course they pay so much of the bill" or its equivalent.

Any of these diplomats would recoil in horror at the idea of being quoted. Yet the central assumption upon which is based the daily activity of most of those who work in the UN, whether they be members of delegations or Secretariat staffers, is that "who pays the piper calls the tune." On the other hand some of the professional diplomats, including most of the good political brains among the delegates, consider too oversimplified this line of reasoning according to which political power over the UN derives from financial support. As a member of the Egyptian delegation once put it during the days of Suez: "If the UN had existed in the 19th century Queen Victoria's England would have had political control over it, just as America does today, but instead of being generous like the Americans, the English would have found a way of making some sort of finan-

cial profit out of it." This somewhat cynical remark underlined the conviction shared by most seasoned diplomats at
Turtle Bay that the US would have an overwhelming influence over the United Nations whether or not it did as much for
it financially as it seems to do.

Moreover, these knowledgeable professionals not only
insist on divorcing overwhelming political influence from overwhelming financial participation; they also like to point out that
United States influence works along three main lines. The first
one is of a negative character; it can best be summed up by
saying that if Washington does not want something to be done
either by the General Assembly or by the Security Council (and
without having to use its veto power), it will simply not be
done.

On the other hand, any initiative of genuine scope taken
by the UN must satisfy political needs and interests of American foreign policy. It is not sufficient that it does not run counter
to American interests, except in those occasional instances
where there is enough of a controversy, of a debate inside the
United States about where the national interests happen to lie.
An interesting corollary of this is that UN action will never
serve the interests of the URSS or of the Soviet bloc except in
those occasional instances when there is a Soviet-American
coincidence of interests; but UN action will (and often does)
go counter to the interests of the Soviet bloc. Another corollary
is that UN actions will not run counter to the interests of US
allies—except when Washington, because of some more urgent
demand in the pursuit of its foreign and domestic policies,
feels that its allies should be badly treated by the UN, as was
the case during the Suez crisis.

The third proposition is that any course of action that
Washington feels must become UN policy, does become UN
policy. While Turtle Bay professionals agree on the first two
postulates, there is a wide difference of opinion as regards the
third. Many diplomats are convinced that this is no longer true
in fact, that it ceased to be true as the fifties came to an end
Some mention 1958 and the Lebanese crisis as marking the

change; others prefer to take the 1960 Assembly that brought in sixteen African members; but this is more of a difference about chronology. They all seem to agree that ever since the voting balance was upset by the flood of Afro-Asian states, Washington no longer has the capacity to make the UN adopt a certain course of action, unless it enlists beforehand the support of most of the Afro-Asians.

Yet there is among the professionals a small group of seasoned veterans, mostly from some of the Commonwealth and the South American countries more friendly to the US, who are convinced that Washington's third prerogative has not been lost, or even curtailed, in recent years. All these diplomats will acknowledge is that nowadays the US delegation has to negotiate much more in earnest than was the case before 1960 whenever Washington is intent on pushing through a resolution, and that these negotiations have to be conducted primarily with Afro-Asian delegations. Once a consensus is arrived at, the result is achieved for all practical purposes. It is not merely a question of counting votes; neither the Soviet bloc or Western European delegations, as the case may be, relish standing in open opposition to an American-Afro-Asian alliance in the Assembly or one of its organs, however temporary that alliance may be. Therefore all the maneuvering and the counter-negotiating is pursued before the US delegation has mustered enough support from the Afro-Asians.

Even when there is a visible reluctance on the part of the Afro-Asian delegations, Washington will not feel stymied if it considers the issue at stake sufficiently important, for it can bring pressure to bear on practically every African and Asian capital, primarily by current economic and financial assistance —or, even more effectively, in terms of what is forthcoming in the immediate future in this politically fertile field of American foreign aid.

This does not mean that Washington will always insist on mustering the necessary Afro-Asian votes, but simply that it can if it wants to. Sometimes the political or diplomatic gains will not be worth bringing sufficient pressure to bear

on a majority of Afro-Asian countries who are obviously
opposed in the first place. In this case, incidentally, there usually
is not a complete unanimity in the counsels of US government,
for the State Department will have gauged in advance the
Afro-Asian opposition and a minority of State and White House
advisers will have come to nurture serious doubts about the
wisdom of pushing the issue *à outrance*. One important example of this was offered by the Article 19 crisis. There was
the strongest possible reluctance on the part of almost all the
Afro-Asians to consent to a "showdown" on the Assembly
floor (while the "safe" Latin American votes in this instance
were more than usually safe, since a majority of the Latin
American delegates were not as terrified by the prospect of a
confrontation as were their Afro-Asian colleagues). As the
Afro-Asian feeling on the matter became increasingly evident
during the winter and spring of 1965, those who opposed the
"showdown" in the State Department—a small and not very
influential group at the time—saw their viewpoint being taken
increasingly into account by the White House. Finally, the
administration decided to back down.

The premise, however, remains unblemished. Washington
is able to make the United Nations adopt a certain policy, provided its own determination doesn't waver.

ᘐ   ᘐ   ᘐ

While it is understandable that these facts of UN life are
never publicly mentioned by delegates or Secretariat officials, it
is more difficult to understand why they are almost never
brought to light in independent studies of the United Nations
by US universities or by individual American scholars. On the
other hand, in comparable studies conducted in countries
friendly to the United States—and for that matter in the more
responsible press in these countries—this overwhelming American influence over the UN is often mentioned and discussed,
when it is not simply taken for granted.

There are several explanations for this glossing over, none of them satisfactory in itself, but perhaps sufficient when taken in the aggregate. For one thing, there is not a sufficient detachment on the part of American scholars and serious students of UN affairs. Not in the sense of intellectual integrity, but rather in terms of a lack of perspective induced by their inescapable national background—as well as by literally being too close to the UN, even geographically (the vast majority of learned studies originating in universities, for example, are from New England and Eastern seaboard institutions of higher learning).

Practically everyone in the United States and a great many people in other countries are convinced that the United Nations is supported financially by the US taxpayer. They vary only in estimating the extent of such support. Americans are prone to believe that their money pays for almost the entire cost of the world organization, while people from other countries tend to consider the US contribution simply the largest of all, although they are persuaded that it insures the very survival of the UN.

What is not commonly realized, however, is that the United States economy on balance makes money out of the United Nations. Professor John G. Stoessinger, of Columbia University and Hunter College, says in *Financing the United Nations System*, published in 1964 by the authoritative Brookings Institution of Washington:

> It has often been said that the presence of the United Nations has made New York City the "capital of the world." This prestige has not remained altogether intangible. Indeed, a substantial amount of money flows into the economy of New York City every year as a direct result of the presence there of the United Nations. An estimate of specific items follows for the year 1962.
>
> First, during 1962, the United Nations paid $40 million in salaries and wages to its staff. Of the 4,500 recipients, 3,000 were stationed at Headquarters. Their share was 64 percent, or $26 million. Assuming that approximately 5 percent or 1.3 million was spent abroad, the

amount that flowed into the city was about 25 million. Second, UNICEF paid $1.4 million in salaries and wages. Allowing for a similar deduction, the city gained $1.3 million. Third, staff allowances of $2.3 million were paid. Allowing the same ratios as for salaries and the same deduction, the amount is $2.2 million. Fourth, the United Nations spent $2.5 million for travel of staff including appointments, transfers, and separations. Of this sum, 40 percent, or $1 million, may have been spent in New York. Fifth, the overhead expenses of the United Nations, including equipment, maintenance, operation, rental, utilities, supplies, and services came to $9 million. The cost for Headquarters was about $7 million. Sixth, the maintenance of missions and staff discussed above comes to $25 million. Eighty percent of this amount, or roughly $20 million, flows into the city. Seventh, New York profits from the presence of journalists and representatives of nongovernmental organizations who are accredited to the United Nations. An estimate of $5,000 for each of the 250 permanently accredited journalists and of $1,000 for each transient journalist amounts to $2 million. In addition, 150 nongovernmental organization representatives are permanently residing in New York City. Their salaries plus those of several hundred transients add another $2 million.

Hence, if the above approximations are reasonable, an amount of more than $60 million flows into the economy of New York City as a result of the presence there of the United Nations.

The impact of the Organization on the New York City budget involves items on the plus and on the minus side. The city's obligation to provide added police protection is an example of the latter. During the Fifteenth Session of the General Assembly, an extraordinarily large number of heads-of-states, prime ministers, and other dignitaries congregated in New York City. This posed great problems for the police. The costs involved led to requests for a federal subsidy, which, in turn, led to a congressional hearing and a subsequent report from the city's Budget Director.

The total picture shows then that an annual amount of roughly $82 million accrues to the American economy primarily as a direct result of United Nations Headquarters location in New York. This "hidden saving" is slightly more than the combined United States assessments for the regular budget, UNEF, and ONUC in 1962. The presence of the International Bank for Reconstruction and Development and the International Monetary Fund in Washington, D.C., increases the above "saving."

It does not take a financial expert to realize that the UN, its delegations and its staff, represent a considerable source of income for the country of location; oddly enough this piece of knowledge has not permeated to the general public, particularly in the host country. What is even more surprising is that no inkling of it seems to be available to those who work in the UN. Among the several inferiority complexes of staffers toward Americans, the matter of money looms large. Moreover, the nagging fear that US financial support for the UN might not continue forever has cast its shadow from the early years. In the 1960s, with the UN financial crisis gaining in intensity and drama almost from month to month, this fear increased visibly. Specifically it centers on the attitude of the US Congress. While it is assumed at headquarters that basically the State Department and the US government as a whole are sympathetic to the UN and quite willing to support it, the attitude of the Senate and the House of Representatives is held to be quite another matter.

When a senator or a member of the House requests information about UN finances and their relation to the US, this is at once referred by the UN offices in Washington back to headquarters, where a number of senior officials ponder the matter and decide on how the information should be supplied. This usually means that it should be made to look forthright and exclusively factual, while not forgetting the public relations angle.

≫ 12 ≪

*HOW INTERNATIONAL
IS AN AMERICAN?*

After a committee debate some time ago during which the
Soviet delegate had held forth for the umpteenth time on the
subject of "American domination" of the Secretariat, a junior
member of the Polish delegation had some comments for a
group of colleagues at a dinner party. He had been prodded by
an equally junior French diplomat, whose mission had not received with disfavor the Soviet speech, once more underscoring
that hegemony by "les Anglo-Saxons" to which De Gaulle was
at the time referring quite often. Everyone was in a convivial
mood, and the Pole gaily proceeded to prove that criticism of
the big brother could now be indulged in by another member
of the Soviet bloc. "The thesis is correct," he said, "but the
arguments will make no impression on our American friends.
The Russian delegate was too heavy-handed."

"What argument would impress the Americans, in your
view?" asked his French colleague.

"Quoting the Bible," replied the Pole at once. When the
laughter had subsided, he continued: "Where the Bible speaks
of the original sin. The UN Secretariat carries the burden of
the original sin of those three thousand original members, most
of them Anglo-Saxons."

"I don't recall any biblical passage to that effect," observed
the French diplomat.

"You will if you read once more the book by the first Secretary-General, Mr. Trygve Lie," said the Pole. I assure you he spells out the UN's original sin."

⁊   ⁊   ⁊

When the UN came into being American techniques and methods were adopted as a matter of course, and once the world body had chosen New York for its haven this became even more pronounced. In fact, the introduction of such techniques and working procedures seemed to many of those able to look at it with a sense of detachment a fairly sensible and not overly supine way of acknowledging American leadership.

Similarly, everyone accepted without demurring the flood of Americans sweeping in with the three thousand appointees to which the young Polish diplomat was referring. In his book Trygve Lie says of the episode: ". . . and I appointed some 2,900 staff members in the course of 1946, predominantly from areas of the world where available persons could be found. It should be added that a high proportion of these temporary appointees fully proved their worth and later joined the career service."

The vast majority of appointees were Americans. It surely could not have been otherwise; a very persuasive argument was that during these early years the United States paid an even higher proportion of total UN costs than it does today. The Americans, most of them with a bureaucratic background, brought into the newborn UN all the methods and practices as well as the foibles of US federal administration. Among these peculiarly American administrative practices were the preoccupation with checks and balances and the ensuing fragmentation of authority; the tendency to have an orgy of meetings in order to "bring everyone into the act" and thus dilute responsibility; a fascination with paperwork to the point of making a staff member invariably invest much more time in writing reports about a specific task than in executing the task; an

indulgent attitude toward waste and leisure inherent in an
affluent society. All these are traits easily identifiable in today's
Secretariat; the years have done little to attenuate them.

The irony was that while the UN adopted all of the worst
features of the US bureaucratic machinery, it did not seem
able to assimilate to any appreciable degree any of the good
qualities shared by most Americans, particularly Americans
with a good educational and social background. Things like a
sense of humor, bubbling energy, the will to get things done, a
sympathetic and amused tolerance for exotic ways, an under-
lying respect for European scholarship and experience. The
explanation is that Trygve Lie simply did not recruit the best
Americans. Unlike his successor, Dag Hammarskjold, the first
Secretary-General did not possess discernment and a feeling for
quality to discover persons of the highest caliber; nor did he
possess those qualities of intellect and charm that would make
such persons volunteer their services and be eager to work with
him, as happened so often to Hammarskjold.

It should be added, in all fairness, that Lie was hobbled
from the outset by an amazingly shortsighted lack of cooperation among the higher echelons of the Washington administration, coupled with a conspiracy by certain influential members
of the middle echelons to introduce into the UN Secretariat
Americans who were communists or their fellow travelers. The
first of these twin handicaps besetting the Secretary-General
became visible with the recruitment that would undoubtedly
set the tone for the entire American contingent: that of the
Assistant Secretary-General of US nationality, the senior
American on the Secretariat. Says Trygve Lie on this matter:

> The choice of a qualified American to fill the post
> proved to be a disappointing experience. I turned to Mr.
> Stettinius for help, but it soon appeared that Mr. Byrnes
> wanted to handle this matter himself. Many well qualified
> Americans were suggested in private conversation, among
> them Adlai Stevenson and Milton S. Eisenhower, brother
> of the General. Not hearing from Mr. Byrnes for some
> time, I made preliminary approaches to both; but they indi-

cated they could not accept. Mr. Byrnes finally submitted but one nominee, John B. Hutson, at that time Under Secretary of Agriculture. A native of Kentucky, he was originally an expert in tobacco products, a good friend of both President Truman and Secretary of State Byrnes, with a long record of service in the Democratic party. I cannot say that I was pleased with this procedure of advancing a single name only. I appointed "Jolly Jack" as Mr. Hutson was affectionately called by his colleagues— and he served during the Secretariat's initial, and rapid, build-up until he resigned in the spring of 1947.

Moreover, Trygve Lie was handicapped by the placement of American communists and their fellow travelers in the Secretariat, through the efforts of a few influential middle echelon officials in the Washington administration who were themselves covert party members or sympathizers. Much has been written about this in the United States, often in a highly emotional vein. Yet many of the pertinent facts have not yet come to light and perhaps never will. Many are persuaded that Alger Hiss, who was convicted for perjury, functioned as a Communist agent (according to Whittaker Chambers and others) in Washington, where he was in a position to recommend the employment of a number of Americans by the Secretariat. Hiss had served in important positions at the Dumbarton Oaks, Yalta, and San Francisco meetings. At Dumbarton Oaks, where the big powers met in the autumn of 1944 to hammer out the blueprint for the United Nations, Hiss served as executive secretary of the meeting. At Yalta, where President Roosevelt agreed to concede three UN seats and votes to the Soviet Union by treating Byelorussia and the Ukraine as sovereign and independent states, Hiss was an influential member of the US delegation. At Yalta he was slated for a key role at the coming San Francisco Conference, where the Charter was drafted and signed. Wrote *Time* magazine, in its issue of 16 April 1945:

The Secretary-General for the San Francisco Conference was named at Yalta but announced only last week—

lanky, Harvard-trained Alger Hiss, one of the State Department's brighter young men. Alger Hiss was one of the Harvard Law School students whose records earned them the favor of Professor (now Justice) Felix Frankfurter and a year as secretary to the late Justice Oliver Wendell Holmes. He was drafted from a New York law firm by the New Deal in 1933, joined the State Department in 1936, accompanied President Roosevelt to Yalta. At San Francisco, he and his Secretariat of 300 (mostly Americans) will have the drudging, thankless clerk's job of copying, translating and publishing, running the thousands of paperclip and pencil chores of an international meeting. But Alger Hiss will be an important figure there. As secretary-general, managing the agenda, he will have a lot to say behind the scenes about who gets the breaks.

Someone like Alger Hiss was evidently in a position to sponsor, with a reasonable chance of success, American candidates for employment by the Secretariat. The storm broke a few years later, at the height of McCarthyism. Says Trygve Lie:

Furthermore the situation lent itself to demagogic exploitation by politicians and publicists not encumbered with principles or a sense of responsibility. That Communist spies for Russia were capable of doing great damage to the country, the atomic spy cases fully demonstrated. If so trusted and respected a government official as Alger Hiss could be convicted for perjury in denying he had spied for Russia, was any government official above suspicion, especially if he had been associated with the New Deal and the wartime alliance with Russia under Roosevelt? If there was one Hiss, might there not be a hundred more who had cunningly wormed their way into positions of influence and authority? Therefore many otherwise sensible people thought Senator McCarthy might be right when he launched his red-hunting by charging there were twice that number. . . .

Then, in October 1952, the Internal Security Subcommittee of the United States Senate Judiciary Committee moved to New York and held a series of public hearings.

In these a total of eighteen United Nations staff members pleaded the Fifth Amendment. As I read the transcript of the testimony in each case I was more and more convinced that these staff members had gravely and irresponsibly transgressed the Staff Regulations. . . .

The public outcry in the United States, whipped up by elements of the press which had never been friendly to the United Nations, grew to appalling proportions, while the morale of the Secretariat slumped badly.

Even adding resignations by American staff members to dismissals by the Secretary-General, the total number of Americans suspected of subversion was a small fraction of those employed by the Secretariat. But the damage done to the organization, as pointed out by Trygve Lie, was considerable, and its repercussions were felt for many years. Even today much of the ill-will toward the UN in American conservative circles can be traced back, at least in part, to those episodes of 1952 in which irresponsible accusations became inextricably entwined with a legitimate concern for national security. The investigation and clearance procedures established at the time by the US federal government have since then made it highly improbable that an American considered a "security risk" will be able to find employment in the Secretariat. In fact, nowadays it is much easier to locate a genuine Marxist-Leninist among the Latin-American staffers than among those of US nationality.

The real handicap for the UN, at present, is that the caliber of the individual American staff member, which was never high, tends to drop a little lower every year while the American contingent in the Secretariat continues to be by far the largest. Many observers attribute this to the bitter memories of the McCarthy days, which tend to discourage the more enlightened and educated American from seeking employment in the world organization. In reality this explanation no longer accounts for the trend. Two factors are prominent in making it ever more difficult for the UN to recruit well-qualified Americans. The rising achievements of American diplomacy in recent years tend to attract the best type of university graduate into the US foreign service, while the discouraging performance of the United Nations has had the opposite effect. As American corporations are becoming increasingly involved in overseas ventures there has been a demand for young men with about the same academic and foreign language assets that would make them potential UN material. American big business offers these young men financial incentives that could not be matched outside private enterprise.

The prospects for quality and performance among UN personnel are melancholy as regards future recruitment of Americans for the Secretariat. Nor is it much of a consolation to point out that the level of intelligence and educational background of the vast majority of Afro-Asians, Latin Americans, and Eastern Europeans who join the United Nations Secretariat is even lower than that of their American colleagues.

⫸ 13 ⫷

LESSER ANGELS SPEAK GERMAN

When the Security Council met early in 1963 to discuss the admission of Kuwait to membership in the United Nations, several of the representatives around the horseshoe-shaped table voiced their approbation, but made pointed remarks about the little country's affluence and their hope that some of its millions would trickle down into the depleted UN coffers. The general tenor of such remarks was held at the time to be in questionable taste, coming from a body as august as the Security Council, whose central preoccupation is war and peace, and who was then exercising one of its ancillary functions, that of favorably recommending to the General Assembly an application for membership.

There was refreshing candor in the wistful and tactless manner in which some delegates harped on the wealth and the expected generosity of the oil-gorged Arabian sheikdom. UN finances were at the time already tumbling toward their nadir as the dispute over Article 19 grew shrill. Here was someone wanting to join the club who could set things right if he had a mind too; a hundred million or so dollars would hardly make a dent in Kuwait's enormous riches, while it would make all the difference in pulling the world organization out of its bleak financial morass. The epilogue, was anticlimatic, as is not unusual in such cases; Kuwait did produce some cash as a gift to the UN, but it turned out to be a small sop (five million dollars) to the hopes that had been expressed in the Council Chamber.

It would be fascinating to speculate on the kind of speeches to be heard around the horseshoe-shaped table if Germany were to apply for UN membership. Kuwait, a prospective Maecenas, ultimately dashed everyone's hopes; but the Federal Republic of Germany has over a number of years been proferring substantial backing in cold cash for a considerable number of worthwhile activities pursued by the UN family. Bonn is aware, however, that it cannot realistically aspire to be received into the fold because of the stand maintained by the USSR.

Still, a reversal of the Soviet position is not altogether unthinkable, in which case welcoming speeches around the Council table would not be in a wistful vein, speculating on what could be contributed, as in the case of Kuwait. Permanent and non-permanent members could cite hard facts on gifts, grants, and loans that bring German voluntary contributions to an impressive total, and which stand comparison with those of the affluent UN members, and in fact surpass most. Moreover, the Federal Republic is a member of all of the UN specialized agencies, and one of the five largest contributors, together with the United States, USSR, Britain, and France. During the Congo operation Bonn subscribed freely to the Congo Civilian Fund, and purchased ten million dollars worth of the bonds issued by the UN. This was the third largest purchase (the United States matched all other purchases and the United Kingdom bought 12 million dollars worth), and it came at a moment when its political and psychological impact was as welcome to the UN as the ten million. The bond issue was a stopgap measure engineered by the Secretary-General, under the coaching of Washington, for the purpose of weathering the heavy financial pressure on the organization at a time when the United Nations was spending 10 million dollars every week to keep UN Congo Operation going. The German pur-

chase of bonds came at a time when a number of member
states had already made it clear that they would not even pay
their assessments for the Congo operation, let alone purchase
bonds. During the sixties the Federal Republic has tended to
increase its voluntary contributions. For instance, at the annual
pledging conferences for the Expanded Programme of Technical Assistance and the Special Fund (now known as the UN
Development Program) the German Observer announced on
almost every occasion that his government was increasing its
contribution by a generous percentage.

This continuing generosity on the part of the Bonn government should not be attributed primarily to altruistic motives. Very few members could claim to extend financial
support to the UN for purely altruistic motives. The Scandinavian countries come closest to this admirable motivation,
for their readiness to donate has become proverbial and in the
aggregate their contributions represent more on a per capita
basis than those of any other group of countries.

In the case of the Bonn government, however, there are
compelling considerations of foreign policy. In the first place
its largesse has enabled it to secure a *sui generis* position
inside the world organization.

Since the number of countries who actually support the
UN financially does not reach an even dozen (over one hundred
member states contribute ludicrously small sums), the Federal
Republic has joined a very select company that wields considerable power inside the UN. And in reality the status of
the German Observer is not too far beneath that of the envoy
of a major power. Even though protocol denies him most out-
ward signs of prestige, next to the US permanent representative, he is the Western diplomat most courted by the Africans,
the Asians, and some Latin Americans. Moreover, his fellow
Western ambassadors will always seek his views when a question of any importance is under debate.

Yet the growing influence of the Federal Republic inside
the United Nations does not prevent Bonn from considering

the world body with grave misgivings and to have an ambivalent attitude regarding eventual membership. For while the Africans and Asians can be kept friendly by a sagacious distribution of grants and loans, Soviet hostility will undoubtedly take an acute form when Peking gains it seat within the UN. Since presumably Washington would not permit Formosa to be expelled simultaneously, the presence of two Chinas in the UN will give Moscow a persuasive precedent for the admission of Eastern Germany were the Federal Republic to become a full-fledged member state. This eventuality has worried Bonn over the years, but at long last the obvious conclusion has been accepted: Germany could gain little by formally joining the UN; the risk of having Ulbricht's puppet state join would be considerable. Thus for the foreseeable future a German Observer will continue at the United Nations, and he will continue to rank in importance with the permanent representatives of the great powers.

PART III
THE PLAYERS

⋙ 14 ⋘

TOGETHERNESS AMONG DIPLOMATS

No political show on earth is as abundantly covered and tele-vised as the one at United Nations Headquarters. Yet, most of what occurs at Headquarters of genuine political significance is never displayed to the public eye on a printed page or a TV screen. One reason is that much more happens at closed meet-ings of committees than at those open to the press. For that matter, even the Security Council, in its search for consensus, holds many more closed meetings than it officially admits, for the most part scheduled immediately in advance of an official session. In recent times the Council tends to eschew public debate unless a measure of consensus has been attained before-hand in a closed session or in informal negotiations among individual members. This has emerged as one of the more encouraging aspects of the tacit cooperation between the United States and the Soviet Union in the years following the missile crisis.

In the sixties a different kind of private gathering has achieved a high political status: the meetings of "groups." They usually take place in conference room 5 or 6 in the first basement of the General Assembly building. Until 1960, the Latin American group of twenty countries was virtually the only one which met with regularity, and its meetings acquired a semi-official status. As Cuba began to be ostracized by a growing number of its hemisphere neighbors, these meetings were shorn of any formal trappings, so that the representative of Havana could be kept out without too much embarrassment. Cuba's tacit expulsion brought the membership down to nineteen, but Jamaica and Trinidad and Tobago became independent two years ago and demanded to join the Latin American group. The Spanish-speaking majority could not think of any good reason why they should not, so it was agreed to accept these English-speaking Caribbeans as honorary Latin American on strictly geographical grounds.

After 1960, as the Afro-Asians soared in number to gain consequence in the UN hierarchy, they began to meet frequently as a group. The accredited correspondents began to give increased coverage to meetings of the Afro-Asian group (although in their dispatches they never used the title of "African-Asian group" as requested by the Africans). Ever more cognizant of their numerical advantage over any other continent, in the last three years the Africans have taken to meeting among themselves while continuing to participate in the Afro-Asian meetings.

The vogue for group meetings gained a new dimension with the "group of 75." This outwardly impressive supergroup is not confined to any geographical or cultural background, but rather gathers in its fold all members of the underprivileged *tiers monde*. It comprises the Africans, the Asians, and the Latin Americans—plus a few odd gate crashers—and represents a direct outgrowth of a mammoth gathering for the purpose of discussing the injustices of foreign trade as they affect the chances of the poor countries ever becoming less poor; this was the UN Conference on Trade and Development, convened in Geneva in 1964 with the reluctant participation of Western countries.

The "75" could have come to mean more than a mere agglutination of countries with common grievances in the crucial field of international commerce. At one point they were about to develop into a massive pressure group against the rich Western powers. This potential nuisance value of the "75" did not go unnoticed in the world's great trading centers; in fact, when a Trade and Development Board was set up to follow through on the Geneva conference, the West insisted on a voting procedure that would in effect circumvent the supposedly sacrosanct United Nations doctrine of "one country, one vote." There was an outraged outcry from the *tiers monde*, but the West stuck to its guns, politely pointing out that ten members of its group, who could be out-voted seven to one by the "75," nonetheless had a bigger participation in global trade than all of Africa, Asia, and Latin America. (As a matter of fact these ten Western countries account for over ninety percent of all the world's commerce.)

A true confrontation between the West and the *tiers monde* never took place at the UN, because this Afro-Asian-Latin American entente of the "75," which had never been too convincing, began to split asunder as Latin American countries, led by Brazil and Argentina, gradually realized that they had indeed very little in common with the Afro-Asians and decided to align themselves more closely with the United States and the West in general.

Today the "75," which at their emergence during the final and dramatic phase of the Geneva trade conference had been hailed as a closing of ranks by the world's underprivileged and over-exploited nations, have deteriorated into a brittle and unwieldy cohort. These delegations find it increasingly difficult to stand together even when a question which is obviously to their common interest comes under debate.

During that same week of August, 1965, when the United States made its peace with the Soviet Union over the application of Article 19, the Latin American group took a position against the Africans by formally opposing the pretensions of Quaison-Sackey of Ghana to be re-elected president of the General Assembly. Although the issue had nothing whatsoever to do with trade and development, many observers felt that it had sounded the deathknell for the "75," as it was indicative that the Latin Americans were fed up with the black continent in general and its UN representatives in particular.

ᗣ   ᗣ   ᗣ

There are other groups at the UN that actually coordinate their policies and tactics much more effectively than the Africans, Asians, or Latin Americans, and whose meetings usually turn out to be much more productive, even though they rarely yield headlines. For these several groups, however diverse politically and ideologically, all share in a passion for discretion and reticence.

Politically, the most cohesive of these is the Communist group, which meets often and for long hours at the headquarters of the Soviet mission. Delegates from communist countries (communist is a word definitively barred from UN jargon; these countries are always referred to as Socialist), when summoned to the modern apartment building on the East Seventies purchased by the USSR, show up punctually. All those summoned are accounted for; there is no playing hookey, as some Latin American delegates are noted for doing at their own caucuses. The Yugoslavs have not been invited to these meetings since 1948; and the Albanians have been conspicuous for their absence in recent years; no one seems to know exactly when Peking's spokesmen at the UN ceased to be welcome at their big brother's mission.

Coordination and smooth teamwork achieved by meeting regularly are by no means a monopoly of the Soviet bloc. Western delegations can be equally effective by the same device. The Scandinavians have been meeting since 1947 (Denmark and Norway, founding members of the UN, were joined on November 19, 1946, by Sweden and Iceland, while Finland was not admitted until the "package deal" of December 14, 1955).[1] Their superb performance at the UN over the years

[1] New members are admitted upon the recommendation of the Security Council endorsed by a two-thirds majority of the General Assembly. As the result of a bargain struck in the Council between

owes much to the fact that all Scandinavian delegates are accustomed to functioning unobtrusively as members of the same team when important issues are at stake (this includes the Finns, much to the annoyance of the Russians).

Other Western countries did not feel the urge to meet regularly in early years, since Western points of view were seldom successfully challenged inside the UN. With the numerical superiority of the Afro-Asians emerging, however, the need for presenting a common front became evident on many occasions, and frequent group meetings evolved as a necessity. These Western meetings used to gather delegations along almost exclusively political lines, with the NATO countries feeling more than any others the need to confer often. However, with an ever-widening band of economic and trade issues appearing in the spectrum of UN activities, Western meetings began to follow a pattern of economic rather than political alliances. Thus, UN representatives of European Common Market countries began to meet.

With the advent of the Geneva Trade Conference two non-Europeans grafted themselves onto the European group. Japan, one of the world leaders in foreign trade, joined with Western Europe to discuss a common strategy for resisting sweeping demands by the "75"; and then South Africa (also an important trading nation) demanded to be included and was quietly accepted. Not so quietly, nonetheless, that this intelligence did not leak out to infuriate and frustrate the Afro-Asians.

Arab delegations also meet frequently among themselves, but in spite of the sentimental drivel about Arab brotherhood, usually included in their speeches, there is no such thing as a common Arab front at the UN. They do not even gather to

---

the Soviet Union and the Western great powers, on December 14, 1955, a group of sixteen countries, including communist, anti-communist, and non-aligned states, was admitted to the UN: Albania, Austria, Bulgaria, Cambodia, Ceylon, Finland, Hungary, Ireland, Italy, Jordan, Laos, Libya, Nepal, Portugal, Romania, Spain.

oppose Israel, since the Maghreb countries, and in particular
Tunisia, show some reluctance in matching the hysterical anti-
Israel virulence of their Middle Eastern "brothers." As a
matter of fact, even among the Middle Eastern countries a
measure of consensus is not often reached, since most of the
countries of the Arab peninsula, beginning with Saudi Arabia,
show no visible enthusiasm for accepting Nasser's leadership.

        ᔭ   *ᔭ*   *ᔭ*

Unlike the Russians, the Americans do not often promote
meetings of delegates representing countries in their orbit of
influence. True, the head of the United States mission will now
and then attend a meeting of the Latin American group; but
this is usually at his own request (sometimes one of his aides
will discreetly suggest that an "invitation be extended" by the
Latin American ambassador chairing the group). The presence of the United States permanent representative means that
Washington wants to rally the support of the hemisphere on
a question of some importance; the Latin American delegates
on the whole feel flattered, as is intended.

    Along similar lines of seeking tactical support the US
delegate will occasionally attend a meeting of "old Commonwealth" delegations. The British do not particularly welcome
this, since they attach importance to these gatherings at which
they like to be the senior partner or host. But the American
delegate will have no difficulty in getting himself invited; all
he has to do is drop a word to his Canadian colleague. Because
of their unique position in regard to the Americans and the
British, Canadians like to be in on all discussions between
the two, and they realize that sometimes this can be achieved
in a tactful but effective manner within the fold of an "old
Commonwealth" meeting.

    But on balance participation in meetings and caucuses
remains for the US delegation an infrequent and an ancillary
mode of transacting diplomatic business—be it with the Latin

Americans, the English-speaking white nations, the Western Europeans, or any others among their friends and allies. Curiously enough the Americans, who dearly love all and any kind of meeting, prefer to conduct their negotiations with delegations at the United Nations almost exclusively on an individual basis. This is one of the few valid explanations for the size of the U.S. delegation. A host of junior and senior diplomats are needed for maintaining contact with the other delegations and conducting negotiations at all levels except the highest. It would be impossible for the U.S. chief delegate to maintain contact and conduct individual negotiations on a day-to-day basis with his dozens of fellow delegates.

This approach has a number of drawbacks. Not only is it questionable whether the Americans are wise in shunning group meetings; the overstaffing of their UN delegation, which they justify by the need for maintaining a running dialogue with all other countries, is considered by many senior diplomats as a diffuse and confusing method. Washington is frequently more bewildered than informed in regard to what really goes on at UN headquarters.

The British are particularly critical of their American allies in this respect. "I say, they pack in their diplomats like sardines across the street," was the observation of a newly arrived member of the United Kingdom delegation after his first visit to the United States mission on First Avenue and 45th Street.

It should be said, however, that packing diplomats like sardines would be even more noticeable at the headquarters of the Soviet mission to the UN, in the east sixties. (That is, if Western diplomats were welcome to visit the offices in the ample premises, which they are not.) In January, 1966, the USSR listed 53 members of its UN delegation, while the United States listed 42. Great Britain and France listed, respectively, twenty-two and seventeen.

SEVEN HUNDRED LOVELY PARTIES

For United Nations diplomats and high officials, social gatherings are indispensable adjuncts to formal debate. Political and diplomatic intercourse are as much a feature of parties given by delegates as they are of sessions of the General Assembly and the Security Council. Exchanges of views, soundings, consultations, and even commitments and decisions will often be set at a reception, an infomal luncheon, or a black-tie dinner. On many an occasion delicate negotiations have been conducted during a weekend at an ambassadorial mansion on Long Island Sound or in upper Westchester County.

Those who have never been to a diplomatic party will often say, with a tinge of envy, when they make the acquaintance of a delegation member: "Do you really go to all those UN parties? How lucky. Such interesting people. So sophisticated. You must have such fun." In point of fact, these social affairs are seldom glamorous or fun; as to their degree of sophistication, it varies widely. Only relatively few UN delegations know how to entertain gracefully and with genuine elegance: the French, the Italians, the Brazilians, the Poles, the Spaniards, the Argentinians, the Yugoslavs, the Pakistanis, the British among them. Many others spend an enormous amount of money to entertain ostentatiously, in an unimaginative, almost heavy-handed manner—for instance most

Arab delegations, the Russians, the Africans (English-speaking Africans being further removed from the social graces than their French-speaking colleagues). The Americans, the Canadians, the Australians, the Scandinavians entertain in an agreeable manner, without dash but also without pretention.

Giving a party always represents an enormous amount of hard work for the host UN delegation, and neither the ambassador nor his wife have any illusions about finding time to enjoy themselves. However, these parties are in a special category because the guests also harbor no illusions. Going to a UN party is grinding and earnest work for everyone concerned.

To begin with, the cumulative effect of parties amounts to a serious physical drain; considerable stamina is required to stand up to some seven hundred social functions a year. That is the estimated number of cocktail parties, luncheons, and dinners an ambassador or a senior Secretariat official should attend through the year; this figure takes into account parties he feels he can safely skip now and then, without allowing a useful source of information to dry up.

It is true that there are some diplomats and UN officials who apparently enjoy going to parties and even make a point of not missing any. Apart from digestive fitness this requires resilience and planning. The arithmetic is in itself staggering, for while anyone can attend only one official luncheon and one dinner a day, the number of cocktail parties often runs as high as three a day, or even more when the General Assembly is in session. However, the eager beavers have their logistics firmly in hand; they first study carefully the several addresses, then dart from one cocktail party to the next in a sequence closely patterned on the topography of the streets of Manhattan. And almost to a man these indefatigable party-goers wear no overcoat, even during the coldest winter months, since not having to line up at the cloakroom saves a considerable amount of time.

The ritual of UN social functions is quite rigid, since practically everyone is there for purposes of work rather than leisure. Drinking, for instance, is not approached in the same way as it would be in a normal party. Only irresponsible diplomats will indulge in several drinks. Certainly no ambassador or high UN official would conceive of drinking to the point at which he might enjoy himself and actually have fun at the party; for this could mean that his senses would no longer be sufficiently alert to pick up useful information from a stray bit of dialogue or interpret a facial expression giving special meaning to otherwise bland words. Worse still, if he allowed himself a couple of extra drinks he might well drift into a congenial, expansive mood, and feel inclined to speak his mind, express an opinion, or say something witty at the expense of some stuffy colleague. No, there is not much drinking at UN parties, not in any case by the important guests, the heads of delegations, and their political counselors. Those who say "Thank you for a lovely party" seven hundred times a year usually do not have many more than seven hundred drinks a year. Nothing is more common at a UN function than an intent diplomat circulating all evening from one group to another with the same glass in his hand, from which he sips infrequently. Drinking for enjoyment is reserved for a few private occasions, among trusted personal friends.

Some ambassadors never touch an alcoholic drink at a cocktail party, particularly in times of crisis, reaching rather for the tomato juice that is always on the trays together with the two standard drinks, Scotch and martinis. Even the Russians, well known for holding their liquor, will select tomato juice at most of these parties.

At luncheons and dinners the same abstemious rule is followed by ambassadors of high professional caliber. Most delegations still observe the sanguine custom of serving cocktails, two wines, champagne, and brandy not only at dinners but also at many luncheons. (Only the French and the Brazilians follow frequently the more civilized custom of serving only champagne "d'un bout à l'autre".) The best diplomats take only the smallest sip of each of the wines.

Paradoxically, these same delegates who are so careful about keeping their drinking to a minimum complain that the Arab delegations do not serve liquor at their parties. Actually the Arabs tend to abide by the Koran's ban on alcohol only at the annual formal reception on their national holiday and to serve drinks at other parties. In any case, even when only orangeade can be had, the food is always of unusual quality at any of the Arab parties. Together with some ten to twelve delegations from Western Europe and some three or four from Latin America, they represent the minority of those who care and know about food.

The admission of numerous African countries in 1960 raised the standards of UN parties, not necessarily in taste, but certainly in ostentation. Perhaps because they come from desperately poor countries and because they feel inferior about their color, the Africans give the most expensive parties in the most expensive Manhattan hotels, usually the Pierre or the Plaza. At one of the first of these parties, during the 1960 General Assembly, a junior member of the French delegation, after surveying the sumptuous arrangements, remarked to an American correspondent: "If France can afford this kind of party for so many African delegations she can't be in such bad shape as your press is saying daily." At the time the Algerian war was at its height, and articles had been appearing in the US press pointing to the strain on the French economy. The joke got around and eventually it reached the African delegations of the French-speaking African countries, all of which are heavily subsidized by France. Gradually these African parties were toned down in their lavishness.

~ ~ ~

The true purpose of a luncheon, dinner, or cocktail party— the transaction of political and diplomatic business—is conducted in several stages. Upon arriving at a cocktail party, for example, the seasoned diplomat will first spend a few minutes standing at a point from where he can survey the whole gathering. He will single out fellow ambassadors with whom he must discuss a pending matter, extract a piece of information, or drop a hint to be conveyed to higher quarters. He will then mentally establish an order of priority, since he may not be able to tackle all of them if the party is too crowded; then he sets out to buttonhole the delegate highest on his priority list. Although the smile and the handshake always conform to standard UN warmth, few words are wasted on greetings or social amenities. The item of business is then brought up and as soon as it is disposed of the diplomat excuses himself and sets out in search of the next person on his list.

Sometimes things don't work out quite so smoothly and the purposefully wandering delegate may himself be intercepted by someone on whom he can't afford to invest time. One accepted stratagem for a graceful disengagement is to tell the bore: "My wife is over there. She has been wanting very much to talk to you ever since I told her about your remarkable speech on apartheid." And then he propels the bore toward his wife, of whom he has had never lost sight in the crowded room just for such an eventuality; she will at once engage the other man in animated conversation; after a few moments the husband skilfully fades away, to continue circulating according to plan.

Many delegates do not map out for themselves such rigid itineraries at a party, nor rely on self-discipline for abiding by them. Rather they follow the mood of the gathering, joining this or that group more or less at random; engaging in a general discussion with a large group of colleagues; later sitting in a corner with one or two key delegates; in the intervals flirting perfunctorily with one or two attractive women. Indeed, the casual observer would assume that diplomats of this school actually enjoy themselves at diplomatic parties. Perhaps they do, but that would be merely a welcome dividend. They choose the relaxed rather than the earnest approach at

Hundred Lovely Parties* [117

parties; experience has taught them that in the long run they achieve better results. For one thing, a remarkable amount of useful information breaks up into small fragments and floats around, so to speak, at a gathering of UN professionals. To flit from group to group, indulging in a little banter and gossip, turns out to be an efficient manner of absorbing useful tidbits of news. Items of information often fall into a pattern such as to elucidate the trend on a current political debate or to indicate the position that will be taken by an important delegation on a touchy question. The gregarious, carefree diplomat often puts to better use a social occasion than his plodding colleague who enters a ballroom or a drawing room as though he were stalking into his office for a hard day's work.

♫ ♫ ♫

In a way, the wife of a diplomat has an even more important role at social gatherings than her husband. She does not attend committee meetings or make speeches on the floor of the Assembly, so her contribution to the performance of her husband and her husband's delegation is made exclusively at parties. And it is a rather important one; a diplomat's career depends more on his wife than that of a man engaged in almost any other kind of activity. Curiously enough, it seems that diplomat's wives usually perform at one of two extremes: she is either a glorious asset or a leaden burden for her husband.

Feminine performance at the UN is rendered more fascinating by the fact that there is much greater variety among the delegates' wives than among the delegates themselves. Some Asian and African delegates make their wives walk two or three steps behind them, a habit that finds some solid justification on educational grounds. When the top Indian at the Secretariat, who also indulges in this habit, went as far as making his wife sit one row back while he sat at the side of Jacqueline Kennedy during the Human Rights Day concert on December 10, 1964, there were raised eyebrows. But a member of the French delegation commented: "How very prudent of him."

The main problem afflicting UN wives is one of communication. Some of them literally cannot communicate, since they speak no civilized language. This is the case of a number of wives of African ambassadors, who know only an obscure African dialect. One of these wives did not hesitate to accept a dinner invitation at one of the Western missions even though her husband was away on a trip. She arrived all smiles, ate ravenously, and was among the last to leave. The host made a valiant effort to engage her in conversation; she seemed very amused and answered volubly in her own African dialect.

Even when they have learned some English the problem does not necessarily become more simple. Standards of education for women are so much lower in most Latin American, Asian, and African countries that most male delegates, including the ones from the *tiers monde*, must rely heavily on good manners in order to engage the ladies in conversation. Sometimes one of them comes up with a brilliant solution, however, as was the case of a member of a Commonwealth delegation, now called "Mr. Cartier" after he described his technique to a group of fellow diplomats after a particularly boring dinner, where he seemed to be about the only man enjoying himself:

> Tonight I was seated between two tiers monde wives as usual, one Asian and one Latin American. It seems that it always happens to me. At the beginning I would grope desperately for subjects of conversation, until one day it dawned upon me that one thing they have in common is that they all wear a great deal of expensive jewelry. I have an old friend who has been with Cartier for many years and is considered one of the top experts in jewelry in this country. So I had him over to my place in the country for a week end, explained to him my usual predicament at dinners, and asked him to teach me enough about jewels to enable me to discuss her ornaments with the lady on my right, and then with the one on my left. I guess I was a good pupil, for by now I can carry on a debate on diamonds

or rubies right through from first course to dessert. [He mused for a moment and added:] Funny thing is that I have become interested in the subject myself. Particularly in Egyptian pieces of many centuries back.

There are, however, a few exceptions among *tiers monde* wives; women who not only wear beautiful jewelry, but are also intelligent and well bred. More than a match for the most glamorous Western ambassadresses, they are almost always Egyptian, Indian, or Pakistani women.

Wives of diplomats can help their husbands not only by going to parties, but even more by giving them. There are many pitfalls of protocol to avoid, and the list of guests must be finely attuned to the political conjuncture. It is no simple matter for a hostess to plan a dinner. For instance, she should not invite an Arab ambassador and his Israeli colleague on the same occasion, nor the envoys of South Africa and any other African country.

There is much a knowledgeable wife can do not only to further her husband's career, but also to promote her delegation's interests, by bringing together for a social occasion representatives of countries that happen to be in bitter opposition to each other on a current question, and whose envoys would welcome the opportunity of meeting on neutral ground. Some of the smaller Western European countries have ambassadresses who are particularly adept at this subtle diplomatic game, and who actually enjoy gathering for an evening under the mission's roof delegates who on that same afternoon were tangling grimly on the floor of the Security Council.

わ　わ　わ

The working week of social occasions does not end on Friday. Weekends are also set aside for entertaining by many delegates and senior officials who have a house in the country or by the seashore. Such invitations are highly prized when they come from the small group of ambassadors with comfortable mansions and the civilized habit of actually letting their guests enjoy themselves—go sailing, play tennis, or just be utterly lazy during the day, leaving shoptalk for the late afternoon and evening.

Some delegations, however, have over the last three years evolved a "poor man's weekend." They invite their guests only for the day to some remote corner of Westchester County or Long Island which the host invariably describes as "only forty-five minutes by car." Usually it turns out to be a ghastly experience. The guest will invariably get lost, especially if the host has mailed to him a mimeographed but always incomprehensible map of how to get there. When he does finally arrive the cocktail hour is almost over and he is ushered in to a "rustic" luncheon, which means eating some badly barbecued meat while sitting on prickly grass at the feet of a bejeweled and garrulous old hag who owns the estate down the road and is thrilled to meet a "real foreigner diplomat." He will have to drink, and praise, some very indifferent California wine which his host must serve in order to be a member in good standing of the exclusive local country club to which the watery-eyed dowager and many other rich Americans belong. When a blessed somnolence begins to set in, it is time to start on the long trek back to Manhattan. The one consoling thought is that he will not get lost on the return trip.

⟫ 16 ⟪

AFRICAN MYTH ON FIRST AVENUE

A capacity for euphemism marks those who work for the UN and reaches its peak in absurdity when Africa is spoken of. Nobody dares say anything resembling the truth about the black continent. Only someone with a black skin and sufficient stature among his fellow Africans can afford to bring out unpleasant but unavoidable facts. One of those few is Robert Gardiner, the head of the Economic Commission for Africa, who did just that when speaking to a group of African information leaders at the African Roundtable in Dakar. "Africans go on criticizing conditions on their continent as if they were still under a colonial government," he pointed out, then added: "But we are really criticizing ourselves." Gardiner knew first-hand from his activities with the Economic Commission for Africa how difficult it was to profit even from the offers of fellowships from the rich countries to help train Africans. He observed: "African governments cannot avail themselves of all the fellowships offered. There are countries in the West who would be ready to sign agreements with us for training some of our people over the next five, ten years. And every year I have to apologize and say that we don't have enough people qualified to take advantage of the fellowships offered." Then he asked his audience: "Who is keeping you back in training people in industry, for instance, if not yourselves?"

Among the Africans there are not many Gardiners, men capable of searching self-criticism while themselves making a valid contribution. More common attitudes are those of African UN ambassadors who were officers of the Special Committee of 24, charged with reporting on decolonialization. When the UN information services prepared in the early spring of 1965 a booklet called "The United Nations and Decolonialization," the ambassadors insisted on having their photos included—a rather unusual procedure—and then held up publication until each of them chose the most becoming photograph. During the weeks preceding publication it was not unusual to find a permanent representative of one of the African republics in the photo library of the information services, with photos of himself spread out on a table and furrows of concentration on his brow as he tried to decide which was the most photogenic reproduction of his statesmanlike features.

ᴒ   ᴒ   ᴒ

During the late fifties and the early sixties the Africans played the cold war card, presenting outrageous demands which usually started with a steel mill and an international airline, two status symbols of the underdeveloped country. It was then that the under-secretary of state at the German foreign office used to refer to the *sowietische Stahl Ofen vom Dienst*, a mythical steel mill which purportedly the Soviet government was holding in readiness for a particular African nation the moment it became apparent that the Western democracies were dragging their feet. Throughout these years, there was a heavy traffic through Bonn, Washington, London, and Paris of African dignitaries demanding steel mills, airlines, industries, or just plain cash—ready with broad hints that their excursion might wind up in Moscow, where the Russians would undoubtedly be delighted to see what they could do to help a deserving and emerging African republic. Late in 1960 the story got around about the exasperated German cabinet minister in charge of development who heard the war threat once

too often and blurted out to the visiting representative of a
French-speaking African republic: "By all means, do go to
Moscow. We shall be delighted to provide the airplane ticket.
You will have to change planes in either Copenhagen or Paris.
It's a bit shorter through Copenhagen but you may prefer to
stop in Paris. Please let me know when I should issue the
necessary authorization to our travel section."

These were the years when fair British royalty would be
photographed dancing with jet-black African potentates and
their wives. In Paris every month or oftener the towering flag-
poles on Place de la Concorde would fly an obscure flag side
by side with the tricolor, as one more French-speaking African
president payed homage to De Gaulle and received reassurance
that his country's development as well as its budget would be
buttressed by the French treasury. This was also the time when
President Kennedy during one of the more tense moments of
the missile crisis found time to keep his appointment with an
African premier.

The Soviets were no less ready than the Western big
powers to court the Africans. When Khrushchev came to the
1960 General Assembly—and in his wake a score of heads of
state and heads of government—he found time to dash to a
party being given by the Togolese at the Plaza Hotel, there
to be photographed with a mildly astonished Sylvanus Olympio
(one of Africa's most moderate leaders, whose senseless assas-
sination two years later was to deprive the emerging continent
of one of its few responsible and capable statesmen).

ๆ   ๆ   ๆ

The situation has changed beyond recognition in the five
years from 1960 to 1965. For all their rantings in the General
Assembly, and the collective bad manners such as walking out
on Prime Minister Harold Wilson when he addressed a plenary
session in the autumn of 1965, African influence as such has
virtually ceased to exist. Only within the large Afro-Asian bloc,
and then by negotiating beforehand with the US delegation,

can the Africans make their will felt on anything but the most innocuous UN activities.

The basic explanation for the swift African eclipse is that those new countries never made a truly determined effort to secure significant positions within the Secretariat. In the United Nations no country or group of countries—not even an entire continent—can expect to exert influence unless the delegations have the kind of unobtrusive but highly efficient support that only key staff members can provide. Capturing an entire chain of command in the Secretariat, such as the Indians managed to do, is nowadays out of the question for any other country or group of countries.

Africa missed its chance in the Secretariat mostly through negligence. The respectable argument against them is that the new countries lacked highly trained civil servants who could aspire to an important post in the Secretariat. The argument is fallacious today, and was even more so in the early sixties, for then almost any African could have had almost any post regardless of qualifications (a handful actually did). But at the time the African delegations were mesmerized by the high jinks in the General Assembly, where everyone seemed to take them seriously. They neglected to press their claims for positions in the UN's vital center of power. UN veterans observed with some satisfaction this lack of interest in Secretariat posts by the delegations of the new countries, since none of them relished an upset to the existing balance of power, even by Africans who, it was believed, could be fairly easily controlled through flattery or the doling out of material advantages. Nonetheless these senior officials took the wise precaution of attaching to their department or staff a "tame African," of whom there are now quite a few in the Secretariat. They have an indefinable family air about them. Well-dressed, urbane, articulate, and lazy, having a family connection with the prime minister or the president of their country, they are usually the African version of a Western playboy.

The African myth rode high for a period of four years, beginning in the autumn of 1960 when a group of newly independent black republics gained admission to the UN. It was exposed during the Congo debate in the Security Council late in 1964 when many of these same countries clashed with the Western powers over the rescue operations carried out by Belgian paratroopers transported in US planes to save white missionaries and settlers from the Stanleyville rebels.

These were precisely the years when the Negro question reached a paroxysm of debate and crisis in the United States. There was a curious interplay between the African's presence on First Avenue and the militancy of the American Negro minority in the drive that culminated with the passage of the civil rights bill. Scores of black African diplomats spotlighted by American newspapers and television networks brought home to millions of Negroes throughout the U.S. the status and importance that colored people of other countries were being granted by Washington. It ironically underscored the secondary status of persons with Negro blood who happened to be US citizens.

As to the African diplomats, they found themselves in a bewildering situation. On the one hand there was the official adulation heaped upon them by their colleagues in thee UN, and particularly by the US delegation. They were drinking in large gulps the glamour and glitter of New York, but choking on rebuffs and humiliations in the city's hotels and restaurants—some only imagined but others only too real.

African delegates missed no opportunity to chastise their American hosts on the civil rights incidents erupting almost every week in the South and in other sections of the United States. Meanwhile, however, they meticulously avoided social contacts with their brethren in color; most of them would don the national dress or at least headdress to go out in the streets of New York, as did their wives when they went shopping. With the help of American officials many Africans have been able to rent apartments or houses in some (but not all) of the exclusive residential districts in Manhattan, Long Island, and Westchester County.

While these African diplomats are still inclined to compare New York to Geneva, pointing out that in the UN's "other capital" there is virtually no color discrimination, nonetheless a remarkable effort on their behalf has been made by their American hosts.

⇒ 17 ⇐

HOW GENERAL A SECRETARY?

Franklin Roosevelt envisaged such an ample role for the future Secretary-General that he thought that title too restrictive. There is evidence that the President favored the name World Moderator. Even when the more modest title was agreed upon, a consensus had extravagant hopes for the future Secretary-General; the Preparatory Commission pointed out that the post calls for the "exercise of the highest qualities of political judgment," and the man occupying it "more than anyone else stands for the United Nations as a whole."

The Charter reflects this in its famous Article 99: "The Secretary-General may bring to the attention of the Security Council any matter which in his opinion may threaten the maintenance of international peace and security." Even before the ink of the signatures was dry, a number of countries, and particularly the big powers, began to have second thoughts— and to voice them in debate, tending to bring the activities of the Secretary-General down to a safe and humdrum administrative level, as described in Article 97:

The Secretariat shall comprise a Secretary-General and such staff as the Organization may require. The Secretary-General shall be appointed by the General Assembly upon the recommendation of the Security Council. He shall be the chief administrative officer of the Organization.

The history of the Office of the Secretary-General is in a sense the history of the first, and then the second, incumbent to give life and vigor to the promises implied in Article 99, while the present holder of the office has been content, at most, to hold on to the gains achieved by Trygve Lie and by Dag Hammarskjold. U Thant has done even that at times with some hesitancy and misgivings, as though wondering whether his two predecessors had not left him too explosive and controversial an inheritance.

In an organization where precedent counts heavily, it would be up to the first incumbent either to affirm the prerogatives and the political role of the office of the Secretary-General or to be content with merely being the UN's "principal administrative officer." Trygve Lie decided to embark on a stubborn, step-by-step effort to affirm and enlarge not only the influence but also the active participation of the Secretary-General in world affairs. By the time of his resignation (November 10, 1952) Lie had established for the Secretary-General the right to make political statements and proposals not only behind the scenes but also before the Security Council and the General Assembly. Some of these statements embodied direct criticism of member governments; he went so far as to expose deliberate distortions by heads of delegations. He also gained the privilege of direct access to a foreign minister or a prime minister in his own capital, either by going there himself or by sending someone in his name—in other words, going over the head of that country's permanent representative at UN Headquarters. In fact, toward the end of his tenure of office Lie had mobilized a small group of personal representatives who pressed his views in several key capitals.

Oddly enough, at the outset this expansion of the Secretary-General's powers was encouraged by the USSR. And the Soviet spokesman was none other than the present Foreign Minister, Andrei Gromyko, at the time Soviet Permanent Representative. At the beginning of the UN, April, 1946, Lie had made a study of the legal aspects of an Iranian case. His conclusions happened to be favorable to the Soviet point of view, and thus displeasing to the United States. He describes the episode in his book *In the Cause of Peace:*

> Immediately upon completing our draft, Mr. Feller and I tried in vain to find the President, Quo-Tai-Chi of China. Just before the day's session was to open, I met him entering the Council Chamber and said I wanted to submit to him a memorandum on the question of retaining the Iranian item on the agenda. Mr. Quo seemed to be surprised and muttered what may have been a diplomatic version of "What business of yours is this?" He did not accept the memorandum, and so, on the way to my seat, I sent it to one of his aides. As I sat down a latent aspect of my intervention came to mind: the status of the Secretary-General. I believed that Article 99, which empowered him to bring to the attention of the Security Council any matter which in his opinion might threaten international peace and security, was more than enough authority for intervening in the proceedings of the Council in this fashion; in fact, I felt that it was the intent of the Charter that the Secretary-General should have not merely the right to submit legal opinions to the President, of which the latter would take notice, but that he should be able to address the Council on any question it might consider. Mr. Quo's attitude seemed to challenge this conception of the Secretary-General's authority. If the President did not acknowledge to the Council receipt of the memorandum, I decided, I would myself ask for the floor and read it into the record.
>
> However, the President had the memorandum read aloud by an interpreter at the very opening of the meeting. He then proposed that it be referred to the Council's Committee of Experts for examination and report, and it was so agreed. Discussion on the Soviet motion to delete the Iranian question was resumed, and after a short time the President announced that he would put the motion to a vote.

But if Mr. Quo thought he could thus relegate into limbo the Secretary-General's memorandum, the next half hour of debate was to make him realize that he had made a serious miscalculation. He was challenged on a point of order, in rapid sequence, by the delegates of France, Poland, and the USSR. Of the three ambassadors, it was Gromyko who upheld Trygve Lie:

> Since we have decided that the memorandum prepared by the Secretary-General should be referred to the Committe of Experts, how can we vote or take a decision? As regards the functions of the Secretary-General—a question which has arisen in passing—these are, of course, more serious and more weighty than was indicated just now. It is sufficient to recall one Article of the Charter to realize the heavy responsibilities incumbent upon the Secretary-General. Article 99 states: "The Secretary-General may bring to the attention of the Security Council any matter which in his opinion may threaten the maintenance of international peace and security." . . . Thus, the Secretary-General has all the more right, and an even greater obligation, to make statements on various aspects of the question considered by the Security Council.

In this as in other instances, Lie did not hesitate to seek the glare of publicity in order to make one or several of the big powers more amenable to listen to his suggestions. And he would do it where it counted most: in the Security Council Chamber. In fact, he seemed at times to act as if heeding the advice propounded by E. G. Phelan in his book *Yes and Albert Thomas:*

> The success of international organization depends more upon leadership than upon any one thing. . . . You must have an element of international leadership in international organization. . . . What you have got in the Security Council is a multinational discussion. You cannot have an international discussion without an international spokesman. There is a profound difference. That spokesman must be the Secretary-General. Mr. Lie, I think, ought to participate in the discussions of the Council. . . . The leadership of the Secretary-General must be public and manifest. It filters down. And it makes all the difference to the members of the Council. Whether the Secretary-

General whispers to the delegates in private or speaks out in public with the journalists there—this is a great difference. The Secretary-General's activity behind the scenes is useful. But multiple consultations decide nothing. They keep the Secretary-General informed and they exercise a gentle influence. This is not the same as influencing an international, collective decision.

This is of course the opposite of "quiet diplomacy," an expression which came to define the actions of Lie's successor and which Hammarskjold himself was fond of using. It can be argued, however, that during his last years the discreet Swede came to rely on pressure engendered by public pronouncements almost as much as on his own favorite tactics of chess-like maneuvers in the wings. Throughout the Congo operation he combined the two approaches with a subtlety and sixth sense never attained by his predecessor. During one of the most difficult Congo episodes, Hammarskjold was concurrently establishing the UN presence in Katanga by flying to Elisabethville himself with a Swedish contingent, dealing with a restive Security Council by carefully confronting several of the big powers with the wishes of the Afro-Asians, and keeping an ungrateful Lumumba at bay through a rolling barrage of letters meant for immediate publicity through press releases. In fact, Hammarskjold's performance during those days resembled the methods that made Albert Thomas famous as one of the boldest and most successful heads of an international body, and which Phelan describes: "The Governments must be told what they have to do, and told in terms, so far as possible, of their own constitution and methods. . . . He insisted on what he called 'letters of principle' in which the duties of Governments were carefully set out and a method for their performance suggested." The difference was, of course, that Thomas was simply the head of the International Labour Organization. (Says Stephen Schwebel: "If the Secretaries-General of the League are the pale prototype of the UN Secretary-General, the Directors of ILO are perhaps the vivid archetype.")

Yet both Lie and Hammarskjold came to grief in the process of expanding and consolidating what they believed to be the power and influence necessary to fulfill the responsibilities of their office. Lie had to resign under the harsh boycott of the Soviet Union, and Hammarskjold during the last months was confronted with a similar boycott compounded by the active hostility of the British, and to a lesser extent of the French.

U Thant continues to enjoy the confidence and the benevolence of all the great powers. Some serious students of UN affairs believe that this justifies any sins of omission; the overriding objective, they maintain, is to avoid the erosion of the office of the Secretary-General by too much political involvement, particularly when the big powers are in the fray. This line of reasoning is attractive to many of the smaller delegations, who do not relish the prospect of one more Secretary-General thrown to the wolves because he dared defy one or more of the permanent members of the Security Council.

18

HAMMARSKJOLD AND THANT:
A STUDY IN CONTRASTS

Dag Hammarskjold and U Thant have made their mark on
the contemporary world scene. Because of their individual personalities and their differences in approach and style, each of
these two men has come to symbolize an era in the history of
the UN.

Among delegates and correspondents—and discreetly
among Secretariat officials—the study in contrasts between the
two Secretaries-General remains a favorite intellectual exercise.
At a dinner party some time ago, the envoy of a Scandinavian
country remarked: "Many of the problems we face in the UN
have their origin in the fact that Hammarskjold was an
inscrutable Oriental while Thant is an English headmaster."
The *boutade* held a kernel of truth. The Swede's mystical,
hermetic turn of mind is sometimes found in the East; the
Burmese, who had been earlier in life headmaster of a high
school up country from Rangoon, still reflects British colonial
influence.

The behavior of these two men are a contrast particularly in times of stress. For example, Hammarskjold would
not quit under fire, while Thant might. When pressured to
resign "in a chivalrous manner" by Khrushchev during a dramatic session of the 1960 General Assembly, Hammarskjold
countered the Soviet Premier's blistering attack with a state-

ment containing this passage: "It is very easy to resign; it is not so easy to stay on. It is very easy to bow to the wish of a great power. It is another matter to resist. As is well known to all members of this Assembly, I have done so before on many occasions and in many directions. If it is the wish of those nations who see in this Organization their best protection in the present world I shall do so again." His statement was interrupted three times by thunderous applause.

Ever since the resignation of Trygve Lie, brought about by pressure from the Soviet Union, it has been held axiomatic around the UN that no Secretary-General can long remain in office once he has incurred the enduring hostility of a great power. At the time Hammarskjold stood up to its wrath, the USSR was the only big power opposing him; a year later, on the eve of his death, both Britain and France had turned against him and even the United States was wavering in its support, as was made apparent by the political climate in Washington during the Bizerte episode.[1] Yet, in the face of this inexorable deterioration of his political standing and prestige—and consequently of his usefulness as Secretary-

---

[1] On July 19, 1961, bitter fighting broke out between French and Tunisian troops on the outskirts of the big naval base of Bizerte which France still held on Tunisian soil. The Tunisian government immediately turned to the Security Council and President Habib Burguiba made a direct appeal to the Secretary-General for a personal exchange of views. Hammarskjold flew to Tunisia, stating that he considered it "his duty to explore the possibilities of improving this disturbing situation by making an effort to establish immediately the necessary contact between the two parties, the basis for which must obviously be strict compliance with the terms of the resolution and respect for Tunisian sovereignty." While in Tunisia Hammarskjold drafted and sent a letter which was badly received in Paris, and answered in very sharp terms by Foreign Minister Couve de Murville. Reportedly Hammarskjold was advised against sending the letter by a key political aide, on the grounds that antagonizing another permanent member of the Security Council should be avoided at a time when there were indications that Washington was disturbed about any unnecessary involvement by the Secretary-General in Bizerte in view of the continuing crisis in the Congo.

General—Hammarskjold would not quit. But there remained for him one way out.

Those who have read *Markings* have been struck by Hammarskjold's messianic streak, a messianism steeped in mysticism and perhaps nurtured in a sad childhood spent in the depressing shadows of the ancient castle of Uppsala. Overtaken by a sense of destiny from the day he was chosen as Secretary-General, Hammarskjold had come to believe that not only the United Nations needed him, but that he and the UN had become one, in a sublimation that finds its reasonless reasons in the mysticism with which he was imbued. When the situation became untenable, the answer was not to resign, and indeed "it is easy to resign," for so doing would be "throwing the Organization to the winds." Death became, instead, the only honorable liberation, the only legitimate redemption. Until it came he held fast against any odds.

That Hammarskjold had a premonition of death awaiting him as the culmination of the UN crisis is a belief held by some of those who knew him best. That he went forth in search of death remains in the realm of speculation, together with other unexplained aspects of the flight from Leopoldville to N'dola. But if the premises inherent in the political conjuncture and in Hammarskjold's character are accepted, the fatal sequence of events sweeps in with the ominous inevitability of a Greek tragedy.

ری   ری   ری

By contrast, Thant in effect told the world press early in 1965 that he would resign if a solution for the Vietnam crisis were not found through negotiations. He was speaking at a luncheon of the United Nations Correspondents Association; the UN press corps was taken by surprise when he announced that another person would have to be found for his post if he was not able to play a useful role in bringing the two sides together. On previous occasions Thant had said repeatedly that

the Vietnam problem calls for "a political and diplomatic solution, not a military one." But he had never before threatened
to resign.

The radically different attitudes of Hammarskjold and
Thant as each of them faced the major crisis in his career
cannot be ascribed to a question of courage; pride and vanity
seem rather to be the compelling motives.

Hammarskjold had his share of personal vanity; for instance, those closest to him recall with what impish satisfaction
he told how the relatively little-known French poet, St. John
Perse, whom he particularly admired and whose poems he had
translated into Swedish, had been chosen over De Gaulle's
candidate for the 1960 Nobel Prize for literature. In fact, he
considered this literary joust with "le Général" a meaningful
factor in determining the increasing hostility of the French
toward him in the course of the Congolese and the Tunisian
political crises.

But above all Hammarskjold had a pervading sense of
pride; while his reputation for aloofness and arrogance toward
others stemmed more often than not from an introvert's shy-
ness and longing for privacy, he could also be coldly contemptuous when confronted with a vulgar or an unintelligent
person.

For Thant, on the other hand, pride and vanity, as we
Westerners understand them, are integrated into face-saving
that pervading trait of Asians. He is a master of its intricate
ritual, which includes paradox and make-believe. He frequently
preaches modesty. Following Burmese custom, he does no
sign "U Thant" but always "Maung Thant"; "U" is a defer
ential title in Burma, standing roughly midway between the
American "sir" and the British "Sir," while "Maung" is the
equivalent of a plain "mister." He wittily tells the story of how
he once had difficulty cashing a check because of the dis
crepancy.

Of the two men, Hammarskjold was probably the on
less bent on making an impression—perhaps because he alway

did. The comparison carries political overtones, since Thant's thirst for publicity might well be the reason for his sensational press conferences, where he often stumbles into a diplomatic or political *faux pas*. He persists in indulging in the "candid" press conference, in spite of painful experiences in extricating himself from some of his more imprudent statements. Once he told assembled correspondents what he thought of De Gaulle's policies, and several weeks later had to avail himself of the passage through New York of a group of French deputies and senators to explain to them lamely, but for the record, that he had been misunderstood by the world press.

Oddly enough Thant's direct approach in press conferences is not carried over into his private conversations with delegates. The ambassador of a medium power recently complained to a group of colleagues: "I never seem to be able to get a straight answer from the Secretary-General. Even when it is in his own interest to tell me what he has in mind. Otherwise how can I secure the support of my government for his position?"

It is not so much that Thant will not speak clearly in private, but that he will hardly speak at all. He has a way of sitting patiently, courteously, and impassively, letting the other man do most of the talking. But the impassivity is sometimes incongruously broken by an impulsive pronouncement, distinctly of a Western type.

Hammarskjold on the other hand, appeared to be voluble to the point of prolixity. But his style of speech—and of writing, for that matter—had all too often a sybilline, meandering quality. He infuriated correspondents at his press conferences, for usually they could not make out what he was saying, and this was obviously his intention. He carried this capacity for planned ambiguity into discussions with cabinet ministers and envoys. Says the ambassador of a major power who was present at a luncheon given by his Foreign Minister to Hammarskjold when the reelection of the Secretary-General was at stake: "I never met anyone who could talk so well and so plausibly, but always around the subject under discussion, never about it. It was a sort of exercise in surrealist semantics."

৶   ৶   ৶

In any evaluation of the two Secretaries-General, Hammarskjold emerges indisputably as the accomplished and impressive statesman. Yet, by the time he flew to his death the United Nations was caught in a maelstrom of dissension and discredit. Three of the four major powers, Russia, France, Britain, were in varying degrees at odds with the organization and particularly with its Secretary-General. UN forces in the Congo had been embarrassingly outfought by a handful of Tshombe's white mercenaries. The financial impasse was beginning to assume disquieting proportions as the UN disbursed an average of ten million dollars of borrowed money monthly to meet its obligations in the Congo, while the Soviet Union, France, and other countries were moving toward refusal to pay their share.

That Hammarskjold should be held responsible for all or for most that was going amiss remains to this day highly debatable. But he was nonetheless saddled with the blame by a group of politically powerful opponents. He had acted courageously, coherently, and in accordance with what he believed were the UN's best interests. But he had committed the cardinal sin in politics: failure. He was, however, ready to pay the price in full.

৶   ৶   ৶

When the hero dramatically disappeared from the scene, and after the shock and the grief had worn off, an almost audible sigh of relief swept through the corridors and the lounges of UN Headquarters in New York. The non-heroic delegates soon settled down to the serious business at hand: hard bargaining to decide on Hammarskjold's successor. Even before candidates were proposed—or could propose themselves—it was unmis-

takable that the final choice could be neither a politically
forceful nor an intellectually towering personality. Nor could
it be another European. During this opening phase when
several candidates—headed by Ambassador U Thant of Burma
and Ambassador Mongi Slim of Tunisia—were jockeying for
position, the envoy of a Caribbean country remarked to an
informal gathering of Latin American delegates: "Everyone
seems to be agreed that the next Secretary-General has to be
non-white and non-brilliant. But I don't see that this rules us
out. Why necessarily an African or an Asian? Someone from
Latin America could qualify. Why, in my own country there
are several eminent statesmen with Negro or Indian blood and
plenty of people ready to vouch for their mediocrity."

The man on whom the choice finally fell did fulfill the
two basic requirements. His most serious contender, Mongi
Slim, was too Caucasian in physical appearance, too cultured
and Europeanized in upbringing. Ambassador U Thant, on
the other hand, was definitely not white and not brilliant. He
was not necessarily considered a mediocrity, but he was able
to get along with just about everybody. As one who was "non-
aligned" he was acceptable to the Soviets (for the first uneasy
weeks of bargaining it seemed that no candidate would be
palatable to Moscow, which was still insistent on the "troika"
approach), yet he had not shown himself too anti-Western
when chairman of the subcommittee on the Algerian war.
His speeches were conciliatory, his courtesy unfailing, his smile
quick and warm. Here was a man who sought to please and
harmonize; here was a man who would never seek to prod the
United Nations to heroic deeds, nor dare pit the organization
against the stark realities of power politics.

After the election was over everyone settled down in
relief mingled with anticipation to watch the mild Burmese
retrieve the UN from the adventurous heights of precedent-
breaking statesmanship to which Hammarskjold had hoisted it.

Thant did fulfill expectations, but perhaps too well. First he cut his losses by "disengaging" from the Congo. But it was a melancholy withdrawal, unskilfully handled. During the last months his representative was literally not on speaking terms with the government which had beseeched the UN for help. When the commanding general of the UN peace-keeping forces departed, not a single member of the Congolese government came to Leopoldville airport to bid him farewell.

Then came the West New Guinea affair, one of the more indecent colonial grabs on record—with the novel feature, however, that the expansionist colonial power, Indonesia, was neither white nor European. Sukarno had not the shred of a claim on New Guinea and its Papuan inhabitants on ethnic, historical, cultural, or religious grounds. The people were never asked whether they wanted to be turned over to Indonesia. The plebiscite promised by 1969 will obviously never be held unless it is rigged beforehand by Djakarta.

It all happened only a few months after Thant's election, when the cocky Afro-Asian majority was raging in the General Assembly against moribund European colonialism. Thant began by sending identical cables to The Hague and Djakarta, expressing his concern over the outbreak of hostilities; it was of course Indonesian paratroops and naval units who were attacking the Dutch in New Guinea, in the hope of following up with a full-scale invasion. After a few months of negotiations with Thant's representative, the Dutch shrugged their shoulders and let West Guinea be delivered to Sukarno with the Secretary-General serving as midwife; they felt they had done all they could reasonably be expected to do for the welfare of the Papuans and were disinclined to continue a costly military holding operation halfway around the world.

The Dutch public, however, which in past years had nurtured feelings of guilt over Dutch colonialism in the islands of Indonesia, now felt angered and wronged: the clean behavior of their government in the New Guinea affair was being subtly and insidiously distorted. The Dutch press pointed out that the transfer of sovereignty arranged by Thant without consulting the inhabitants—for the good reasons that no segment of the Papuan population wished to come under Djakarta's rule—was in direct contradiction to the principles embodied in the United Nations Declaration of Human Rights.

As a delegate was heard to remark, the United Nations umbrella would never have been spread over the shabby deal "if the Secretary-General had not been so impartially leaning toward his fellow Asians." But once the deed was done the Dutch government was content to call it a day, and devote its full attention to the pressing business of unprecedented prosperity on the home front.

There was nonetheless an aftermath to the affair which hurt UN prestige and self-confidence at a time when the organization, reeling under the big power clash over Article 19, could least afford it. Ironically, the blow came not from wronged Holland but from triumphant Indonesia. As the year began, Sukarno announced that Indonesia was quitting the United Nations, the first member state to do so, and so far the only one. (1965 had been proclaimed by the UN General Assembly International Co-operation Year.)

While Sukarno's bombastic gesture was primarily meant to divert attention from his failure to "crush Malaysia," his anger toward the UN was only too real. He had been misled by the complacency of the membership and of the Secretary-General in the New Guinea episode into believing that the General Assembly would not dare elect Malaysia to the Security Council. But Malaysia was elected, and by March 1, 1965, Djakarta had completed its withdrawal from the United Nations, closed its UN mission, while all the big specialized agencies in Indonesia were told to pack up and leave. All, that is, except the World Health Organization, where Indonesia maintained its membership. By an interesting coincidence, Mrs. Subandrio, wife of the then Indonesian Foreign Minister, was a member of the WHO board, which entitled her to trips to Geneva, all expenses paid by WHO.

∽   ∽   ∽

For Thant, Indonesia's withdrawal meant a loss of face that
only Asian delegates to the UN were able to correctly evaluate.
But the irony of the situation was not lost on the West. A
country literally created by the United Nations, the one country
that had indisputably fared well at the UN under Thant's
stewardship, was leaving the organization, after Sukarno had
contemptuously ignored Thant's pressing appeal to reconsider.
The Secretary-General had lost face in his own region of the
world, where presumably his fame and prestige would be
highest.

There is no doubt that Thant was deeply hurt, and it is
more than coincidence that his threat to resign over Vietnam
came only a few weeks after he had been ignored by Sukarno.
Losing face in his part of Asia is unthinkable. Unless a solution could be found for the Southeast Asia crisis along the
lines he had proposed, a new Secretary-General would have
to be found.

∽   ∽   ∽

Such high hopes had been centered on Thant that neither
the clumsy disengagement in the Congo nor the embarrassing
involvement in New Guinea seriously undermined his standing. Only the more experienced specialists in the foreign
ministries of the world's major powers, and a handful of
diplomatic correspondents, recognized the erosion of the Secretary-General's position.

∽   ∽   ∽

As the Article 19 controversy inexorably developed into an
ominous deadlock that threatened the very survival of the
organization, it became apparent that Thant tended to be help-

less and ineffective in an emergency. He was vague and preachy
in his pronouncements, when he should have been forceful and
pragmatic. He failed to diagnose the problem for what it was—
a major clash of big powers on political concepts of their role
and that of the United Nations in the crucial field of peacekeeping operations. He failed to grasp the fear and the dis-
array of the medium and small powers, and he never really
believed that so many of them would want "to sit this one out."
Like the president of the General Assembly, the Ghanian
Quaison-Sackey, Thant was taken in by the setting in motion
of the ponderous, pompous machinery of the "committee of 33"
talkfests. But unlike some shrewd political observers, Thant
did not realize that the law of diminishing returns had caught
up with the UN, that the bureaucracy creaked with purposes
that no longer existed, that the committee of 33 would not
even begin to solve the imbroglio, and that it did not much
matter whether the committee met or not. Under the stress
and strain of developments Thant was brought down by a
peptic ulcer and repaired to a hospital, then home for a period
of convalescence. He was away for several weeks at the height
of the crisis.

It was not only that Thant talked of "the UN's financial
problem" as if he believed that calling a political deadlock a
mere question of money it would make it easier to solve. Everyone at the UN was repeating the quip of a member of the
British delegation: "Never in the history of human conflict
have so many talked so much about so little money." Even
then Thant continued to behave as though money, rather than
the organization's political life, was at stake. During the
months when time remained for meaningful negotiations at
the summit, he who had merrily flitted between the capitals
of the great powers at the beginning of his term of office
became almost glued to UN Headquarters, although it was
obvious to everyone that the ambassadors stationed in New
York had no power to negotiate what had become a matter of
high policy for Moscow, Washington, and Paris.

An article on the UN financial crisis appearing in the May 6, 1965, issue of *The Reporter* had this passage:

> In good part, this development was due to Secretary General U Thant's conception of the nature of the struggle and of his own proper role in it. From the beginning, he inclined to concentrate on the fiscal and political aspects of the problem to the neglect of the institutional issue that had been raised. Since the money crisis, which he inherited, coincided almost exactly with U Thant's term of office and since it unavoidably grew worse in the course of it, his anxiety about raising funds and paying bills pretty well explains itself. Nonetheless, his numerous critics contend that in contrast with Hammarskjold, U Thant mediated between the major members, as distinct from negotiating on behalf of the organization. As time passed, his attempts to "break the deadlock" and his unwillingness to commit the organization to a stand indicated that he had come to accept the "big power conflict" view of events; and once the Secretariat had bowed out of the conflict, that was precisely what it was bound to become.

Thant should have spent those precious months shuttling between the White House, the Kremlin, and the Elysée. He could, and should, have made a nuisance of himself. If the little Burmese schoolteacher had fought stubbornly for the survival of the United Nations, which his illustrious predecessor Hammarskjold had identified with the weak and the needy nations of the globe, it might not have touched the hearts of cold-blooded statesmen, but it would have made an impact on public opinion in their countries.

As it turned out, Thant did not rise to the occasion. Not only was he no match for Johnson, De Gaulle, Khrushchev; whenever he was given the opportunity to present his case where it really mattered, lukewarm communiqués clearly revealed that he had failed to press home the UN case.

Could Thant have acted otherwise? Of course. During the months when the storm was brewing, the Secretary-General of the United Nations should have made clear that he was prepared to make full use of the prestige and influence of his office in order to have the big powers squarely face their responsibilities. If they had decided to wreck the UN over a matter of a little money, at least they would have to come out and say so. Public opinion everywhere would have reacted favorably to a continuing pilgrimage by the Secretary-General to the world's great capitals to fight for the organization's survival. Even if he were to be rebuffed everywhere, he would have placed UN interests in a much better tactical position when the General Assembly met in its 19th session.

Thant chose "immobilism" instead, and the Article 19 crisis should be ascribed not only to sins of commission by the big powers, but also to sins of omission by the Secretary-General. Yet one should not be too harsh with him; under present circumstances one cannot expect too much of the man who sits in the corner office of the 38th floor. His predecessors had also committed blunders or sins of omission. Trygve Lie's around-the-world junket on his "20-point" peace program was a sad fizzle, and his behavior during the McCarthy offensive against American Secretariat members showed little courage or dignity. Hammarskjold, for all his heroic aura, will probably be judged severely by history on his failure to act when the youth of Hungary was fighting and dying on the streets of Budapest.

The stark reality is that the post of UN Secretary-General—christened by Lie as "the most impossible job in the world"—ideally calls for a combination of qualities of mind and character not easily found: rigorous academic training, a vocation for statesmanship wedded to administrative virtuosity, ability to think swiftly and argue convincingly in at least two of the organization's official languages. And last but not least, personal courage and personal integrity tempered by a sense of proportion and a sense of humor.

There are men in the more civilized countries who possess

these qualifications. The trouble is that under the prevailing system they stand no chance of being elected Secretary-General. For one of such caliber would already have attained a position of eminence in his own country, perhaps in his own continent, by the time he was tapped for "the world's most impossible job." This in itself would make him suspicious in the eyes of other governments in other parts of the world. The Soviets, for one, will never again accept for the position of Secretary-General a person of true stature (unless he is a communist). Not after their unnerving experience with Hammarskjold.

19

THE SECRETARIAT'S STANDARDS

The young lady sitting demurely on the leather sofa in the big office had neatly chiseled Caucasian features and a black skin. She was a granddaughter of Emperor Haile Selassie of Ethiopia. She had come to apply for a job in the United Nations information services, and the UN official sitting across from her in the big leather chair had been asking about her background. No, she didn't have any experience in journalism, radio, or TV, but she was particularly interested in television. No, no other specialized training. Her background was as expected: best schools in England and Switzerland, fluency in several languages, the social graces. She smiled modestly but confidently while she spoke. A princess of the blood should have no difficulty in joining the United Nations.

Her ambassador thought so, too. He had sat on the same leather sofa only a few days earlier and spoken to the same UN official. He had also subtly indicated that the kind of salary that would go with the post would of course be of no interest to Her Imperial Highness. What was not mentioned during the conversation was the princess's real motive for wanting a job with the world organization, although both the ambassador and the UN official were quite aware of it. Obviously the young lady wanted to live in New York for a while, but her grandfather never allowed a female member of the imperial family to stay abroad for any length of time once schooling in Europe was concluded. To work for the UN: that was the one exception; the world organization had enjoyed the Emperor's benevolence ever since it had chosen Addis Ababa as seat for its Economic Commission for Africa.

✍   ✍   ✍

During that same week in 1963, as in any week of any year since 1945, several thousand people from all over the world were, like the Ethiopian princess, trying to get a UN job. The exact number cannot be estimated, since only a minority is on record, those who apply to the UN department of personnel, describing their qualifications and background on the four-page yellow form printed in both English and French, which is distributed with a certain lavishness through UN offices abroad or directly from headquarters in New York. Actually the ones who fill in the application forms have only the remotest chances of being accepted, unless they have influential friends inside the UN or in their own government.

Of these thousands who at any one time are trying to get a job in the Secretariat, the vast majority are sufficiently aware to concentrate their energies on obtaining support in high quarters for their candidacy. Since there are literally only a handful of vacancies in the Secretariat every year, usually a member government will have to exert definite pressure. Obtaining a UN position for one of its nationals is held by most governments to be a matter of some importance; it is usually handled by the permanent representative himself. The ambassador will begin by visiting the head of "personnel" and several influential under-secretaries, reserving for a later stage the 38th floor, where he will concentrate on the Chef de Cabinet but will not neglect to speak directly to the Secretary-General himself.

Applicants are of all sorts and with every kind of background. The black princess with the hypnotic eyes was not the first of royal blood; in fact, the UN has had for the last few years another prince on its payroll, the Aga Khan's brother; and although several millionaires like Paul Hoffman of Marshall Plan fame are on the UN payroll, very few applicants are uninterested in salary scales. In fact, for the thousands of persons who at any one time are bending every effort to get a UN job money is undoubtedly the strongest motivation.

In most professional UN posts, salary plus fringe benefits add up to a handsome total even in comparison with what is paid in New York by private firms. And when the staff member obtains an assignment "in the field," his salary in dollars miraculously multiplies in almost every country in the world. In Yugoslavia, a joke circulates that Marshal Tito is the second best paid man in the country; the head of the UN information center in Belgrade is entitled to a salary considerably higher than that of the chief of state. In practically every single African, Asian, and Latin American country the head of UN technical assistance activities is paid more than a cabinet minister; in many of these countries his salary is higher than that of the president.

Among fringe benefits the pension on retirement ranks high for its generosity. Retirement age is sixty, while most member states set sixty-five for their civil servants. The UN staff member who retires at sixty on full pension will not have to go back to his own country; he can afford the high cost of living on the Côte d'Azur. Many of them do precisely this, buying a house on that magic stretch between Cap d'Ail and St. Raphael as they approach retirement age and going there every year for their vacation, which allows them to brush up on their French. Early in 1965 a Scandinavian staffer was being considered for transfer from an Asian post to Geneva, but versions conflicted at Headquarters about his knowledge of French. The clinching argument was ultimately adduced by a friend who one evening told a group of senior officials who were debating the transfer over a drink:

I wouldn't worry about Gunmar's knowledge of French. Two years ago he bought himself a house on Cap d'Antibes where he is going to retire. Last summer he invited me to spend a week there, warning that we would both be sleeping in the chauffeur's apartment over the garage, as he was remodeling and modernizing the house. Every morning Gunmar would be up and around by eight o'clock, walking around the place, discussing the work in progress with the three masons and the carpenter, and awaiting for the contractor to show up on his daily visit. One day I witnessed him haggling with the contractor and finally bring down by a good twenty percent the estimates for a second bathroom. It takes real fluency in the language for any foreigner to win that sort of argument with a French contractor.

‿ ‿ ‿

If salaries and pensions are attractive, working conditions at the UN are considered even more so. Working hours are from nine-thirty to six, but only secretaries (and not all of them) are expected to show up before ten to ten-fifteen in the morning. A summer schedule has been established from June to September, with working hours of nine to five. This measure is popular, since everyone continues to arrive about ten in the morning, while the daily stampede that overloads the elevators and clogs the two revolving doors on the ground floor takes place at five sharp, instead of at six sharp.

Lunch hour normally extends from one to three. Some like to stretch it to three-thirty and even four o'clock, but this is frowned upon. The morning and afternoon coffee breaks have become sacrosanct institutions; at ten-thirty in the morning, and then again around four in the afternoon, the cafeteria fills to overflowing.

Vacations are thirty working days yearly—Saturdays and Sundays not counted—which amounts to a six-week vacation every year. For staff members in the professional category who are not US citizens every two years brings a "home leave," the UN paying the round trip.

The quality and quantity of work accomplished varies enormously not only from department to department, but also from section to section and almost from office to office. Among the thirteen hundred professionals at Headquarters a few are almost fanatically hard workers; a few more are dedicated to the pursuit of total idleness. However, these are both small groups; work and output are always compared to that of a government bureaucracy, where everyone works at a deliberate pace, output is carefully measured in terms of promotion and transfer prospects, the system resting on the twin pillars of plethoric paperwork and systematic overstaffing.

However, a growing number of the serious students of the United Nations contend that the accepted parallel between the Secretariat and a governmental bureaucracy is too facile on both these counts, since it fails to take into account the high degree of political sophistication attained by the UN in comparison with its member states when it comes to the performance of its bureaucratic apparatus. In the twin fields of plethoric paper-shuffling and systematic overstaffing, political considerations play a role far above and beyond what occurs, for example, in the bureaucratic establishment of a great power.

Unlike the case in most foreign ministries, overemphasis on paperwork and habitual clogging of departments by idle functionaries are not cause but effect in the UN. They are not merely symptoms of a complacent and entrenched bureaucracy, but rather are exploited as strategic assets for the defensive and counterattacking moves planned by the higher echelons of UN bureaucrats in times of stress or crisis. When it comes to defending their vested interests and personal privileges the competence and resourcefulness of these higher echelons, to which the Indian "chain of command" makes a decisive contribution, is of such an order that UN bureaucracy should no longer be dismissed simply as "comparable" to that of any of the member states: in reality it stands much higher in terms of power and influence over the entire establishment.

While this concept of the supremacy of the UN bureaucratic establishment is slowly beginning to be accepted, it is still argued that at least two governmental bureaucracies, those of the two superpowers, could challenge the Secretariat. This argument, however, is academic. While in sheer "paper by the pound" and "number of bodies" both the Washington and the Moscow bureaucratic establishments easily outstrip the one on the East River, actual performance in Washington or Moscow is to a considerable extent sheer waste. It is rather the Soviet and the American bureaucracies which on the whole are apt to indulge in pointless paper-shuffling and in over-staffing purely for patronage, whereas at the UN the "sea of paper" and the "idle hands" may make good copy for news-papers like the *London Daily Express*, which choose to ignore the sound motivation—the promotion of personal and group interests—that underlies the apparent bureaucratic morass on the East River.

That the UN bureaucracy is superior to the US bu-reaucracy is not difficult to demonstrate; that of the US has often been dissected and analyzed. The USSR is another mat-ter, because analysis and exegesis of the Soviet bureaucratic establishment is not easy to come by, although a perusal of *Izvestia*, and above all of *Pravda*, yields many a useful indica-tion. More revealing is the attitude of senior Russian officials who are assigned to the Secretariat under the Soviet quota. They invariably develop an attitude of high respect for the mechanics and the motivations of the UN establishment, and become intent on understanding and absorbing highly devel-oped techniques which are taken for granted at the UN, but which for a Russian who will be going back to Moscow to occupy a high position in his Foreign Ministry will prove immensely valuable, both from an overall point of view as well as in the two key fields of paperwork and overstaffing.

An example of this is given by the episode of memo ST/ADM/SER.A/993 of February 18, 1965, put out by the General Services department, which was extensively com-mented upon and analyzed in UN circles. The Secretariat Rus-sians were clearly impressed, although they carefully abstained

from participating in any of the informal "post-mortem" sessions on the memo held during the following days among
crack UN bureaucrats and in fact also among delegates—
mostly Western delegates, since 993, as it came to be known,
was too advanced in its technique for the Africans, or even the
Latin Americans, to fully understand and appreciate. The Russians apparently chose to conduct their exegesis in Moscow
government departments, for on the following day, a Friday,
a junior Soviet Secretariat official collected fifty copies of 993.

In retrospect it becomes apparent that 993 was blown
somewhat out of proportion and came to be celebrated beyond
its merits, which were at bottom pedestrian and certainly not
unprecedented. The reason for this over-evaluation was simply
the timing of 993, which was as carefully planned as every
word in its text. Thursday, February 18 had been a fateful
day in the history of the UN. Just before 993 was distributed,
the United States delegation and the allies of the U.S. had
beaten a humiliating retreat before the clever parliamentary
maneuver of the lone delegate representing the interests of
Peking, Ambassador Halim Bubo of Albania.

For months debate had raged in the world press on the
"bankruptcy" of the United Nations, and UN finances were
scrutinized more closely than ever. Memo 993 was a typical
example of "defense in depth" by the Secretariat, putting to
useful employ the twin techniques relating to paperwork and
to overstaffing. Its full text read:

UNITED NATIONS   ST/ADM/SER.A/993
SECRETARIAT   18 February 1965

INFORMATION CIRCULAR
To: Members of the Staff
Subject: MESSENGER SERVICE
1. As part of the general measures which need to be taken
to keep expenditures within the limits prescribed by the
General Assembly, certain changes in the Messenger
Service will take effect on 19 February 1965.

2. Regular messenger runs covering the established stops will begin each day at the following times:

9:30 A.M.

11:00 A.M.

1:30 P.M.

3:00 P.M.

4:30 P.M.

3. Material for dispatch by mail or pouch that is not collected by the last afternoon run may be delivered by hand to Room 2050 at any time prior to 7:00 P.M. Cables for dispatch may be delivered to the same room at any time.

4. The special delivery of urgent incoming cables will continue to be effected; however, no other special messenger service will be available except as required by the Executive Office of the Secretary-General. In a few other instances certain non-routine messenger functions will be modified. The Secretariat offices directly concerned will be consulted in each case, and efforts made to arrange satisfactory alternatives.

5. It is appreciated that the changes notified in this circular may cause temporary disruptions of previously established working patterns, and it is regretted that this must occur. The co-operation of all staff is requested in order to keep these disruptions to a minimum.

Director of General Services

ᔐ   ᔐ   ᔐ

On the day 993 was issued, and throughout the following week, emissaries from "general services" went out lobbying among the delegates, calling attention to the initiative they were taking and what it represented in savings for the UN budget. They refrained, however, from saying that the economies were basically due to the dismissal of several members of the messenger service.

In this particular case both plethoric paperwork and systematic overstaffing had been put to good use. Since the bulk of the papers circulated in the building through the messenger service lacked any intrinsic significance, not to mention urgency, delay of their delivery made little difference. And because systematic overstaffing had always been religiously followed by "general services," the dismissal of messengers mattered to individual humans but did not materially affect performance. Moreover, standard operating procedure in all departments in the Secretariat is not to depend on messenger service, since it normally takes many hours—and often two days—for any paper to be delivered from one office to another. Consequently the other departments had over the years improvised their own messenger service. When a paper of some importance has to be sent from one office to another, the custom is to ask a secretary to do it, thus ensuring prompt delivery.

Fundamentally, the 993 episode was interesting only as an exercise of "defense in depth": in a time of crisis a department with a poor record of performance tried to convince delegates that it was intent on both efficiency and economy. In this sense the memo was accorded too much importance, and borrowed significance because it came out on the very day when the financial crisis had reached a dramatic climax. By placing paperwork and overstaffing at the service of its own survival, the housekeeping department was in reality setting an unfair example to all other departments in the Secretariat, which are motivated by political considerations of a higher order. Departments engaged in political or economic activities maintain a plethoric output of papers to keep the majority of their staff members, who happen to be of a very low caliber in terms of academic background and competence, occupied with trivia. The few outstanding staffers can be assigned to any significant project under way at a given moment.

Conversely, the practice of systematically overstaffing a department satisfies political and geographic injunctions, yet allows for the recruitment of at least a few truly competent professionals. Almost all the Africans and a majority of the Latin Americans and the Asians in the Secretariat, for instance, have shown over the years an abysmally low level of performance. But Africans, if not Latin Americans and Asians, have

to be recruited in ever larger numbers under prevailing political pressures, while the recruitment of Western Europeans
becomes more difficult every year. Since as a general rule the
academic and intellectual level of Western Europeans is embarrassingly higher than that of Africans, Latin Americans,
and Asians, the only way to secure the services of a few Europeans who will give a good account of themselves is to accept
cramming the department with *tiers monde* nonentities.

ಉ   ಉ   ಉ

UN department heads who insist on professional rather than
political standards for recruitment usually defeat their own
ends. For instance, the Ethiopian princess was refused a post
in the information services on the grounds that she had no
qualifications. Her delegation's resentment was compounded
by that of other Afro-Asian delegations, who invariably give
a color-line interpretation to any professional evaluation. This
inevitably put additional obstacles in the way of the information specialists in the world body.

»» 20 ««

THE MEMO JUNGLE

Since several hundred Secretariat staff members from the lowly
P-1s to the semi-exalted P-5s, D-1s and D-2s, have nothing to
do, the vast majority of them are dedicated to the parturition
of memoranda as often as feasible, and if possible daily. Their
immediate superiors usually accept with good grace the endless
stream of memos to which they are subjected by their sub-
ordinates. Almost all of these memos are pointless; they will
be quietly filed and forgotten. But while they are being drafted,
redrafted, dictated, typed, originals sent to superiors, copies
generously distributed to other sections, the staff member lives
in a world rich with illusion. And the illusion runs full circle
when, with a little luck, he casually encounters his superior
in a corridor or in the men's room.

"Hope you received my memo."

"Came in this morning. Haven't had time to go through
it yet. Piles of stuff on my desk when I came back from Africa.
Amazing how it just mushrooms."

"I know. It's amazing how it grows."

"Yes, the stuff just piles up. But I put your memo on top.
Want to read it carefully. After six is the best time. Telephone
stops ringing."

"I appreciate it. In case you need any clarification just
ring me up and I'll come over. I usually stay after six myself."

"Good idea."

They say goodbye and will probably not run into each other again for days. But it has been a highly successful encounter for both of them. The subordinate feels elated at having discussed his memo directly with the boss; he believes this is one memo that will be read, and perhaps will not be forgotten. The supervisor will congratulate himself on the fortuitous meeting; having had that talk in the corridor with his subordinate, he can with a clear conscience avoid going through the motions of reading and commenting on the memo. And since he knows that the dialogue will be reported to all P1s, P2s, P3s, and P4s in his section, he can't help feeling pleased at the several points he got across in one minute of dialogue: (a) that he is snowed under with work, (b) that he always stays after six to catch up on his work, (c) that he has just returned from Africa, always considered a virtuous trip, since its pleasures are held to be scarce.

In reality, the supervisor (a) is never snowed under piles of stuff, since he has had the good sense to corner a veteran assistant who enjoys doing paper work, (b) while in effect he stays on after six Monday through Friday, and sometimes as late as eight or nine in the evening, it is almost invariably to have drinks with other senior officials of the department in the under-secretary's boardroom, (c) his trip to Africa was much more pleasant than it sounded, since he managed to stop for several days in Cairo "for consultations" on his way to and from Addis Ababa, in order to fully enjoy the physical assets of a sensual Lebanese secretary working for the technical assistance people.

∽   ∽   ∽

At higher echelons and in the sensitive departments, however, memo writing grows in stature and becomes a weapon of survival. In these exalted realms the very technique reaches heights of complexity and refinement, and it is no exaggeration to describe the very best memo writers of the United Nations as true virtuosi, who have proved their superiority to the best memo writers of the USSR, the United States, and India, the three countries that lead the world in this field.

Most of the memo writers at these higher echelons limit themselves to a defensive or holding operation. They are quite resigned to their P-5, D-1, or D-2 jobs, and prefer to await developments instead of pushing and plotting for fast promotions and choice assignments. Nurturing no great ambitions, they realize that nothing should be taken for granted about their prestigious and well-paid job; for instance, merely to avoid transfer to an undesirable Asian, African, or Latin American outpost calls for continuous vigilance, and memo writing is an important tactic.

Consequently, they will not let a single day go by without working on the production of a memo. The aim is a steady and sustained production, not subject matter. They are perfectly aware that in all probability a memo will not be read by the under-secretary or the department head to whom it is addressed. But it will be "on record," and by the end of the year a thick folder in the departmental files will harbor their memo output. And that counts.

On the other hand, even the more placid among these professionals cannot always manage to remain outside a power clash within the Secretariat. While they aspire at nothing beyond holding on to their jobs, they are sometimes inevitably caught in the cross fire of a power play; much to their distress they may be even forced to choose sides, knowing only too well that their career may be in jeopardy if they pick a loser. But as veterans of many a similar clash, they can usually predict quite accurately who will win and who will lose.

They need time to study and analyze the developing power struggle to correctly evaluate the outcome. To gain this precious time, they resort to memo writing in one of its more intricate aspects: defense in depth combined with probing maneuvers. This category of memo writing calls for a high degree of technical skill and even for a sense of strategy, as can be gleaned from the following instance.

The under-secretary heading the political department decides that a study on Cyprus should be prepared by his staff in order to brief the Secretary-General on the intricacies of a situation in which the UN has become deeply involved. In theory this represents a helpful initiative, originating in the appropriate quarters in the Secretariat: the under-secretary in charge of political affairs is also in charge of Security Council affairs, and the UN happens to be in Cyprus following a Security Council decision.

In reality, however, he happens to be the one Soviet under-secretary in the organization, and his proposed political study has nothing to do with briefing purposes; it is intended rather to impress upon the Secretary-General the Soviet position on Cyprus. In case the Secretary-General declines to be impressed, the study may still serve a useful purpose from a Soviet point of view as a pressure instrument. In effect such a study, carrying the UN imprint, will in the nature of things be taken as a UN position paper, and it will prove awkward for the Secretary-General, and even more so for UN personnel assigned to Cyprus, to ignore its arguments and implied conclusions.

As soon as the Soviet under-secretary announces his intention to the staff of Political, a senior department official will draw up an outline of the paper, based on the under-secretary's suggestions, and assign specific parts for research and drafting to several middle-echelon staffers. Let us assume that among these only two are Westerners; this is a reasonable assumption, since Political is the one department in the Secretariat where Westerners are in a minority. The department has been headed by a Russian from the very beginning of the UN, and it is staffed with a majority of Russians and Eastern Europeans. Let us further suppose that of our two Westerners one is a veteran with considerable skill in the techniques of memo writing, while the other is a comparative newcomer whose only assets are serious studies at a famous university and a doctorate in political science.

The veteran Westerner will immediately realize that both he and his junior colleague have been pushed into a sticky corner. Whatever they write about Cyprus (in other words, if they try to be factual and detached within the framework of their Western background) will be overshadowed by the papers prepared by their communist colleagues, which will follow the anti-NATO Soviet line, already unveiled in the Security Council by the delegate of the USSR.

On the other hand, precisely because the project contains so much political dynamite it is not at all certain that it will be carried through. The NATO delegations will have been alerted by their Secretariat contacts, probably less than one hour after the Russian under-secretary informed his staff of his intention. There will be strong reactions from several NATO delegations, meaning not only the Turks and the Greeks, but also the Americans, the British, and the French.

The situation is fluid and our veteran Westerner will probably end up in trouble whether he carries out his assignment or not. The solution is to prepare a carefully drafted memo for a defense in depth. It reads as follows:

> To: Mr. Vladimir Ilyitch Popov
> Under-Secretary for Political and Security
> Council Affairs
>
> Through: Mr. John P. Goldman
> Chief, Political Studies Section
>
> From: Mark P. Danaos
> Political Officer, Political Affairs Section
>
> Subject: *Study on recent developments in Cyprus question*

This political officer has been assigned the preparation of a section of the study on Cyprus and accorded two weeks to complete his assignment.

In view of complexity and importance of problem, as

reflected in Security Council decisions, detailed research material must be assembled in several languages. The Translation Section has indicated that it will not guarantee early delivery of translations from the Greek and the Turkish languages, even of relatively brief articles in periodicals and dailies.

Since this project has been attributed a very high priority by the Under-Secretary, in view of the shortness of time it is requested that a junior professional be detached to work with this political officer, who will then be able to concentrate on assembling important printed material on the Cyprus question in the Greek and Turkish languages, and submit it at the earliest possible moment to the translation section.

Only if this request is approved could the assignment realistically be completed in two weeks, and the final draft be presented to the Under-Secretary through the Chief, Political Studies Section, for approval.

For all its apparent simplicity and pedestrian approach, this memo is of a very high technical caliber indeed. It was written and rewritten several times by Danaos, and then shown in confidence to an old friend in the economic department who is an expert memo writer and who made a few minor improvements and described Danaos's baby as "a tight little jewel, a tight little jewel on the whole." Danaos was so touched by this compliment that in a moment of unguarded magnanimity he went to see his junior Western colleague, Claude Artemis, and offered to extend to him this umbrella of high-quality defense. He was surprised and hurt when Claude refused without hesitation, saying with a short laugh:

"Why not do the paper? I assure you it's more fun than writing memos. This Cyprus thing is rather fascinating. I have been looking at it closely."

Claude was much younger than Danaos, and basically a decent fellow who had volunteered to give Danaos's eldest son some badly needed coaching in Politics and Government before his college examination. The boy had passed with flying colors, and Danaos was grateful to Claude. Now he felt compelled to insist in order to protect his unsuspecting colleague: "It isn't a question of having fun, Claude. It's a question of hanging on to your job. You can have fun after office hours."

"Hanging on to my job? Why, I was given this assignment, just like you and half a dozen other guys in the department. So it is my job. The fact that I'm going to enjoy doing it, I don't see why anyone would hold it against me. It will be a dandy paper, you watch and see. And with solid scholarship behind it. I'm going to go through the lectures of old man Fowles. He has died since, but I was still in time to be his student at Princeton. I think he's about the best anywhere when it comes to analyzing civil wars. Just what I need for Cyprus."

Danaos shuddered. "That would presumably be the Woodrow Wilson School of Public and International Affairs, Princeton University?"

"Why, yes," beamed Claude. "Great school. Personally, I think it compares to Sciences Pô, although no Frenchman will admit it. Did you know old man Fowles?"

"No, and I don't want to hear about the man, or about your Princeton school," said Danaos impatiently. "That will only get you into deeper trouble with our friend Vladimir. Now read my memo once more."

Claude did as he was told, and when he had finished commented: "It makes no sense to me. You don't need anyone to help you, and you certainly don't need to sit and wait for translations from Greek and Turkish by our translator guys, who wouldn't dream of taking less than six weeks to translate a one-column editorial. Why, Reuters and France Presse will give you the same day a reliable transcription of any article of importance appearing in Athens, Nicosia, Istanbul, or Ankara. And anyway, most of it is pamphleteering and exchanging wild accusations."

Danaos decided to be patient and didactic, instead of losing his temper. After all Claude had been very patient with his boy during those cramming sessions. "You have been with us only four years, Claude, but still it should be long enough to learn about memos. This one requires an answer. This way we can protect our jobs."

"I can see that it requires an answer," said Claude, "and I can tell you exactly what the answer is going to be. They are going to say the hell with you. They are not going to give you an assistant that you don't need in the first place."

"Yes, but by the time the memo goes through channels and Vladimir says no another week will have gone by, perhaps ten days. And by that time I'm pretty sure the British or the Americans will have made a move."

"Sure enough. They will say the hell with this study, what does Political mean by coming out with a position paper on Cyprus, unless it's the one you and I are going to write."

"Do you think we could get away with our version on Cyprus?"

Claude thought for a moment. "It's not our version on Cyprus. But it damn well will be much closer to the truth, to what the situation is really like over there, than what Yuri and Boris are going to write, and that greasy Rumanian chap."

"Don't forget our wild Guinean who has just discovered Marx, and our bootlicking Indian, and our new Pole."

"What new Pole?"

"He hasn't joined yet. Not officially. But he has been included in the writing team. Johnnie Goldman told me. It is they who are going to write the draft that Vladimir is going to accept."

"They shouldn't be allowed to get away with that," said Claude indignantly. "They are just going to rehash the Fedorenko line, over and over again."

"So what? Do you want to be a hero or do you want to keep your job?"

"I want to do a job of cold political analysis. The way old man Fowles taught us."

Danaos exploded: "Then go back to Princeton, damn you.

I don't really want to help you if you don't want to be helped. Me, I have to hold on to this job because I'm paying alimony and I still owe a dozen payments on that boat I keep out in Long Island, and I certainly won't enjoy being transferred to Karachi or Accra or Asunción. So I won't be a hero. But you are a bachelor and you don't have a permanent contract, and you belong in Princeton anyway."

"I don't want to go back to Princeton," said Claude sulkily. "Not yet, anyway."

Danaos was still angry. "That will be strictly up to you. I'm going to leave you a copy of my memo after all, but keep it under lock and key. Think it over and write your memo, based on mine, in case you don't really want to be sent back to Princeton. But use your brains in paraphrasing. I'm not sticking my neck out for you, and Vladimir is no fool."

All of a sudden Claude turned conciliatory. "Perhaps this memo of yours is the greatest piece of political strategy since Kennedy went on television on Missile Monday. But I really don't see why."

Danaos was coldly professional. "Why? Because it gains time for me until the British or the Americans . . ." He halted and reflected for a moment. "For that matter I think it will be the Americans themselves who will move. This could be serious and the West is bound to block Vladimir's power play and the Secretary-General will be under pressure from both sides. And I, who am a lousy P-4, will keep out of the way of the big boys, as I should." After a moment he concluded hopefully: "And Vladimir will not be angry at me."

"That you don't really believe," said Claude. "He's as smart as they come. He's the new Soviet generation, don't you forget it."

"Officially I will be on pretty solid ground and I will have given him no offense. I'm only a P-4, and Vladimir doesn't take it out on the small fellows. He plays a hard and ruthless game, but he doesn't play dirty, unless he is given no choice. I'll be all right." He walked to the frosted glass door, stopped for a moment before stepping out of Claude's cubicle: "Don't get me wrong. I'm all for academic freedom and for what Fowles stands for. And I think your Princeton school is not bad. Not in the same class with Sciences Pô, but not bad at all."

Before he closed the door Claude sang out to him gaily: "Do you know what an assistant professor gets at Princeton?"

"It's more than a lowly P-2 like you gets at the UN. Yes, I know that. But you won't make it to an assistant professorship. You're not that good." He mused for a moment. "Not yet, anyway. Another two years and you will be ready for teaching at Princeton. Go ahead and write that memo, Claude. For God's sake, don't make it look as if you have copied mine. As I say, Vladimir is no fool, and he's not a treacherous guy, but he hasn't got a sense of humor. No Russian has, not even the new generation ones. Don't try to sound as if you're making fun of him. Try to sound as if you are the dumb one. It shouldn't be too difficult."

He gave Claude a knowing wink and closed the door softly.

HE HAS A PROBLEM FOR
EVERY SOLUTION

The definition of a UN staff member as someone "who has a problem for every solution" is often heard at UN headquarters, at the delegations located in its neighborhood, and even at parties. It is usually brought up by someone who has just gone through a particularly frustrating experience in tangling with the East River bureaucrats.

The paternity of the expression is attributed to a junior member of the United Kingdom delegation, who of course denies it. He is not being modest, because the expression was in existence for many years before the UN was born; while its origin remains unknown, it is believed to have been coined in English, and thus to have been aimed presumably at either the American or the British bureaucracy. Actually the definition applies to the members of any government bureaucracy, irrespective of language or country.

In this sense the definition, though amusing, does not really help to understand the UN bureaucratic establishment, and consequently the functioning of the world organization. In point of fact it is rather misleading when applied to the members of the United Nations Secretariat, since it places undue emphasis on the sluggishness which any bureaucrat worth his salt will endeavor to introduce into the executive machinery. While a UN bureaucrat will of course refrain from taking an initiative or making a decision (and within the limits of prudence will prevent anyone else from so doing), this by no means constitutes a central objective for him. Actually he is a much more accomplished and indeed a much more sophisticated practitioner of the techniques of bureaucracy than his counterpart in a governmental establishment. Blocking decisions is but one phase of his activities.

The true complexity of the UN bureaucratic establishment, and hence of the operations of the Secretariat of the United Nations, is revealed in the following question-and-answer discussion between a former UN official and a journalist friend who wanted to write an article on the Secretariat. Because of political pressure the article was not published.

Q. "It is generally accepted as one of the UN facts of life that executive power is concentrated in the hands of the so-called Anglo-Saxons, who share it only with the Indians. Do you agree?"

A. "It depends on what you mean by the Anglo-Saxons."

Q. "Primarily the Americans, then the British, with the Canadians and Australians having much smaller influence. The Americans of course hold by far the largest number of posts, but I'm not interested in numbers but in key positions. For instance, there is an American as Executive Officer in practically every department. Wouldn't that in itself mean a controlling network of officials in key positions?"

A. "It is actually much less significant than it sounds. Americans in the Secretariat are by no means as well articulated among themselves as the British or the Indians."

Q. "There is of course another theory that has been gaining ground, according to which it is the Indians who have seized power within the Secretariat, operating as a well articulated group, to use your expression. Would you rather subscribe to this interpretation?"

A. "I don't see why I should. I have a great deal of respect for the Indians, for they have shown much skill and resourcefulness in infiltrating the Secretariat. I will go

even further and say they have the best intelligence-gather-
ing system within the United Nations; confidential information is usually tracked down by them at a very early stage
and passed up to their top man on the 38th floor with
remarkable speed. But they are not in control of the Secretariat, nor is that the trend."

Q. "Will you agree, however, that at least one Indian
is entrenched in a strategic position in every department
of the United Nations, without exception?"

A. "There is no question of agreeing. This is common
knowledge, I might even say trivial knowledge. But it does
not amount to a seizure of power by the Indians. For one
thing, they have never been able to overcome intense
rivalries and dislikes among themselves; for instance, the
southern Indians from the Madras area, who are by far
the better political operators, resent being looked down on
by their countrymen from the northern provinces. What
is even more serious is that the Indians have never been
able to develop a truly effective system of public relations
to overcome the general dislike and distrust in which they
are held. Unless they overcome these twin handicaps, which
I seriously doubt, they will never be able to seize power
in the sense of actually running the show. My personal
opinion is that the present system will prevail during the
years ahead."

Q. "You mean the sharing of power between the
Americans, the Indians and the British?"

A. "If I were to accept that listing, I would place the
British first and the Americans last."

Q. "But haven't the Indians been losing ground in the
Secretariat ever since they lost face in 1962 when the
Chinese beat them on the Himalayan border?"

A. "Let us not confuse the two things. They lost an
enormous amount of face, but very little ground. They lost
face with the Afro-Asians and with the Soviet bloc, which
is bad for the pursuit of India's foreign policy, but matters
little in terms of power realities within the United Nations,
since neither the Afro-Asians nor the Communists have any
substantial influence on the Secretariat."

Q. "How about the Westerners? Do you mean that the
Westerners were the only ones to overlook India's decreased

influence and prestige after the Chinese routed the Indian frontier army and threatened to sweep into the plains of Assam?"

A. "Of course the Westerners were fully aware of the new situation created in Asia by the 1962 Himalayan campaign. After all, don't forget the Americans and the British reacted more swiftly than anyone else since they had more at stake in the area. It was primarily because of them that the Chinese withdrew quietly to the contested border areas on the Northeast Frontier Agency, even though they could have staged an unopposed military march all the way into Calcutta. But we are not discussing grand strategy in Southeast Asia but merely controlling influences within the Secretariat. Since the British and the Americans hold the balance of power together with the Indians, it was not in their interest to have the Indians suffer the consequences of their Himalayan defeat also here in the UN."

Q. "My information is that the Americans had been fed up with the Indians in the Secretariat for some time and were rather eager to begin cutting them down to size in 1962. Is that correct?"

A. "What matters is not what the Americans wanted to do, but what they finally were persuaded to do by the British. The British persuaded their American allies to agree to preserve the Indian position of strength inside the UN."

Q. "Are you implying that the British have a dominant role when it comes to deciding joint US-British policies regarding the UN?"

A. "I used advisedly the word 'persuaded,' in its genuine sense, not as a diplomatic euphemism. The British persuaded the Americans that it was not in their interest, or in the interest of the Western alliance for that matter, to have the Indians lose substantial ground in the Secretariat."

Q. "Why not? Wouldn't that have left the Americans and the British in a dominant position by themselves inside the UN, without having to share their power with the Indians?"

A. "Nothing of the sort would have happened and the British, with their uncanny political wisdom, knew it all along. Suppose senior Indian officials had actually been wrenched from their strategic posts on the 38th floor and in the departments that count. The vacancies would not have been filled by Westerners, but by other Afro-Asians. What guarantee could the Americans and the British have that they would be able to instal an acceptable Afro-Asian, such as a Liberian, for instance? None whatsoever; in fact, they would run a real danger of having some of the posts filled by wild Ghanaians or Malians. Indians are much more dependable."

Q. "Dependable? The Americans are always complaining. Aren't the Indians supposed to play the non-aligned game?"

A. "The Indians know on what side their bread is buttered. They dislike the Westerners, of course, but then they dislike all colored races, too, and are cordially disliked by them. But make no mistake, it is the Indians who are the real Westerners of Asia, not the Japanese, as it has become fashionable to say. Besides, they depend so much financially on the Americans, and to a lesser extent on the British, that they have to side with them when the going gets rough. The fact that the Indians are devious and whenever possible treacherous upsets the Americans, who insist on mixing ethics with politics, but it does not in the least disturb the British, who have known the Indians for several centuries. The best proof of this is that although the British have a lot more respect for an Arab than for an Indian, they will go a long way to block an Arab from a senior post in the Secretariat, while they will push an Indian. And I agree with their explanation, which is that while an Arab is not as untrustworthy as an Indian, on the other hand the Indian frightens more easily when he is in a tight spot, and thus becomes easier to handle. Believe me, the Indian chain of command inside the United Nations will survive for quite a few years the political and economic decay of India. The British will see to that and the Americans will go along with them. Reluctantly, I grant you, but they will go along."

Q. "All right, let us accept that the Indians will maintain their grip on power inside the Secretariat, by courtesy of the British and the Americans. Doesn't this mean that in effect the balance of power within the UN will be held by

the Americans and the British, or perhaps by the British
and the Americans, since you seem to think that is their
order of importance?"

A. "I think we should first agree on some fundamental
semantics. These concepts of power structure, balance of
power and grab for power by this or that nation or this
or that bloc are really romantic exaggerations. The realities
of power in the Secretariat are much simpler and more
pedestrian. There is no over-all power structure as such,
but simply in-fighting among cliques. It so happens that
one of these cliques, the Indian chain of command, represents a single nation and operates vertically, from the 38th
floor down. But that is due to the special circumstances we
have just discussed and in effect constitutes an exception.
All other cliques operate horizontally, with their members
holding senior posts in every department. It is basically an
'old cronies' setup, and Anglo-Saxon control is merely due
to the fact that almost all of them come from white English-
speaking countries. Of course the British and the Americans are predominant, but don't forget the Canadians, the
Australians and even an occasional New Zealander. And
if they serve the interests of the United States and the
United Kingdom it is simply because their background and
their political convictions lead them inevitably in that direction. While there is a pro-Western political climate that
pervades the Secretariat, there is very little that is sinister
about the actions of the Anglo-Saxon senior officials responsible for this climate. In fact among these few dozen
senior officials I doubt whether there is a single one who
receives instructions from his delegation daily, as is the
case with the Russians. Technically they conform to the
ruling in article 100 of the Charter, the one that says they
shall not seek or receive instructions from any government."

Q. "We all know about the cliques. Their purpose,
according to the research I have already done, is rather to
promote the interests of the members of the clique, like
getting soft assignments, trips to Europe, rapid promotion
and that sort of thing. As you say, the cliques are composed
of old cronies who will look after each other's interests. But
that is just picturesque detail. How effective can they be
in the UN's day-to-day operations; above all, can they be

effective when the organization faces a crisis, if these cliques are basically mutual welfare groupings?"

A. "You are confusing the operational and the survival functions of the clique. In fact, I would reserve the name of clique for the operational aspects, and use the concept of fief for survival. On the operational level the clique functions with sufficient effectiveness. While the UN bureaucrat avoids making a decision, the clique does not. In fact it insists jealously on its power to make decisions. Every time an important move is made in the house, the Under-Secretary who proposes it to the Secretary-General, and the Secretary-General who approves it, have usually had very little to do with the actual decision, which is always taken by a compact, homogeneous group of old-timers who reach a consensus among themselves long before the problem is formally submitted to the Under-Secretary or to the Secretary-General himself. That is the operational aspect of the clique. But since there are several cliques in the Secretariat, they have organized themselves, for survival purposes, in a sort of feudalistic structure of fiefs, each one under its own baron or suzerain. The rules for belonging are few and simple. Loyalty to the baron and to fellow members of a fief, promotion of the material welfare of fellow members and of the prestige of the fief inside the Secretariat. The one unforgivable crime is to work out an individual, unilateral pact with another fief."

Q. "Is it true that there are alliances and even non-aggression pacts negotiated between the different fiefs?"

A. "Certainly. Since the balance of power is fluid in the Secretariat, the baron at the head of each fief maneuvers to obtain the support or at least the neutrality of other influential barons. This is particularly true when something of importance is developing. For instance, when the new trade and development outfit was being set up, there were so many new jobs available both here and in Geneva that there was serious concern among the fiefs, especially since there was an organized attempt to give most of these jobs to outsiders, on the pretext that they were better qualified for the highly specialized functions."

Q. "Wasn't that true?"

A. "I don't know what you mean by true. There was

a plan afoot for having a number of highly desirable jobs
gobbled up by outsiders. This represented a pressing danger for fiefs within the Secretariat, particularly those
operating in the economic branches. The fact that some of
the candidates from outside were prominent in the economic field was irrelevant; a member in good standing of
a fief in the Secretariat can be made to look as good on
paper as a professor at the Sorbonne. But there was no
doubt that a crisis was looming. So the several fiefs in the
economic sections of the UN 'buttoned up,' as they always
do in times of danger, and went to work."

Q. "What do you mean by 'buttoning up'?"

A. "It's an expression handed down from world war
days. I think it means an armored vehicle preparing for
action. They like these dramatic names. Actually what it
means in practice is for everyone to shut up so as to avoid
leaks, and to speed up the flow of inside information
through the umbilical cord every fief maintains with the
38th floor, so as to be able to plan in advance a sensible
strategy."

Q. "What you call a sensible strategy in this case was
pushing that little Czech into the number two position in
Geneva, I presume."

A. "Very sensible. In fact I'm inclined to think it was
a brilliant move. Do you happen to know that little Czech,
as you call him?"

Q. "Smetana? I have known him for years. Every
correspondent knows him. He is very helpful about briefing
us discreetly on what went on in closed sessions of his committee. I mean the floor fights and that sort of thing. When
it comes to straight economics he doesn't understand much,
but he has sense enough to have assistants who are gradu-
ates of top universities. But his appointment to Geneva to
such a high position created quite a flurry. I know because
I cabled a special story. Apparently the Russians were
upset; they don't trust Smetana. For that matter, the Czech
delegation doesn't trust him either. He has managed to be
on both sides of the fence ever since the Communist coup
in Czechoslovakia in 1948. Why was he appointed to such
an important post in this new trade and development
outfit?"

A. "As you say, Smetana is not really trusted by the Communist delegations, and much less by the Western ones. Consequently, appointing him gave a political coloring to the staffing of the trade and development organization, which was just then being planned. The delegations from the major countries, who had thus far agreed with the technical approach, now considered that political appointments were called for. Each delegation came up with its own candidate, and as was to be expected most of the candidates were old-timers in the Secretariat, men who knew their way around and who could keep a close check on Smetana."

Q. "You mean that the heat was off for appointing these famous economists from the outside?"

A. "Of the new posts created by the General Assembly for the trade and development outfit, almost all have gone to old-timers here in the Secretariat. There is no longer any question of canvassing the great universities and ministries of planning and economic development to find brilliant people. All that is forgotten and the establishment is secure once more."

Q. "Do you mean that it's impossible for the United Nations to enlist the services of first-class people?"

A. "Someone of course may always join from the outside if he is backed by one of the powerful cliques. But the type of person who can make a brilliant career in the outside world has really no incentive for joining the Secretariat, unless he comes from an underdeveloped country and the pay in dollars represents a fortune for him."

Q. "Then the conclusion is that the Secretariat is condemned to mediocrity?"

A. "I don't understand the question."

Q. "It seems pretty obvious from what you tell me that only someone who has been a failure in the outside world will want to join the UN."

A. "There you are introducing moral judgments that have no place here. The purpose of the Secretariat is not to function but to participate in power plays. There are four thousand people in this building, another thousand in Geneva. There is nothing for them to do in terms that would be understandable to a private firm, for instance.

But it would be very unjust to call anyone of them a para-
site. They are engaged in a number of political maneuvers
and activities that should not be dismissed as of no consequence merely because they take place at a trivial level. In
point of fact the struggle for power among the different
cliques, the push for survival and expansion among the
fiefs, have a repercussion on the world's chancelleries that
is out of all proportion to the caliber of the people who
constitute the establishment in this building. In this sense
the Secretariat is playing a significant role in international
relations."

*   *   *

Appended to the questionnaire answered by the former UN
official was a text known as the "decalogue." It was not prepared by the official; he merely gave a copy to his journalist
friend. In fact, it has no known author, and from its uneven
and somewhat discursive style must have been written by
different people, probably at different times. The decalogue
is never openly circulated, and senior officials who have access
to it will describe it as "irreverent" or even as "impertinent."
   No one in the UN, however, challenges the soundness of
the advice it gives. As a matter of fact, nowadays the decalogue is much sought by officials at the director level, and even
by under-secretaries. Over the last two years, and perhaps
even earlier, delegates from a number of countries have made
efforts to get a copy of the decalogue, which apparently would
prove a useful guide of conduct in many foreign ministries.
(In February, 1964, it became known that one of the Western
ambassadors sent a copy of the decalogue by diplomatic
pouch to his foreign minister.) This has not been a welcome
development, since it has tended to glamorize the decalogue
and lend it an exaggerated importance. Because members of
delegations, including ambassadors, have become interested
in the decalogue, there is now a tendency to forget that after
all this is merely a set of useful rules of behavior for lower

echelon officials, and should not be treated as a significant document with policy overtones.

The text of the "decalogue" handed to the journalist read as follows:

1. Never commit yourself in writing on anything of any importance or relevance, and be careful not to state an opinion in writing on something that looks insignificant, until you have proven to your satisfaction that it is truly insignificant. Above all, never commit yourself in writing to a course of action that could conceivably be establishing a precedent. On the contrary, express immediately your reverence and respect for tradition, and indicate in your memorandum that you would not presume to propose establishing a precedent, and that it would be more prudent to follow the traditions of the United Nations, established over a period of almost twenty years.

2. Always commit to writing everything that doesn't matter, but draft it in such a way that your colleagues will be wary of assuming authorship. Try to develop a clouded style with ominous overtones, indicating that a serious or even critical situation may develop in your department at any moment. Since in any case this happens often, you will gain a reputation for foresight with your superiors. Even if nothing happens your memo will be treated with respect because of its sibylline style and will be passed from hand to hand for exegesis among the higher echelons. This will add slowly but perceptibly to your standing in your department.

3. In daily dealing and verbal exchanges, including casual talk in the corridors, try to develop the talent for making the trivial seem pregnant with mysterious possibilities, and for making the irrelevant sound recondite. The best way to develop this talent is to listen carefully to senior members of the Secretariat who are respected in this field, and to try to speak exactly as they do. After a few years you will develop a style of your own, and don't worry in the meantime. The fact that you imitate one of the higher-ups in the Secretariat will be interpreted by most of your colleagues as if you had become his protegé, an assumption that will not hurt your career.

4. Cable as often as possible and make your cables "confidential no distribution," since that will give you status. If your post is not high enough to permit your sending confidential cables, try to obtain a special dispensation from your boss. Sending too many cables may of course get you some rapping on the knuckles from the controller's office, but it's worth it, especially if you get the "confidential no distribution" dispensation. Since this type of cable always leaks, this means that your name will come to the attention of a number of highly-placed officials. Send also as many airmail letters as possible marked "Personal and Confidential," and at least once every month send one letter marked "Strictly Confidential" but not personal. Unlike the confidential cables, confidential letters are not primarily a means of gaining status, but rather of securing information. Have at least one ally in Geneva, London, Paris, and write to him regularly, sending scraps of useful information. He will return you the favor. Remember that when the investigating committee appointed by the General Assembly went around the world in '58 checking up on the information centers, everyone along the line was both alerted and briefed in time by a "Personal and Confidential" as the committee moved from one country to the next.

5. At meetings take the floor either at the very beginning or towards the end of the session, but never fail to make yourself heard. If you have something to say that is of interest to the other participants prepare it carefully, be clear and terse. If you have nothing to say and are not well briefed on the subject under discussion, then be lengthy and diffuse, adopt a doubtful and slightly baleful tone and introduce a pessimistic note. However, if the interests of your department or of your group are involved in the debate, then be optimistic to the point of euphoria.

6. Whether at large meetings in a conference room or small gatherings with senior officials present, when asked a question always answer by asking another question. This will throw the other fellow off and will allow you time to think how to avoid answering the question if pressed. Never answer a question unless the answer promotes your interests or those of your group.

7. Never volunteer information. Don't forget that in-

formation is a valuable commodity and should not be squandered. Remember also that you are not necessarily the best judge of how valuable is the information in your possession. What looks to you like a trivial and well-known item may represent the missing link for someone in another department, and thus be for him worth bargaining for. Establish and consolidate, on the other hand, exchange of information with as many other officials as possible, and with at least one in every department. This must be conducted on a "stock-market" basis, so that the information you negotiate should increase its rating over the months and be traded against ever more valuable items.

8. If you have been promoted to a post at the decision-making level, never take a decision. Every time you are asked to decide say you are going to think it over and use the next 24 hours to consult with your allies in your department. If you are pressed for a decision, being told that the matter is urgent, be even more careful. There is probably a power play under way and you should consult also your allies in other departments and find out if the 38th floor is involved in any way before making a move. However hard you are pressed, be dilatory and postpone taking any stand, lest you be caught between two opposing factions. Don't make exceptions to this rule.

9. The warm handshake and the perpetual smile are basic tools for your job and should never be taken for granted. Avoid lapsing into routine or carelessness like having the *sourire figé* of so many of your colleagues. Smile to yourself in the mirror while shaving in the morning and smile in the mirror during the day at the UN every time you go to the men's room and wash your hands afterwards. Don't worry if someone is washing his hands next to you and looks puzzled at your smiling at yourself, even if it is a delegate. He will never guess that you are merely exercising your smile, and if he does he will respect you for it. As to the warm handshake it is better to train with American colleagues. Americans have by far the firmer, warmer handshake, although oddly enough they don't indulge in as much handshaking as the Europeans and the Africans. Try also to give a personal touch to your handshake perhaps by holding the other man's hand for a linger-

ing moment. If that is misunderstood, it won't do you any harm; it might even gain you potential allies.

10. Worry and keep on worrying. If you don't you will not have a successful career or fast promotions, however skilful you may be at flattering, maneuvering or planning. They will tell you it will mean an early ulcer or heart attack, but that is a risk you must take. If you relax and stop worrying for one single day, you will lose valuable ground. If you relax and stop worrying for a full week, you might as well resign.

››› 22 ‹‹‹

THOSE UN RUSSIANS

In speeches at the UN the Soviet delegation has often attacked the Secretariat power structure and the exclusion of Soviet citizens from posts of any significance. Nobody paid much attention to their speeches and the Soviets, who were always under-represented despite the terms of Article 101 of the Charter, which refers to the "importance of recruiting the staff on as wide a geographical basis as possible," did not seem really to care.

Recently the Kremlin finally awakened to the key role played by the Secretariat, and began more strenuous and specific efforts to obtain its share of influential Secretariat posts. On two occasions over the last couple of years the Soviet ambassador to the United Nations addressed long letters to the Secretary-General, complaining about the exclusion of Soviet personnel from the Secretariat and making specific demands for posts, particularly for senior ones. The ambassador went as far as to indicate which posts the Soviet government claimed in which departments. In the first of those letters he meticulously staked out a claim for a post in a newly created service handling economic and social information (the political content of such information had not gone unnoticed in Moscow), while listing a number of senior posts at the director level which he also claimed for Russian nationals. In several cases

he had predicted a forthcoming vacancy to the day by calcu-
lating the retirement date of the person occupying the post.

The Soviet Union and the other communist countries had
a good legal case, since they were patently under-represented
in the Secretariat. Also, after 1960, when African nations
joined the UN en masse, and began to hanker for Secretariat
posts, this added leverage to Soviet demands.

Directives were issued from the 38th floor ordering the
personnel department to pay more attention to "geographical
distribution." This department contained one of the Secretariat's tightest little cliques of old cronies, mostly from Anglo-
Saxon countries, and it had in the past always dragged its feet
when it came to hiring Russians; its response to the new drive
was notably lacking in enthusiasm. But under the political spot-
light it had to go through the motions, and as a result there
are today many more Soviet nationals in the Secretariat than
there were only a few years ago, several of them occupying
posts that look important on paper.

Two questions should be asked about Russians in the
Secretariat. In reality how do Soviet staff members fare at
present in the UN? Secondly, since it cannot realistically be
expected that a Soviet citizen will conform to the Western
concept of an "international civil service," how effective are
these Soviet staff members in serving both the immediate and
the long-range interests of the Soviet Union during their stint
of duty at the Secretariat? The answers are not simple, but
rather an amusing but instructive array of contradictions, from
which the Russians do not necessarily emerge as unqualified
traitors to the cause of international peace and friendship.

One should perhaps begin by trying to look at the questions from their point of view. First of all, Moscow is still
reluctant to assign first-line candidates to the United Nations.
This is no longer a matter of policy, but rather stems from the
attitude of a score of top Soviet officials: the men who actually
run, in the administrative sense, the Ministry of Foreign
Affairs, the several technical ministries, and the Academy of

Sciences of the USSR, each of which has men qualified for UN positions. But those top Soviet officials are loath to lend their bright young men to the UN, even when the order comes from august quarters in the Kremlin. So they procrastinate, and think up urgent tasks that cannot be finished if Sergei Ivanovitch is taken from their team to be sent to New York. On the other hand, Sergei Ivanovitch, who is on his way up in one of the key ministries or in the Academy, does not relish the thought of being shunted to the UN and have his promotion prospects jeopardized by the time he is pulled back to Moscow.

Not long ago one of these Sergei Ivanovitchs, a young diplomat who clearly had a bright future ahead of him, told a Western friend: "This is my second year at the UN, but only because I have not been able to get myself assigned to a really good embassy where my work would be recognized."

"What do you consider a good embassy?" he was asked.

He laughed and gave an unusually frank answer: "Last year I was offered the number two position in our embassy in Yemen, as minister-counselor, but I begged the Ministry not to pull me out of the UN. You see, one of my best friends served in Yemen and he told me it's as bad as most of the African countries. I'm not experienced enough to get a good post in Western Europe, but I think I can get into one of the Latin American embassies." He shook his head and concluded: "Don't misunderstand me. I like being in the UN, one learns a lot. But it is hurting my career."

He was an exceptional case, having stayed for two years at the UN because he wouldn't accept the first embassy post proffered. Often a Soviet staff member is recalled abruptly, sometimes after only months of service. The reason given is almost invariably "illness in the family," the sick person being, by order of preference, mother, mother-in-law, father. A heart attack is usually chosen as the sudden illness. Unlike the trend in most other countries, Soviet ladies seem more prone to heart disease than their menfolk. (Recently there seems to be a trend toward a longer tenure by Soviet officials at the UN.)

This Soviet policy is of course self-defeating from their own point of view. The official they assign to UN duty does not have the time to accumulate valuable experience, nor to exert any influence on the work of the Secretariat, before he is recalled to Moscow. On the other hand, even were the Kremlin to pursue a more intelligent and persistent approach, it is doubtful whether it would achieve results. There are today dozens of Russians in the key UN departments, occupying positions ranging from director down; but today, as always, all Russians in the Secretariat are neutralized, except in one small department headed by a Soviet under-secretary. In that specific case, it is the department itself that is neutralized.

This hallowed system of neutralizing all Russians inside the Secretariat has been in operation from the beginnings of the United Nations. For older staffers it is one of the accepted "UN facts of life"; but it does come as a surprise—and a shock—to new staff members coming from the outside world and bearing the Russians no special grudge. But even someone with no cold-war background—someone from a country of Latin America, say—who joins the Secretariat and witnesses the systematic discrimination against his Soviet colleagues, is at first outraged, but soon begins to understand, and even accept, the valid if tacit justification of the shabby system.

The Soviet citizen who joins the United Nations remains flagrantly and clumsily at the service of his government. There is never any question of his having joined the service of an international organization; he continues to be an earnest, plodding, tirelessly dedicated member of the Soviet government bureaucracy. He contacts the Soviet delegation daily and presumably passes on any scrap of information he may have gathered; he receives instructions at frequent intervals, if not daily. He industriously preaches to his colleagues the party line on the main political event of the moment.

And sometimes he is literally left speechless until the party line is doled out to him after descending a long bureaucratic ladder all the way from the Foreign Ministry in Moscow. Many a UN staffer has had amusing experiences with a Soviet colleague whom he would stop in the corridor to ask for his views on a political development that had suddenly burst into the headlines. More often than not, all he would get would be a reticent, evasive comment. But on the following day, sometimes later the same day, for that matter, he would be stopped in another corridor by the same Russian colleague, and given an analysis of the situation which reproduced faithfully official Soviet reaction (which sometimes would not be carried by Tass until a day or two later); the Russian colleague had meanwhile made his daily report to his delegation and been properly briefed.

Sometimes, incidentally, on events that are not of burning concern to the Soviet delegation, Soviet staff members are not properly briefed and continue to deliver a quaintly anachronistic version, no longer current in Moscow.

So much of the Soviet staff members' time is set aside for reporting to his delegation (perhaps they have to do it in writing). Most of them have a reputation for sloppiness and laziness in regard to their official tasks. A wise old section chief who has two Russians working under him once said: "One of them is very good in his field, first-class university training in Leningrad. The other Russian is a dope. But neither of them is of any use to me. I can't really get mad at them. The poor fellows are serving at the same time the world's two worst bureaucracies, but they have to give priority to their own people back home and here at their delegation. I would probably do exactly the same if I were in their shoes, but since I'm not I neutralize them as all of us do."

Neutralization of the Russians takes two main forms. In the good old days, it meant purely and simply bypassing systematically any Soviet staff member in any department. However important his post, a Russian would never be told anything of what was going on. This held true for all levels, including the very highest. The best known example is that of Georgey Arkadiev, Under-Secretary for Political and Security Council Affairs during Hammarskjold's last year in office, who used to go around bitterly complaining that in spite of his position he had nothing to do and was told nothing by the Secretary-General.

Arkadiev, known as "Georgie" to his colleagues, had recurrent and celebrated skirmishes with Hammarskjold, usually in the presence of a number of his fellow under-secretaries, who followed the exchange with the fascinated attention one accords an international sporting event—which in a way it was. Georgie showed himself no match for the rapier-like thrusts and feints of Hammarskjold's political *escrime*, but he was no fool either. Despite his thickset, bullish, peasant appearance, Arkadiev possessed enough mental agility to make the Secretary-General enjoy the jousting.

Georgie's Waterloo came only after Hammarskjold's death, during that famous Security Council session when he openly and brazenly sent little notes to Ambassador Valery Zorin, to help the Soviet delegate hold his own with Adlai Stevenson in a crucial procedural debate.

It was an absorbing performance, recorded for the world public by the cameras of UN Television and of American, Canadian, and European networks that also occupy booths in the "television row" which overlooks the Council's horseshoe-shaped table. It shocked delegates of countries not members of the Council, occupying their reserved seats inside the Council chamber, and the accredited correspondents watching from the press section.

As customary when the Council was in session, Arkadiev sat on the left of the Council's president, whom he is supposed to advise, in his official capacity, on technical matters. What he actually did was to scribble one note after another (first consulting the Council's booklet on rules of procedure). It was too much for any one to stomach; the Kremlin did not venture

stiff opposition when told that Arkadiev could not continue as
under-secretary. He was quietly withdrawn and replaced by
Evgeny D. Kiselev. Until the day he left, however, he never
ceased complaining of being bypassed and ignored.

๛   ๛   ๛

During the Thant era a more sophisticated technique has
been developed toward Soviet staff members. Systematic bypassing is now considered too crude, and too dangerous in
terms of eventual reprisals. The new technique, known as
"snowing-under," has been perfected primarily by senior Western staff members. Essentially it consists in keeping all Soviet
staffers minutely informed of everything that happens within
the Secretariat, provided it is of no consequence. Since in the
Secretariat's daily activities so much of what is glorified by
the name of "work" is sterile and pointless paper-shuffling,
this technique has proved diabolically successful.

The poor Russian Secretariat official is snowed under
piles of irrelevant documents and masses of innocuous memoranda. Since he usually is a newcomer, fresh from the ponderous Soviet bureaucracy, he happily plunges into the sea of
paper; it takes him a while to realize that he is never given
access to anything of importance.

Under a modified form the same technique is applied to
meetings. In fact, the very character of a meeting changes
when the Soviet participant is not present; matters of significance are at once brought under discussion. If the Russian
comes in late (Soviet staffers are not celebrated for their
punctuality) the meeting smoothly and swiftly lapses into an
earnest and protracted debate of trivialities.

Not everyone in the Secretariat is party to this conspiracy of silence against the Russians. Apart from those who
have ideological affinities with the Soviet Union, there are quite
a few staffers, sometimes known as "the internationalists,"
who are sincerely concerned with a genuine international ap-

proach within the UN; they are convinced that dealing in a forthright manner with the Russians would pay in the long run. These "internationalists" maintain that the Soviet staff members should be integrated, since the Secretariat ought to reflect such an obvious political reality as the communist world. They like to say: "The Russians should be made to feel they are members of the team."

How would these good intentions of "the internationalists" work out in practice? In a few scattered cases they actually seem to work out well. A few Soviet staff members, mostly in technical or highly specialized posts, do put in an honest day's work, make a valuable contribution to the output of their department, and are pointed out with pride by their colleagues. But they are the exception. The bulk of the Russian contingent in the Secretariat invariably mixes ideology and propaganda with the work at hand, at times with considerable skill. They tirelessly push the Soviet line and try to orient the work of those they supervise along lines that would presumably bring some minor advantage to the communist cause. The "internationalists" are willing to put up with this—to a point. They will say: "We are trying to educate the Russians in that international co-existence of which they keep talking. It's the long pull that counts. Of course they will spout propaganda and try to slip in their political approach; but don't we Westerners do the same, except that we do it with so much more detachment and finesse that it's harder to pinpoint? Give these Russians time and they will arrive at some sort of acceptable compromise between their convictions and what is expected of an international civil servant."

Curiously enough, the Soviet government appears to agree with this hopeful reasoning by the "internationalists." The Kremlin has given evidence that it is seriously concerned lest its UN officials, particularly of the younger Soviet generation, acquire the perspective and the spirit expected of an international civil servant. Consequently, they pull back to Moscow those who begin to do useful work for the UN even faster than others. This fills the "internationalists" with disappointment. But when chided by their colleagues of the "don't-give-those-Russians-an-inch" line, they will stoutly answer: "Give them time. The situation is already much better than it was during the Stalin years."

Alas, the "internationalists" feel the chill of despair in their souls when confronted with the ugliest reality of Soviet participation in the UN: espionage. At frequent intervals a Russian staff member, usually one held in high esteem by his colleagues, is flushed out by the FBI and has to return home precipitately. Every time this happens one can almost hear the "internationalists" sighing in the corridors: "How could he do this to me?"

PART IV

THE STAGE

23

SITTING ROOM ONLY

United Nations Headquarters, known to its inmates as "The Glass House on the East River," is in effect a conglomeration of buildings adroitly pressed together on a sliver of ground between First Avenue and the river. Unmistakably identified by the domed profile of the General Assembly building and the soaring 39 floors of the Secretariat, since the inauguration of the Headquarters in 1950, there has been added to the compound the squat structure of the Dag Hammarskjold Library.

From newspaper and magazine photos and television, the General Assembly hall and the Security Council chamber, have become in the public mind the symbols of the UN at work. The Assembly's blue-and-gold expanse with the huge UN emblem perched over the green marble podium, and the Council's horseshoe-shaped table encased by a double row of television and interpreters' booths are by now familiar to people in the farthest corners of the world. Actually these are not necessarily the two meeting places which are most often in use at Headquarters; in fact, many more meetings take place the year round in the dozen-odd committee rooms spread around in the first basement.

The work of any parliament should be done in committee. But while most parliaments transact real business at committee meetings closed to the press, at the UN this is often not the case. In fact, the larger committee rooms in the first basement, with seating arrangements capable of accommodating all the delegations, have their own press gallery. Because of this indiscreet glare of publicity, delegates prefer to conduct off-stage the more meaningful part of their day-to-day activities, and reserve committee meetings for formal speech-making and establishing their government's position for the record.

Off-stage means primarily the North Delegates Lounge, a high-ceilinged room of generous proportions with wide windows opening on the East River along one side and graced at its far end with an imaginatively stocked bar. Behind the bar is tucked away a quiet cafe-espresso den.

Quite a good deal of UN business is conducted here by delegates standing in front of the bar, glass in hand, or sipping a cup of coffee, or sitting in one of the wicker chairs or the leather sofas. The most formal claim to a niche in history for the Delegates Lounge remains to this day the famous conversation between Ambassador Jacob A. Malik, then head of the Soviet delegation, and Philip K. Jessup of the U.S. delegation, at which was dropped the first hint that the USSR was willing to negotiate the lifting of the Berlin blockade. Oddly enough, this major international crisis, which had isolated Berlin and led the United States, aided by Great Britain, to run an airlift for months on end into the beleaguered city, technically had nothing to do with the United Nations and had never been formally debated at any of its meetings.

On a less spectacular plane, the lounge serves as a relaxed meeting ground for delegates and visiting statemen, where views are exchanged, compromises explored, bargains struck for a impending ballot. What goes on in the Delegates Lounge closely reflects what is happening at the world organization.

Seasoned correspondents are well aware that a carefully mapped-out stroll through the lounge, stopping to talk to selected delegates, never fails to yield information. Bureau chiefs for the wire agencies and the most experienced correspondents make it a point of going to the North Lounge at

least once a day; if they can't make it they will send one of
their staff. Most of the delegates who wish to be contacted or
interviewed by the world press will unfailingly be found at
the bar during cocktail hour; conversely, an ambassador engaged in particularly delicate negotiations will not even saun-
ter through the lounge.

On the frivolous side, correspondents come to this marketplace of Headquarters to pick up the latest rumors and bits
of gossip, or simply "sniff the air." Also, many a delegate has
been seen sitting in a corner, earnestly conducting negotiations,
which will certainly not affect the state of the world, with a
comely young lady whose profession can be surmised to be
much older than that of the ambassador. Periodically UN
housekeeping authorities will launch a drive to keep the North
Lounge off bounds to ladies of easy virtue, particularly after
one of the more lurid New York papers runs a story on "UN
call girls"; but it is no easy task, since the bright young things
are brought into the Lounge under impeccable auspices, usually
a status-seeking African delegate for whom any blonde is a
blonde.

ري *ري* *ري*

At the other end of the group of buildings is the South Delegates Lounge, much smaller and contiguous to the Security
Council. Delegates to the Council, however, are not often seen
there; they go either to the North Lounge, like everyone else,
or stay in the protected seclusion of the antechamber to the
Council (no one is admitted during the consecutive translation
of a long speech). There they consult with members of their
own staff or other delegates to the Council, while sitting under
a Picasso.

This does not mean that the South Lounge remains
deserted. Its bar, so ingeniously located that it is quite possible
to walk through the lounge and onto the Council chamber
without suspecting its existence, is regularly patronized by

some of the really serious drinkers in the house, mostly Secretariat officials and a sprinkling of delegates. The few tables are usually taken by couples who prefer the relative seclusion of the South Lounge. Not all of the women, are bent on romantic pursuits; some of them are charter members of the drinking brigade and are quite able to keep pace with the men with whom they sit.

The North and South Lounges are connected by a long, wide corridor from which branches a shorter passage leading to the General Assembly hall. It is mostly in these corridors that the "conversations de couloirs" take place between delegates to coordinate procedural maneuvering, swap information, or simply gauge the climate of a developing political crisis. Often it's only the briefest of exchanges between two diplomats who meet, stand for a few moments together, talk in low tones, and then go their separate ways. If they become immersed in their subject, they will automatically drift to one of the many leather-and-metal easy chairs of modern design strategically placed along the corridors. A steady stream of delegates, correspondents, and UN officials continues to flow in front of the two, but under one of the tacit rules of the house no one will ever attempt to interrupt. However, the roving correspondents will make a mental note of who is sitting with whom, and for how long. As one once explained: "When I have to file a story predicting the outcome of the crisis of the moment, I like to wander around seeing who is talking to whom in the corridors, and particularly whether they are standing or sitting. If they stand the situation is still fluid, but if they sit for a while it means some sort of arrangement is in the wind. So I go after my regular sources to find out what kind of deal is under way."

∽   ∽   ∽

The topography of UN Headquarters makes unavoidable a certain amount of chumminess among delegates. They keep running into each other in the corridors, touching elbows at the bar, queuing up to have a café espresso. Even the short elevator ride up to the restaurant—only two floors—becomes a minor social occasion, since everyone goes up at about the same time. And of course the rubbing of shoulders continues through the evening at the inevitable parties.

Such a surfeit of personal contacts through the day and into the night could be expected to breed boredom and even irritation, but the glittering environment outside the UN has a neutralizing influence on the excessive coziness of the inner environment. New York waits outside, cold, impersonal, and throbbing with synthetic excitement. The newly arrived UN diplomat plunges thirstily into it at first, but after a few weeks he comes up for air, saturated with the dubious pleasures of the big city after dark. He then reaches out with relief and even a certain sense of anticipation for the conviviality of his colleagues, the clannish gatherings, the shoptalk of a working day stretching endlessly into the night. The relentless and feverish life of the world's biggest city becomes a pleasure to be held in abeyance for special occasions.

The UN diplomat becomes unabashedly provincial in terms of his little world centered on "Headquarters and adjoining areas." He even develops a fondness for the cocktail parties held in the delegates' dining room, with some of the luncheon tables whisked away and others pushed against the walls. He will contentedly sip the watery drinks proffered by the same affable middle-aged waitress who served him a starchy "plat du jour" at noontime. He will even follow the trail of the hot-snack cart rolling ponderously through the big room, and nimbly appropriate a fried shrimp while still a few are left. He begins to feel secure and contented in this inner environment, somehow protected against the metropolis outside, which he has found to be aloof if not condescending. He begins to hanker for the tepid domesticity of his little UN world, and to think of most of his colleagues as pals.

This clubby effect of UN Headquarters on the diplomats

assigned there carries with it some curious political overtones. For one thing, the best professionals among the delegates swiftly acquire a capacity for reading each other's minds, which cannot be developed by serving even in the world's key political capitals. The unique "UN togetherness" develops a political sixth sense in gifted diplomats. Sometimes an impending shift in policy by an important country will be sniffed out at the UN while it is still under tight security restrictions. The confidential instructions of even Soviet delegates, the most secretive of the lot, are sometimes guessed by some of their more perceptive colleagues; the chummy intimacy that the atmosphere at Headquarters exudes has proved capable of eroding and to some extent mellowing even the dour and suspicious Russian diplomats assigned to the UN.

24

THE OTHER UN CAPITAL

Squeezed in between First Avenue and the East River, the group of UN buildings hangs precariously on the edge of Manhattan, and seems to reach eagerly upwards as if in need of breathing freely from the top of its 39-story Secretariat skyscraper. A Latin American delegate of the old school, whose rolling, melodious speeches had been a feature of debates for almost two decades, first at the League of Nations and then at the United Nations, surveyed with obvious dismay the Headquarters compound shortly after it was inaugurated in 1950 and confided to a small group of colleagues: "I don't like this modern architecture, and if everyone says it's because I'm old-fashioned and nostalgic for the League, I will say: that is true. Here they have pushed us against the river, and if we don't watch out we will fall in one of these days. The Palais was of another world, it had a green amplitude around it and was not crushed by the big city."

ᔅ ᔅ ᔅ

Geneva's Palais des Nations, which the UN inherited from the League of Nations and today serves as European headquarters for the world organization, belongs indeed in another world.

The differences are only too visible architectonically; psychologically they are subtle but unyielding.

Motionless and unimaginative, the five contiguous buildings of the Palais spread and sprawl over 16,800 square meters. But for all its massiveness there is a feeling of space and freedom because of the vast, peaceful park surrounding it. After lunch, weather permitting, many of the thousand international civil servants who work there can stroll under the trees. A few of them, perhaps more conscious of the bulging waistline that threatens deskworkers, walk at a brisk pace, circling the immense structure. This is known as "fare les deux kilométres," for the perimeter measures two kilometers, well over a mile. Those addicted to the "deux kilométres" are considered as mildly fanatic by most of their fellow workers, for everyone who works in the Palais maintains that he walks much more than two kilometers during the course of a day's work. The endless stretch of corridors is in fact considered by many as an unnecessary handicap placed upon efficiency, and there are those who believe that the Palais should have been planned in height, like the UN Secretariat building on New York's East River, with banks of fast elevators.

Actually, the Palais is not quite as squat as it looks; it stands eight floors high, which in Europe is a respectable height for a building. On the eighth floor is the restaurant with a pleasant terrace where tables are set out in summer and the view on a clear day stretches over Lake Leman to Mont Blanc, Europe's highest peak. The sense of space and leisure, of old-fashioned elegance, is so pervading that it comes as a surprise to learn that the Palais also houses a very modern communications network.

The central switchboard permits the polyglot telephone operators to dial directly a telephone call not only to anywhere in Switzerland but also to nine other European countries, including Britain, France, and Italy. Among the girls who operate the telephone exchange at the Palais five know Russian, Spanish, and Italian, while knowledge of French, English, and

German is obligatory. On a typical working day the telephone exchange will handle some two thousand incoming calls, and twice as many outgoing ones, of which several hundred are international calls. In a normal year the total traffic handled by the Palais des Nations switchboard totals over two and a half million incoming and outgoing calls.

Geneva is also the main relay point of the UN telecommunications network, which spans half the globe. The network connects the Palais by radioteletype with UN Headquarters in New York and with UN offices in London, Paris, Rome, and Vienna. From Geneva the network stretches eastwards to Karachi, from there to New Delhi and to Bangkok. From Bangkok it goes on to Seoul in South Korea, serving the UN Korean Reconstruction Agency.

Geneva is also linked, through another line, with Naples, which serves as the main assembly and supply point for the UN Emergency Force (UNEF) in Palestine. It then connects with Jerusalem and with Gaza, headquarters for the battalions from nine countries that patrol the uneasy border between Israel and Egypt. There are several other substations in the Middle East, among them Beirut, Damascus, Tel Aviv, Tiberias, Nablus, Bouteha, Juneitra.

In July, 1960, at the very beginning of the Congo operation, a team of UN communications specialists moved into Leopoldville and within a few days set up radio-teleprinters, almost at the very moment the first contingents of "blue helmets" were deplaning at the Leopoldville airport. Said the head of telecommunications at the Palais: "We made communication history by connecting the Congo with Geneva, and through Geneva with Headquarters in New York. Until the arrival of our troops the Congo was connected only with Brussels."

For an emergency UN technicians can branch onto this far-flung network mobile stations operating from jeeps and station-wagons in remote areas of the world. In the event of a political crisis sole dependence upon radio telecommunications

from Headquarters in New York with and through Geneva
may fail, so a secondary system has been set up as protection
against adverse atmospheric conditions. In radio there are
eleven-year cycles during which reception varies from very
good to very poor. For the contingency of poor reception the
UN has on lease duplex transatlantic telegraph cables available
twenty-four hours a day.

ා   ා   ා

The Economic Commission for Europe, commonly referred
to by its initials, ECE, is in some ways the most important UN branch operating within the Palais. It is also one of
the few operations of which the thousands of visitors who are
taken daily through the building on conducted tours are aware.
As they stream past the ornate committee rooms aligned on
each side of the marble-floored Salle des Pas Perdus, they rarely
miss seeing a sign announcing a session of ECE. The sign includes a succinct reference to the matter under discussion and
many a tourist has been heard to ask: "What do they mean by
'ECE—Inland transportation'?" A visitor one day turned to the
guide and inquired facetiously: "Is this the world's super-
market by any chance?" pointing to a sign at the entrance of
Salle IX which said "ECE—Olive Oil."

These cabalistic bilingual signs, on display almost every
day, are one indication of the work carried on by the Economic
Commission for Europe, which deals with questions as vast as
foreign trade, agriculture, and power, but will also concern
itself with as housewifely a commodity as olive oil.

But apart from the tourists' passing curiosity, ECE's work
is too highly specialized and studded with statistics and charts
to arouse active interest among the general public. Yet governments follow its activities closely, for ECE is the only all-
European forum available for a joint approach and discussion
of economic development in both Western and Eastern Europe.
In this sense it is a sensitive barometer of current attitudes in
the communist states toward the West.

Those committee rooms in the Palais are neutral sanctuaries where specialists from both worlds discuss mutually profitable forms of trading and doing business together. Most of the discussions are conducted in closed meetings. ECE economists and technicians from the two opposed worlds of Marxist and free-market economies have nonetheless gained a reputation for approaching the subjects under discussion in a down-to-earth, no-politics fashion. In the field of housing, for instance, there are annual study tours out of Geneva to many European capitals. As a result of these excursions by ECE experts, techniques for low-cost housing projects developed in the Soviet bloc, such as prefabricated apartment buildings, have been adopted by Western European countries, while many of the sophisticated Western advances in construction equipment and methods have been brought to the attention of communist builders.

A Western delegate was once asked whether political sparks never flew behind the closed doors of Salle IX or Salle X, the two committee rooms where ECE meets most often. His answer was revealing: "When you start discussing how to speed up railway communications through the breadth of Europe you find out that the fellow sitting across the table seems to have forgotten all about his Marxist dialectics and all of a sudden the discussion turns businesslike. After all he is, like me, a specialist in railways. We become immersed in solving the technical problem at hand, and suddenly we find ourselves in agreement." Then he added, smiling: "For that matter, many a time the discussion is carried on after business hours over a drink or dinner in one of those little restaurants in the Vieille Cité. Why, we sit around with these communist fellows for hours, and believe it or not, we only talk shop. No one brings up the cold war."

In recent years ECE has come to grips with the development of tourism in Europe and has done much to simplify matters. A traveler who nowadays can cross almost any frontier in Europe without being held up more than a short time by immigration and customs has ECE to thank for it.

∽   ∽   ∽

The Palais is first and foremost a place where statesmen, diplomats, and experts congregate for specific purposes in meetings that vary from tight little gatherings of specialists discussing something as specific as the flow of a minor commodity across customs barriers to conferences dealing with problems of war and peace which concern every nation and perhaps every human being.

In the ten last years, the Palais was host to several epoch-making symposia in the political domain: summit meetings of heads of state of big powers, gatherings of foreign ministers, conferences on diasarmament, on Berlin, on Indo-China, on Laos, on switching the atom to peaceful uses. Recently President de Gaulle proposed that the big powers meet in Geneva to decide the future of the United Nations.

Not all of the big conferences have dealt with political problems. Last year and the year before, two of the largest conferences ever to assemble in Geneva, one on Science and Technology and the other on Trade and Development, were dedicated exclusively to questions that have to be solved if the have-not nations are ever to develop. At each of these two meetings, more than a thousand delegates gathered to discuss practical ways of helping those countries where three fourths of the human race live.

The Science and Technology Conference has been described as the most encyclopedic gathering of modern times. It laid the foundations for a survey of what new methods and techniques could do to accelerate the emergence of the world's under-developed nations into the twentieth century. The Conference on Trade and Development also aimed at helping under-developed countries by finding ways to enable them to profit more from international trade.

Another conference at the Palais has met almost continuously for the last few years; everything else depends upon it. This is the Eighteen-Nation Conference on Disarmament which, in the view of many diplomats, will go on for years until world disarmament has been achieved—unless, of course, our planet decides to blow itself up in the meantime. This is perhaps the most important continuous political symposium ever to meet in Geneva although its sessions are remarkably undramatic. They are held behind closed doors in the Salle du Conseil, the same chamber where in the thirties Europe's most famous statesmen sought in vain to stave off the Second World War.

This Eighteen-Nation Disarmament Conference does not even particularly insist on taking credit for the tangible results already achieved. It is no secret, however, that the test-ban treaty, the "hot line" between Washington and Moscow, the agreement not to place atomic weapons in orbit, all these were decisions first discussed, prepared, explored, and to a large extent painfully negotiated during long months at the Palais des Nations.

✍ ✍ ✍

For all its bigness, the Palais is only one among the group of buildings which together comprise what is sometimes known as the "international compound." Only from a helicopter can one take in the expanse of this compound hugging the shores of Lake Léman. It includes the Palais and the headquarters buildings for the International Labour Office (ILO), the International Meteorological Organization (IMO), and the International Telecommunications Union (ITU). And now it also includes the headquarters of the World Health Organization (WHO), inaugurated early in 1966.

The International Labour Organization (ILO) has a history which antedates by a year the birth of the League of Nations. It was set up in 1919 to bring together governments, trade unions, and employers, for the purpose of raising the standards of workers and promoting the cause of social justice. To date, it is the only world body which brings together, in its assemblies, delegations composed of representatives of labor, management, and government, each entitled to an equal voice and vote.

Throughout the period between the First and the Second World Wars, ILO functioned as an agency of the League of Nations, but with full autonomy. In 1946 it became the first Specialized Agency affiliated to the United Nations.

ILO is concerned with matters as diverse as working hours, radiation protection, migration for employment, and paid holidays. It also has become increasingly involved with working conditions for women. In its broad approach it encompasses the protection of basic human rights such as freedom of association, collective bargaining, abolition of forced labor, discrimination in employment. Many agreements in this field have been signed by many countries, and to date there is a total of nearly four hundred ratifications. As a matter of fact, ILO is the only international body which has taken principles set forth in the UN Universal Declaration of Human Rights and incorporated them into binding international instruments duly signed and ratified. Indeed, the Convention and Recommendations from the International Labour Organization, which now amount to two thick and heavy volumes, are the equivalent of an international common law for labor practices which slowly but steadily is spreading over the globe.

In recent years ILO has become increasingly active in labor questions in underdeveloped countries and nowadays such questions account for more than half of all the work carried out at its Geneva headquarters and in the field.

The World Health Organization (WHO) is another of the international agencies of the UN with headquarters in Geneva (its headquarters were in the Palais for years, until its own building was completed). WHO is at present engaged in what might be the decisive stage of a global campaign to exterminate malaria. Already three hundred and ninety million people have been saved from the scourge, and a further seven hundred million people live in regions where the campaign against malaria is being actively pursued by WHO and the local government.

Yaws, an even more crippling disease, is also under sustained attack everywhere in the tropical areas of the world. WHO has already examined 285 million persons afflicted with yaws and in cooperation with the local health authorities has given penicillin treatment—miraculous in its effect—to thirty-eight million men, women, and children.

The list of diseases under sustained health campaigns on a world-wide basis by WHO also includes smallpox, tuberculosis, leprosy, trachoma, bilharziasis, sleeping sickness, hookworm. To man these far-flung campaigns, WHO is training what amounts to an army of health workers—doctors, nurses, midwives, sanitary engineers, and technicians. It offers over two thousand fellowships a year to less-developed countries, and it maintains a far-flung service of day-by-day information on the outbreak of epidemic diseases by cabled reports from governmental health authorities all over the planet.

ᵔᵔ   ᵔᵔ   ᵔᵔ

The International Telecommunications Union (ITU) is housed in a modernistic building just outside the enclosure of the Palais. Its new headquarters were inaugurated only as recently as 3 May 1962, but ITU goes back more then a hundred years. In fact, it is the oldest of the international organizations which are now part of the UN family, for it was launched on 17 May 1865. At that time, the necessity of agreeing on common standards for newly developed telegraphic communication led twenty countries to accept the invitation of Emperor Napoleon III to assemble in Paris. Out of this meeting was born the International Telegraphic Union, which became ITU in later years.

One of ITU's most delicate responsibilities is to assign radio frequencies to countries, and to prevent any country's broadcasting stations from causing harmful interference with a neighbor's broadcasts. The frequencies allotted are duly recorded in the huge Master International Frequency Register. ITU further provides advice to member countries to enable them to operate as many radio channels as possible effectively, but without interfering with another country's operations. This can be a delicate matter when overcrowded parts of the radio spectrum are involved.

With the advent of the outer space age the scope of ITU's work has been radically transformed. It is now delving increasingly into the possibilities of extensive international communication facilities through satellites.

There is yet another specialized agency in Geneva, also housed in a modern headquarters, not far from the Palais: the World Meteorological Organization (WMO). Like ITU, it undertakes activities which also reach into outer space, for WMO has become increasingly concerned with weather satellites. It was at WMO's futuristic headquarters that a few years ago two eminent meteorologists, one from the United States and one from the Soviet Union, met and worked together for months. They planned, in cooperation with WMO officials, how to put the progress achieved by the Americans and the Russians in placing satellites in orbit at the service of weather reporting for all countries.

∽   ∽   ∽

There is also within the Palais a UN body dealing with refugees, whose humanitarian work many people hold as second only to that of the international Red Cross whose headquarters are a stone's throw away. The Office of the United Nations High Commissioner for Refugees is actually many years older than the United Nations. In fact, the functions and the very idea of a High Commissioner for Refugees were born at the League of Nations. In 1921 the Norwegian explorer and philanthropist Fridtjof Nansen became the League's High Commissioner for Refugees. Nansen then, with hardly any staff to assist him, tackled the enormous refugee problem stemming from the First World War. Before he was through he had given his name to the famous Nansen Passport for stateless people.

The Second World War brought in its wake new waves of homelessness and destitution. By then, Nansen had died, and under a new High Commissioner the UN in 1947 set up in Geneva the International Refugee Organization. By 1951 more than one million persons had been resettled; yet the High Commissioner for Refugees still had as his responsibility the fate of one and a quarter million refugees of whom more than 300,000 were in a state of abject poverty. Worse than that, there were still some 120,000 living in camps in Europe, many of them former concentration camps.

The problem was so vast and anguishing that the United Nations General Assembly proclaimed in 1960 a World Refugee Year, a vast enterprise for fund-raising commanded from the Palais des Nations. By 1962, enough funds had been raised so that, for one thing, all the former concentration camps were virtually cleared of their occupants. But the ebb and flow of world conflict thrust new burdens upon this small group of people working at Geneva. Beginning in 1962, new waves of refugees were cast on the shores of hospitable countries. In less than two years, more than half a million persons on four continents became refugees. Among them there were hundreds of thousands of Algerian refugees in Tunisia and Morocco, now repatriated since Algeria's independence. Refugees streamed out of Communist China into the tiny Portugese enclave of Macao, a few miles from Canton, and into Hong Kong. One celebrated refugee shuttled back and forth on the ferryboat between Macao and Hong Kong for several years before the governments involved accepted the good offices of the High Commissioner to stop the journeying of a man who had by then become, if not the most famous traveler in the world, certainly the most persistent one.

Other cases which have made fewer headlines: those

Tibetan refugees flowing into Nepal and Angolans into the former Belgian Congo. Recently the massacres in Rwanda set waves of refugees seeking asylum in Tanganyika. In fact, the present High Commissioner for Refugees described the problem of these 150,000 refugees as "the largest and most burning" of those now facing him. For it involves among other things a five-hundred mile migration by men, women, and children, driving thousands of head of cattle, from their temporary refuge in Burundi to a permanent resettlement site in the Mwesi Highlands of Western Tanganyika.

This work has attracted people who by their background and family fortunes were not in need of jobs but who were fascinated by the possibilities of helping their fellow men under the most adverse and geographically remote conditions. One of the sons of the Aga Khan, for instance, has been a moving spirit in this program of UN work. The handsome young prince, educated at Oxford and speaking fluently several European and Asiatic languages, moves around incessantly to mobilize private and public support. His name and rank open the doors of high government offices and the purses of affluent donors.

PART V

THE REHEARSALS

⇒ 25 ⇐

WHY THE POOR BECOME POORER

The current United Nations Development Decade aims to increase the growth of the world's underdeveloped countries by five percent a year by the end of the decade. There could hardly be a more modest goal; it would mean that in most of the world's eighty poor countries most of the population would have crawled away from the edge of a subsistence economy. It would not imply anything faintly resembling access by 1970 to the kind of food, schooling, housing, and entertainment that is taken for granted by even the very poor of Europe and North America.

In fact, the goal was so modest in terms of the gap between rich and poor nations that until 1965 UN circles believed it was attainable; the general tenor of the reports to be issued in 1965 was anticipated along lines of restrained self-congratulation. Much to the dismay of those eager bureaucrats, when appraisals became available in 1965, prepared not by report fiends but by some of the world's leading authorities on development, the tone and the supporting facts and figures were invariably sobering if not dismal. The DD, as the UN decade had come to be almost pharmaceutically known, was beginning to look uncomfortably like the flop of the century.

The Secretary-General had warned all along that the rich nations were getting richer, and the poor nations poorer. But at Turtle Bay it had become fashionable to take U Thant's pronouncements with a grain of salt: "Keeps those rich boys on their toes . . . imagine the U.S. talking of withholding its technical assistance contributions . . . and the Germans could cough up more money . . . not to mention those conceited French . . . they are the worse of the lot, putting enormous amounts of dough on the line, but it all goes bilateral . . . good for the SG . . . let him keep at it . . . he can rouse the Afro-Asians and put the heat on the Western fat cats. . . ."

Then all of a sudden the DD was named a failure by people under no political compulsion to prod the "fat cats," but who on the contrary had spent a lifetime on very good terms with them; in fact, these authoritative voices belonged to persons who were not altogether alien to the breed. A feeling of growing uneasiness swept over the bureaucratic bastions of Turtle Bay. To have the decade declared a failure even before it was half over might jeopardize their own jobs; through the sixties much of the staffing and the spending at headquarters and in the field had been brought under the magic umbrella of "trying to do something for the developing countries." ("Underdeveloped" is considered bad form around the UN; in official jargon a country is either "developed" or "developing." Both these terms are misleading, for there is no such thing as a truly developed country. Even the affluent societies have quite a few tasks in development ahead of them. As to the poor countries, some of them are indeed developing, but others are not; whereas every poor country is visibly underdeveloped.)

The big blow came midway in the decade, and from an unlikely quarter—the World Bank. Over the years the UN had become reconciled to being totally ignored, or at most distantly patronized, by this affluent but ungrateful offspring. In theory the World Bank was part of the "United Nations family" and would graciously condescend to make an appearance, although not always in the person of its president, when the Secretary-General once a year gathered around him in

Geneva the heads of the fourteen affiliated agencies of the UN
and went through the motions of behaving like a *primus inter
pares*. The Bank was one of the fourteen, but even on the
annual pilgrimage to Switzerland seemed only vaguely aware
of this.

At least that was the way it had been through the years
when Eugene Black was the Bank's president. But now they
had a new man, called George Woods, who seemed concerned
with the fate of the poor countries—that is to say, with most
of the UN membership.

At the end of September, 1965, finance ministers and
leading bankers gathered for a week in Washington. It was
the annual World Bank—International Monetary Fund meeting, at which financial luminaries would avail themselves of
the opportunity to voice mildly whatever complaints their countries had against the Bank or the Fund. They would be assured
of a courteous but aloof hearing, and then they would disperse.
But the 1965 session was different from all others. George
Woods took the floor and instead of delivering the usual gra-
cious and vacuous address, he lashed out at the world's rich
countries. He placed on them an uncomfortable share of the
blame for the misery in which most of the world continued
to wallow.

Speaking with the authority of his position, Mr. Woods
remarked that for over half of the world's eighty underdeveloped countries and more than half of their total population, the
five percent annual growth proposed by the UN was not in
sight, nor was there any prospect that it would be reached in
the years ahead. In fact, in fifty countries the growth had
barely been one percent, or less, in many cases, which meant
that the dismally low standard of living in these countries
would not even keep abreast with the soaring birth rate. Added
the president of the World Bank: "The average per capita
income in this group is no more than $120 a year. At a one
percent growth rate income levels will hardly reach $170 a
year by the end of this century. In some countries it will be

much lower . . . if the present trends are allowed to continue
there will be no adequate improvement in living standards
in vast areas of the globe for the balance of this century."

Mr. Woods pointed out that the rich countries are simply
not coming through with sufficient capital investment in the
poor countries in either the public or the private sector; moreover, in many cases the rate of interest charged on loans is so
high that a substantial slice of the money received is needed
merely to service the debt. Between 1956 and 1964 the external
debt of the underdeveloped countries jumped from ten to
twenty-four billion dollars. One half of actual flow of foreign
capital to these countries is eaten up by high interest rates,
amortization, and dividends paid out to foreign companies.
The president of the World Bank concluded by remarking: "In
short to go on doing what we are doing will, in the not too long
run, amount on balance to doing nothing at all."

Earlier in the year, at a ministerial meeting in Paris of
the Development Assistance Committee of the Organization for
Economic Cooperation and Development (OECD), Woods had
pointedly noted that the conditions under which the United
States was helping underdeveloped countries had become
stiffer; there had been a shift from grants to loans, usually
repayable in dollars at pretty high interest rates. Nor were the
rich countries of Europe being more liberal; in fact most of
the European governments and bankers had a worse record
than the Americans.

OECD's Development Assistance Committee has for its
proclaimed goal the channeling of one percent of the gross
national product of the rich countries into assistance to the
poor underdeveloped ones. Almost all of the Western powers
have failed to meet this target; one of those who indeed does
spend abroad a little over one percent of its GNP, De Gaulle's
France, does this for reasons intimately related with the pursuit of continuing political influence and economic sway over
its former African colonies. The sort of thing that African
delegates in the UN like to stigmatize as "neocolonialism."

Furthermore, the problems of underdevelopment cannot find a solution purely in economic terms. George Kennan said perceptively in an interview published in *Encounter* in 1960: "Anyone can see why the underdeveloped countries are terribly interested in the problem of economic growth. . . . I personally think that they are making a great mistake to wish to change their societies with the speed with which they actually seem to wish to do this. It is my own belief that if you change the lives of people so rapidly that the experience of the father, the wisdom of the father, becomes irrelevant to the needs of the son, you have done something very dangerous—you have broken the organic bond of the family, and you have created emotional trauma in the minds of young people."

WHEN "UNITED" NATIONS
MAKES SENSE

There are no real prospects that any significant flow of capital for economic development will be handled through the World Bank, and even more implausible through the UN. The International Development Association, affiliated to the Bank, has a somewhat better chance, particularly since the wealthy donor countries know that in IDA their interests are protected by the system of weighted voting. The amounts that IDA will have at its disposal in the foreseeable future, however, would still be quite modest.

But in the field of technical assistance, the United Nations should, and perhaps could, take upon itself the principal role. This is one area where an international organization commands an inherent advantage over even the richest of the donor countries. Any of the world's eighty-odd poor countries of Asia, Africa, or Latin America, while engaging in a desperate quest abroad for applied science, modern technology, and industrial know-how (and for securing the services of foreign scientists, experts, and technicians to show how it's done and to train the natives in their skills) is invariably torn between suspicion of these foreigners and their motives and the pressing need for their services. But if the foreign scientist, expert, and technician does not serve under the auspices of any of the world's affluent powers, but rather under those of the international organization—to which the poor country belongs like everybody else—he cannot be suspected of promoting, even indirectly, foreign policy objectives of one of the powers.

In this sense the United Nations enjoys a decisive advantage in the field of technical assistance that it would not command to any comparable degree if it were furnishing capital instead of technicians. Moreover, very many underdeveloped countries readily accept, while they do not particularly relish, grants or loans by an affluent Western power (or for that matter a newly affluent Eastern power). And some of these countries have shown themselves capable of applying the sums received in their economic infrastructure with a reasonable degree of discrimination and efficiency. When they receive technicians in any numbers from the same affluent land there are psychological and emotional barriers to putting to good use the specialized knowledge and skill of these foreigners—but not if they are sent under United Nations auspices. For one thing the foreigners are from a number of foreign countries, which seems to make a difference, and they are provided by the world body, which makes even more of a difference.

This does not mean that the specialized agencies have always known how to make the best use of their intrinsic advantage as members of the UN family. To begin with, the agencies have not adapted themselves fast enough to the overwhelming needs of the poor countries, nor have they yet understood how fast the scene has been changing in the *tiers monde*. But above all, the UN specialized agencies leave much to be desired when it comes to working together, as can be gleaned from these passages of Andrew Shonfield's book *The Attack on World Poverty* (1960):

> Their work [UN specialized agencies] in the underdeveloped countries ought to be one integrated operation, responding flexibly to changing needs, with a single responsible authority answering for the direction and performance of each project. In practice, the specialized agencies negotiate together over any piece of work involv-

ing their collaboration in the high manner of independent
sovereign states, whose basically friendly relations are
constantly in jeopardy because their spheres of influence
abut on one another. It is not that they fail to collaborate
in the end; they do get together. But too often it requires
the most elaborate formal preparations; there are delays
while the commanders parley with one another and the
battlefield waits; and finally when the allies do join up for
the battle they will surrender no power at all to a commander: each insists on retaining complete control over his
own troops. There are certain conventions about seniority,
but they affect status rather than power. At the United
Nations in New York, officials set great store on a convention that in any inter-agency work that includes the Technical Assistance Office of the United Nations Headquarters
(UNTAO), the latter can automatically claim the senior
role. But in practice any pretensions to leadership from
New York are vigorously rebutted by the other members
of the UN family.

The best that can be hoped from this procedure of
coming together as independent entities to collaborate on
a project, which ought to have been conceived from the
start as a single piece of business, is that it does ultimately
produce a reasonable working arrangement in the field
between the technicians who are trying to get on with the
job. At its worst, it results in years of delay while a problem
clearly recognized as crucial is tinkered with, instead of
being tackled. This is the sad story of the United Nations'
effort on "community development"—one of the most strik-
ing examples of wasted opportunity. The term "community
development" suffers from vagueness, but it broadly covers
any program of leadership and education in primitive villages which uses labor and other resources readily available
on the spot to raise the standard of living. An obvious
example is the introduction of a cooperative system of
contributing work by villagers towards the construction
of a local road or a rat-free warehouse for storing grain,
which will serve them all. The outside technical expert
comes in with advice about methods and materials—but
also, if he is to be effective, in a much more awkward

role, as the original pebble cast forcefully into a stagnant pond.

Plainly this kind of work, by its very nature, involves an element of quasi-revolutionary activity in the village, since its over-riding aim is to force the pace by bringing in untraditional and more productive methods of agriculture—and that in turn almost inevitably involves social change, disrupting first of all the old patterns of behavior and respect towards the landlord, the trader, and moneylender. To be successful it requires special talent in the man on the spot and a very carefully thought-out campaign by the organization in charge of the program, with lots of tactical variations in readiness to deal with special circumstances. The idea is, after all, to find a voluntary answer to the problems which the communists solved by forced collectivization of farms, backed up in China by the further military regimentation of the peasants. There could hardly be anything more ambitious than the attempt to set up a free working alternative to the juggernaut.

It has not been done. The idea of a controlled and non-violent agrarian revolution has attracted a lot of attention, particularly in India, but the results of several years of much publicized effort are extremely meager. Of course there are show places where the visitor can see with his own eyes that peasants have struggled out of their apathy and got together to create a village hall or school. But judged in terms of the effect on average living standards— and that must mean, in Asia, its effect in helping to increase the output of food—the experiment has got nowhere. And one of the reasons is that each country has been largely dependent on its own local experiments and blunders in going forward with the program. The mass of information that might have been brought to bear on the problem, through an intelligent use of data drawn from the big agrarian changes that have taken place in other countries, has not been effectively applied.

As late as 1959, seven years after the big Indian community-development program was launched, one finds a mission of international experts, sent by the United Nations, pointing out the following things to the Indian government. First, the program has failed to concentrate sufficiently on

the main object, which is to raise agricultural output, and
has allowed the energies of its officers to be diverted into
marginal activities of a social and cultural character—
partly no doubt because these seemed easier to do. Secondly,
and connected with this, the program has not made contact
with the minds of the poorer peasants. Because the official
coming from outside tends to look for people with a
modicum of education to make the cultural and social
bridge between himself and the established order in the
village, community development comes to be viewed by the
ordinary villager as an alliance between the government
man and the existing ruling class. The report concludes
that if the program is to succeed in raising agricultural
production, "it must win the confidence of the majority of
the people by avoiding too exclusive dependence on the
more well-to-do persons in the villages and by not being
afraid to take up the cudgels against social abuses, against
infringements of the law—such as the kind of share crop-
ping in which the farmer receives one-third of the crop—
and against usury and speculative sharp practices.

Here is precisely the kind of issue on which the
United Nations should have been in a unique position to
provide expert guidance and direction right from the start.
It is bound to be a delicate operation, trenching as it does
upon sensitive areas of a nation's cultural heritage and on
its spiritual inadequacies; to be of any value, an outside
adviser must feel strong enough to use the critical freedom
and the sharp practical approach to the problem of stirring
up the villages, which is so well expressed in the independent report from which I have just quoted. Yet most of
the time the various agencies of the United Nations, which
have made their piecemeal and separate contributions to
community development, have tagged along behind other
people's ideas, almost as if they were afraid, more than
anything else, of being accused of wanting to exercise
leadership. It is noteworthy that the Ford Foundation, finding this obvious gap waiting to be filled, has now decided
to put some ten million dollars into a series of big experi-
mental projects in Indian community development with the
aim of answering a number of urgent questions on policy
for the future. . . .

The defenders of the present United Nations family system point out that the agencies do, in fact, work together successfully on a number of projects and that there are very few examples of complete stultification through overlap. It is true that the open quarreling is much less— and so is the covert sabotage—than it was some years ago; the machinery for dealing with demarcation disputes, which now operates under the control of a committee of the heads of the independent agencies and the UN Secretary-General, meeting twice a year, works pretty well. And it is supported, lower down, by the working groups of departmental heads from different agencies, who meet together informally in Geneva once a year. The trouble is that each one of these acts of coordination is a tour de force, and what emerges is a series of compromises about the way to handle a tricky development problem, rather than a single vigorous push for development itself.

∽ ∽ ∽

In the last few years there has been some improvement in the behavior of the agencies, spurred not so much by the governments, oddly enough, but by the United Nations itself, in the person of one of its more dynamic and imaginative personalities, Paul Hoffman. When the Special Fund was established in 1958, one of Hoffman's first decisions was that in regard to anyone of his projects he would deal with only one of the specialized agencies, which would then be responsible for securing services needed from any other agency. This was the opposite of the loose approach then prevalent at UN headquarters of bringing as many people into the act as could conceivably be justified. Because the Special Fund kept firm control of its funds it was able to impose this sensible system on everyone.

Hoffman is now taking on added responsibilities as the head of the new UN Development Board, which is in effect a merger of the Special Fund and the Expanded Program of Technical Assistance. This means he will carry even more

weight with the specialized agencies and will in effect be in a
position to do something which has seemed an impossible dream
all these years: make the whole system of specialized agencies
and UN economic and social bodies operate as an integrated
machine for the benefit of the poor countries. On the other
hand, Paul Hoffman is now in his seventies and there will come
a time when he will have to slow down. There is no one in
sight who can command anything comparable to the respect
and the grudging allegiance that the specialized agencies are
willing to extend to him.

⫸ 27 ⫷

ALPHABET FOR FOUR

In any discussion of the specialized agencies in their overall aspects it has become customary to single out the "big four": International Labour Organization (ILO), World Health Organization (WHO), United Nations Educational, Scientific and Cultural Organization (UNESCO), Food and Agriculture Organization (FAO).

The term is somewhat deceptive, for if the concept of "big" is to be interpreted as meaning influence and importance, the World Bank and the International Monetary Fund far outweigh any of the "big four," or even all four taken together. However, it almost never occurs to anyone to consider either the Bank or the Fund as full-fledged members of the United Nations system, which is hardly surprising, since this disturbing thought is not often entertained by officials of these two aristocratic and copiously endowed institutions.

In another and more profound sense "big four" is justified, however. ILO, WHO, UNESCO, and FAO are indeed the big ones in that they alone are in a position both to influence decisions of governments in fields of considerable importance, and to participate to a degree in carrying out these decisions. The Bank and the Fund are at least subconsciously aware of this, at their planning echelons, and it is not without a tinge of envy that these echelons maintain an attitude of

contemptuous aloofness toward what a former head of one of
the two institutions used to refer to as "those alphabet agencies
who manage to spell inefficiency with only five letters and
overhead with only three." Incidentally, it would be unjust to
conclude that the Bank and the Fund are the severest critics
of the "big four." In recent years there has been a growing
concern, on the part of those governments who pay most of
their budgets, for financial austerity, effective coordination
among the agencies as well as a minimum of subordination to
supervision by the United Nations. Thus, in 1964 the 63-
million-dollar budget of UNESCO was approved by a large
majority of member countries who together contributed less
than twenty percent of the total. The important contributors
abstained from voting, including the United States (30%),
the Soviet Union (14%), Great Britain (7%), Federal Republic of Germany (7%), and France (5.7%).

However justified the need for these changes, the fact
remains indisputable that in their own feudalistic, free-wheeling way each of the "big four" has nonetheless, time and
again, presented politically uncomfortable realities in such an
authoritative and detached manner that governments could
not avoid taking their views into account. Then the specialized
agency has proceeded to participate in the tackling of such
realities, providing a catalytic element which on certain occasions could be decisive in terms of results achieved. Thus,
UNESCO's bold program for fighting illiteracy in the underdeveloped world could prove to be a dynamic factor in many
countries that so far have been unable to teach their masses to
read and write.

An example of this type of influence by one of the "big
four" is furnished by FAO in the matter of birth control for
the *tiers monde*. On October 4, 1965, Pope Paul VI addressed
the General Assembly of the United Nations. The most controversial point made by His Holiness was his statement against
birth control, coming at a time when many voices in the
Catholic Church—and many of the bishops then gathered in

Rome in the final phase of Vatican Council II—were apparently convinced that the Church should modify its intransigent attitude, since the "population explosion" was perhaps the most anguishing problem confronting the underdeveloped world. The Pope seemed to dash these hopes when he told the United Nations: "Your task is to ensure that there is enough bread on the tables of mankind, and not to encourage an artificial birth control, which would be irrational, in order to diminish the number of guests at the banquet of life."

A mere forty-eight hours later the UN Food and Agriculture Organization published a report, "Food and Agriculture, 1965" showing that the impressive increase in the production and export of food over the last ten years had been virtually wiped out by the population explosion in the poor countries; in these, the underdeveloped countries, the amount of food grown per capita had increased only by one percent. In the rich, developed countries, where an abundant table was taken for granted by the average citizen ten years ago, the growth in food production had nonetheless been fourteen times greater than in the poor countries. The FAO report went on to say that during these last ten years "it is indeed a considerable achievement that it has been possible to cope with this population explosion without widespread starvation." (It is doubtful, however, that the people of the underdeveloped countries are quite as eager as FAO to congratulate themselves for the considerable achievement of not having starved to death.)

The FAO report went on to say what could be expected up to the end of this century: "Merely to keep pace with the expected population increase without any improvement in diets would require total food supplies to be almost double by the year 2000, but present dietary levels in the developing countries are so inadequate that actual needs are far greater than this. . . . FAO studies . . . indicate that the total food supplies of the developing countries will have to be increased four-fold in the next 35 years to give their vastly increased populations an adequate, though in no sense a lavish, diet."

Obviously, a leap of 400 percent in food production by the poor countries in the next few decades is out of the question, when in the last ten years they have managed only a one percent increase. What FAO was pointing out, in the carefully guarded language of an official report, was the sheer impossibility for the underdeveloped countries to grow enough food for domestic consumption in the foreseeable future. Consequently the governments of these countries, so long as they refuse to introduce birth control as a national policy, will be ever more dependent on the charity of rich countries in order "to cope with this population explosion without widespread starvation." Since then, the 1966 famine in India and the appeals by New Delhi to the United States and other countries has underscored the grim prediction.

There is nothing new in these sobering statements. In fact, many poor countries have been dependent for a number of years on the charity of the United States to hold "widespread starvation" at arm's length; for instance, a number of Asian and Latin American countries. It may be true that Public Law 480, which permits the U.S. government to virtually give away millions of tons of food, may serve as a useful tool of domestic policy in solving some of the more annoying aspects of relations between the administration and the farmers. It is even plausible, as has been argued, that it is better to get rid of millions of tons of surplus wheat by shipping it overseas to the starving masses of India than to spend millions of dollars in storage costs in the United States. But the fact remains that this is global charity by the United States, in the true biblical sense of "feeding the hungry," on a sustained yearly basis.

In this case, FAO carried out a basic task by pointing out that governments of the underdeveloped countries are unable to fulfill a primordial function—assuring adequate food supplies—and they will be unable to do so in the foreseeable future unless they adopt certain policies to restrain population growth. The alternative is an indefinite dependence on American charity, a solution which is probably not unpalatable to the rulers of quite a few *tiers monde* countries, but which they realize is not without political risks.

Obviously, such a warning could only be given by an organ that would be both technically knowledgeable and in theory unbiased. That the warning followed the papal pronouncement by only forty-eight hours could scarcely be considered fortuitous.

⇛ 28 ⇚

CLOAK AND DAGGER SECTION

Of the four thousand employees of the United Nations family in Geneva, about three fourths work for the specialized agencies with headquarters in town: World Health Organization, International Labour Organization, World Meteorological Organization, and International Telecommunications Union. Another thousand persons work directly for the UN inside the Palais des Nations, engaged in an amazing variety of occupations and preoccupations.

Some notes jotted down not long ago by a staffer stationed at Headquarters who was sent to Geneva on a working trip give an inkling of this microcosm within the Palais. He wrote:

> Quite a chat I had yesterday in that cavernous cafeteria, somewhere in the bowels of the Palais. Walked endless corridors to get there but got lost only once. Had been quite often to cafeteria but always in good weather months and I would get in from the park. Cafeteria is quite different then, looking almost like restaurant in resort town, miraculously opening up its tall glass doors on an outside lawn. Had holiday mood.
>
> No such mood yesterday. Day was grey and bleak, the bise had swept across the lake and was swirling outside. Not that you could see it from the inside. Glass doors completely steamed up, cafeteria felt cozy, almost like

bistro. Particularly since well past lunch hour, only little groups huddled at a table here and there.

Decided it might be good occasion to conduct personal sampling; chose a table where I knew one of the four men sitting, social affairs guy by the name of Dupont, now arranging this coming seminar on welfare problems. He waved as soon as he saw me and asked me to come over and sit down. Not surprisingly, it turned out that Dupont had a little business to discuss with me; his colleagues thought the seminar needed some publicity, he said. Perhaps some interviews for the papers, or on radio or television, for those countries where it seemed they couldn't care less. So could I arrange it?

Naturally I gave him the usual pep talk, that was what we were interested in and I would talk to my colleagues and see what we could do. Always glad to cooperate and that sort of crap. But I warned him at the same time about a few facts of life when it came to newspaper space or broadcasting time for any UN activity that was not political. Unless he could guarantee a good free-for-all at the seminar, the headlines would keep going to the political tangles in which the organization seems to get involved all the time. Very few managing editors interested in social welfare.

He shuddered at the idea of the delegates to his seminar getting into a good fight; also, he was unconvinced by my healthy skepticism. So I said, "Let us ask our colleagues sitting around this table. I bet they are engaged in interesting work. Let's ask if what they do gets the publicity it deserves."

"Certainly not," said a studious-looking young man sitting across the table. "I do simultaneous interpretation for this debate on tariffs going on now, and I hear the delegates complaining all the time about indifference in the press."

"Do you yourself think the debates are newsworthy?" I inquired. He shrugged. "It's just another job for me. At the beginning the words they use seem awfully technical, but after a while you get used to it. By now I find some of the debates interesting, but I wouldn't blame the correspondents for not agreeing." Then he added, nudging his

neighbor, a tweedy and older man who looked unmistakably English, "Donaldson here is the one who handles
glamor. He is documents officer for outer space."

"For the legal aspects of outer space," Donaldson
corrected. "Believe me, old boy, that makes all the difference. No correspondents hanging around our subcommittee.
It's the chaps on the other, the technical subcommittee, that
have the press fellows clustered around them."

"Anybody at this table who feels he gets any publicity
for what he is doing?" I looked around as I asked the question, and a man in his forties, sitting right in front of me,
said quickly: "Count me out. I never want to see a correspondent again." The others all laughed, then Donaldson
explained for my benefit: "Nielsen is a chemist with Narcotics. But by now he probably wishes he had never left
his university in Sweden to join the UN."

The Swedish chemist nodded gravely. "Those journalists, they never want to know how the work is done,
and they can make themselves quite unpleasant."

We were all listening. Nielsen went on: "We are
using certain methods for tracing the origin of opium samples. New methods, very advanced. A lot of research had
to be done first just to work through the techniques. My
university of course, but also other universities and research
institutes in Europe, in America. . . ."

I interrupted: "Why are the newsmen quite unpleasant? What do they want to know?"

Nielsen shook his head sadly. "Only political questions. Which countries are violating the international agreements and how they smuggle the drugs into Europe and
North America. And whether countries in Asia and the
Middle East make a big profit from narcotics, big enough
to show in their balance of payments. Can you imagine me,
an international civil servant and a scientist, answering
such explosive questions?" Then he added, as an afterthought: "Besides, I don't know the answers. I'm a laboratory man."

At this point the fifth person at table, a very young
looking fellow with a brown skin and aquiline features
spoke out: "Well, I got myself interviewed. My picture
taken, too. And my chief said it was all right."

It turned out that he was a Pakistani named Husein, working in telecommunications. Dupont immediately urged Husein to tell his story, remarking to me accusingly: "You will see that it's possible to get the press interested. Husein did a very good job with the correspondents here."

Husein clearly thought so too. He was pleased to tell everyone about the event. "It happened last week when things again got a bit rough in the Middle East. They wanted to see how our teletype system works to send instructions to the UN troops in the Gaza Strip. Two of them represented British papers."

"But that has nothing to do with Geneva," I interjected. "Any instructions for the troops come from Headquarters. It's highly political and it's always handled by New York. Anyone knows that."

"That is so," agreed Husein. "But it all passes through Geneva. We are the relay point for all UN telecommunications. Everything goes through our Geneva facilities, coming and going."

"But then you could tell them only about routine operational details," remarked the Swedish scientist with lofty contempt.

Husein held up his two hands, fingers spread wide apart. He was smiling and showing dazzlingly white teeth, but his tone was aggrieved: "Perhaps the higher authorities in New York will have to ponder about how to stop the fighting. That is after all their appointed task. But once they have decided, the instructions would never reach the commander of the Force if I didn't see to it that the relay system is working properly. One day last week I sat in the communications center half through the night. There was something wrong with the equipment and New York was concerned that the messages were not getting through fast enough. But with these ten fingers I kept everything under control."

I told Husein that the accredited correspondents undoubtedly got wind of the breakdown and that was why they wanted to interview him. I thought I was making my tone sarcastic but Husein continued to be pleased with himself. "The very next day, yes," he said proudly. "The very next day they wanted to interview me. Several of them, including two British correspondents. Then my chief said it was all right, as long as I discussed only the equipment. But then they also took a photograph of me, and then another one just of my hands repairing a piece of equipment." He turned to me and explained: "Unavoidably that was what you and your colleagues would call a doctored photograph. The real repair job had been done during the night. I just went through the motions for the UN photographer who took all the shots and then made them available to the correspondents."

At this point the Swedish chemist stood up to leave, and when he shook hands with me he said I should come and see his Narcotics Division one of these days. I'm going to do that, but I wish I had been told in time about the breakdown in communications so we could have handled the press ourselves. As usual the news leaks out to the correspondents but not to our own press services. I got hold of the clippings and the way they presented the communications breakdown didn't make us look too good. Not that I really blame them. There are quite a few accredited correspondents here at the Palais, we don't realize in New York that they amount to a full-fledged press corps, with all the wire agencies and several of the major papers represented the year round. But believe me, they are a frustrated lot. They feel they're entitled to news, they insist that they keep getting only the crumbs. They keep repeating to each other this joke that appeared in *The New Yorker*, about the dowager skimming through a newspaper and remarking to her tycoon husband that something seems to be going on in Geneva all the time, but she can never figure out what it is. One of the old hands in the press corps actually showed me the cartoon, and then he said to me: "When something is really happening here in the Palais you guys are most careful about not letting the press get its teeth into the news." I joked with him about us being kept in the dark just about as much as the press corps, which is partly true, but it didn't make much of an impression.

We better watch out because these Geneva correspondents are getting to be a frustrated lot."

A week later the UN information man had jotted down some more notes. They read:

> Yesterday took up invitation from Swedish scientist and spent most of afternoon speaking to him and fellows who work with him in Narcotics. We went the rounds of the laboratories and I had to stand and listen to a lot of talk, most of it dull. As I suspected, Nielsen wants to get some publicity. He's scared of the correspondents, sure enough, but he wants us to dream up a nice, interesting story that will do credit to him and his outfit. I'm not sure we can get the news media to use it, but I'm putting down these notes, just in case. There might be a chance on a TV show, even at network level. Better to try for a splash in something like this. We stand just as good a chance.
>
> So after they had me thoroughly exhausted we went to the lounge on the third floor and those low-slung leather chairs felt even more comfortable than ever. All they offered me was cafe espresso but I didn't really mind, since by that time I had pencil and paper in hand and my work was just beginning; I'm not complaining, but I just want it to be known that I'm putting in long hours and it's much harder to get a free drink in Geneva than it is in New York.
>
> Besides myself and Nielsen, there was Nielsen's senior administrative assistant, an American called Latham.
>
> So I sank into that big, broad leather chair (excuse me, I see I sank already about five lines ago, but I was dead tired and I was not wearing my best walking shoes, which is a mistake, since no one should even enter the Palais without his best walking shoes, and my feet hurt and I don't want to see another laboratory, narcotics or otherwise, in a long, long time.) So as I settled into the leather chair I told the two of them in my best diplomatic manner: "I have been listening to both of you for the last two hours, and believe me it has been fascinating. But I hope you will now allow me to ask questions about a couple of things that I think would interest one of the information media, in case we can get them interested, that is."
>
> "Go ahead," said Latham, with a smug expression on his face. "But before you start I will bet a week's ration of

cafe espresso that I'll guess what the first question is going to be."

I was foolish enough to say the thing that one is expected to say. So I said, "It's a bet." And he said just the word: "Interpol."

I lost the bet, because of course that was the word I had on the tip of my tongue and both Latham and Nielsen knew it and they smiled to each other.

At this point another of their narcotics people joined us, a junior assistant of Nielsen from some obscure country in Latin America who spoke English with a singsong accent; he listened obsequiously while Nielsen repeated the whole story to him, and how I had lost the bet. Then he sat down, but he didn't lean against the back of the leather chair but sat on the edge and sort of bowed to his boss, Nielsen, and then turned to me and spoke quite superciliously: "They all want to hear about us and Interpol. Professor Nielsen says it's because of the Iemmebon influence."

I asked him who was Iemmebon and there were complicated explanations until I finally grasped he meant James Bond, but apparently Iemmebon is the way they pronounce it around the Caribbean area. So I said: "Now let's hear about this cloak-and-dagger stuff. What's in it and what is precisely the relation with Interpol. How do you two work together?"

It was Latham who answered, quite sententiously. "We in the United Nations Narcotics Division cooperate closely with Interpol, but of course we don't work together. As a matter of fact, our relations with Interpol are a projection of our relations with member governments. We serve as a coordinating point and a clearing house for information. The governments communicate to us regularly their new regulations on drugs and the problems they face in curbing illicit production and traffic. Similarly, we receive the reports from the International Criminal Police Organization, which is commonly known as Interpol, on seizures of drugs shipped by one of the international narcotics smuggling rings."

"Is that where the cloak-and-dagger stuff comes in?" I asked.

"Precisely. We issue these reports from Interpol as UN documents, and of course the style is not quite like that of other documents of the organization."

Then Nielsen interposed: "But in all modesty we ourselves could claim some kinship with James Bond. Our narcotics division is engaged right now in evaluating the drug addiction problem throughout the entire world, the causes of addiction, the best approach to cure and rehabilitation. And in my own laboratory we spent the last few days tracking down the geographic origin of samples of drugs Interpol had seized in Marseille the week before. Our conclusions might help in breaking up one more international gang."

"We also furnish technical assistance to member governments," said the young Latin American.

Nielsen shook an admonitory finger. "Let us not use this bland UN language. We are dealing with something sinister, on an international scale."

"Technical assistance? What kind of technical assistance," I asked.

"Let me give you one example," the Swedish chemist continued. "Let us take Iran. Up to 1955 the opium poppy was grown legally in Iran, as it had been from time immemorial. And of course drugs for legitimate use were made from the opium poppy, we were told. But then, because it was impossible to prevent the big harvests from leaking into illicit channels, and because drug addiction had become a major problem in the country, we persuaded the Iranian government to ban altogether cultivation of the opium poppy."

"Which is all to their credit," remarked Nielsen. "They were giving up exports estimated at six million dollars a year."

"But it was not easy to enforce the ban and eliminate drug addiction," Nielsen went on. "So one year later the Iranian government asked for technical assistance from the United Nations. One of our experts was sent to advise the government, draft a new narcotics code, start a nation-wide drive."

"They even had jeeps with loudspeakers to publicize the campaign," said Latham. "Some of our specialized agencies advised the farmers how to switch from their cash crop, the opium poppy. And are trying to help solve the social and medical problems of addicts who have lost their source of supply."

I was not sure there were TV possibilities, but it was worth a try. "How easy is it to get a television team into Iran?" I asked.

Nielsen looked uncomprehending, but Latham knew at once what I was talking about. "Nothing is easy in Iran."

"You mean it has to go up to the Shah?" I inquired.

"That is our experience, when something of any significance is being considered," said Latham cautiously.

"I wonder if the Shah has any time left to run the country," I said. "I have never talked to any UN outfit operating in Iran without being told that only the Shah could decide."

PART VI

THE WORLD PREMIÈRE

29

HUNGARY: WHAT MIGHT
HAVE BEEN

By informal understanding the presidency of the General Assembly rotates among the different regions of the world, and 1965 was to be a European year. Moreover there was a genuine possibility that the president of the 20th Assembly would hail from a Communist country. If "rotation" really meant what the term implied, electing a member of the Soviet bloc would be justified. No Eastern European country had ever gained this recognition in the United Nations, while there had been three presidents from Western Europe, of which two came from NATO countries, not to mention three from the British Commonwealth.

As it turned out, the selection fell once more on Western Europe. The visit of Pope Paul VI, which had been announced only a matter of days before the opening of the General Assembly, may have decided the outcome, for it mobilized the support of many still doubtful delegations, who felt it would be particularly appropriate to have an Italian in the presidency to receive His Holiness. And so Foreign Minister Amintore Fanfani of Italy was chosen.

The presidency bestowed once more upon the West, it was quickly agreed that the chairmanship of the most important of the seven committees, the First or Political Committee, should go to an Eastern European. (There are those who

maintain that the man who presides over the Fifth Committee,
which handles finances and budget, has in reality more true
leverage at his disposal than his colleague in the First.) But
the Soviet bloc proposed for the chairmanship of the Political
Committee not Yugoslavia, but Hungary, whose permanent
representative was duly elected. Of all the members of the
Soviet bloc, Hungary is still by far the least respectable in the
eyes of many delegations. Memories of 1956 still rankle, and
until a very few years ago it would have been inconceivable
that the head of the Hungarian delegation could command
enough votes to be elected to any office in the United Nations.

There was an added irony to the episode, since the only
reason there were elections for the several committees in 1965
is that the United States gave in on its Article 19 position.
A few weeks before the Assembly convened the head of the
US delegation announced that it would not demand that
countries more than two years in arrears should have their
voting rights taken away from them, as that ill-fated article of
the Charter stipulates. Hungary was among the small group
of countries, led by the Soviet Union and France, that had
refused all along to pay for the UN's peacekeeping operations.
Moreover, it was the only country that had the dubious distinction of actually having been deprived of its voting rights
because of falling in arrears in its payments to one of the
specialized agencies, the International Labour Organization,
during two consecutive years (1954 and 1955).

The whole episode shows, if nothing else, "how con-
veniently short memories can be here at the Assembly," as a
junior member of the American delegation put it.

                        ✌   ✌   ✌

The Hungarian revolution remains to this day not only one
of the least honorable chapters in the history of the United
Nations, but also one still surrounded by unanswered questions and unexplained episodes. It has never been submitted

to the searching exegesis that dissected all facets of the Congo operation, or for that matter of the Suez crisis, which ironically overshadowed it.

The first question that comes to mind is whether the Secretary-General could and should have done more during those fateful days when the Soviet Union hesitated and Hungary had literally a fighting chance of escaping from the oppressive Soviet embrace into a neutral limbo not too unlike that in which Austria lives (perhaps Finland provides an even better analogy). It seems that Dag Hammarskjold asked himself the same question. Some feel there was a barely disguised effort at self-justification on Hammarskjold's part when he later explained that during the decisive week when it seemed as though the Soviet Army might pull out of Hungary (and did pull out of Budapest), no suggestion was made to him that he fly to Budapest. The Secretary-General then goes on to say:

> And if you will read the records of the Security Council and the General Assembly for the week which started the twenty-eighth and in fact went up to, let us say, the fourth and fifth of November, you can very well see why there was not any such proposal. There was certainly not a single member of the Secuirty Council who at that stage felt that the situation was clear enough to make such a proposal or felt that it was a good idea to send the Secretary-General away. There was never any choice from that point of view.

Was there not? Hammarskjold suggested that there had been no spontaneous suggestion that the Secretary-General take action and that in any case action on Hungary would be blocked by the Soviet veto in the Security Council, as indeed it was. But only a few days later action on Suez was blocked in the Security Council by the British and French vetoes, and Hammarskjold still found ways to play a dynamic and effective role in the crisis.

The possibilities open to the UN, acting through its Secre-

tary-General, begin to emerge when the events in Hungary
are recalled in terms of press dispatches by international news
services, coupled with the dramatic appeals to the UN in radio
broadcasts from Hungary.

A summary of these press dispatches reads as follows,
from day to day:

Tuesday, October 23, 1956: Student demonstrations
in Budapest take place in front of the statue of General
Bem and the Polish Embassy. Students demand reforms,
democratization, the return of Imre Nagy.

Police try to disperse the crowd when students attempt
to be heard over Budapest radio. Tear gas is used and then
students are arrested. The crowd attempts to free the students and the police open fire. The demonstration turns
into a riot and street fighting breaks out.

Martial law is declared, a call for Russian troops
issued, and, during the night, Soviet tanks and jets are
reported used against the demonstrators.

Wednesday, October 24, 1956: Additional Soviet military units enter Budapest at the request of the Hungarian
government. Fighting breaks out between Soviet troops
and the Hungarian people.

Changes in the Party Central Committee and in the
government are announced. Imre Nagy replaces Andras
Hegedus as Premier, but Erno Gero remains First Party
Secretary.

Nagy appeals to the people to stop fighting. Surrender
deadlines are announced as fighting continues. The deadlines are moved forward several times, and finally altogether abandoned. Rebels capture factories in Budapest.
Fighting reported in Debrecen, Szolnok and Szeged. Government troops recapture the Ganz Machine Works and
the Csepel Iron Works.

Thursday, October 25, 1956: The Nagy government
claims its forces have restored order in Budapest, but
admits fighting continues. Erno Gero is relieved as First
Party Secretary and replaced by Janos Kadar. Nagy and
Kadar announce that, following restoration of order, negotiations for withdrawal of Soviet troops will be initiated.

Nagy promises to reconvene parliament and to consider a reform program and reorganization of the government.

Friday, October 26, 1956: Fighting continues throughout the country. Insurgents take the entire area between Magyarovar and the Hungarian frontier of Hegyeshalom.

The Party Central Committee pledges: 1, election of a new government based on the Patriotic People's Front (PPF); 2, correction of past mistakes; 3, negotiations with the USSR for withdrawal of Soviet troops and the establishment of relations between the two countries on the basis of complete equality; 4, acceptance of workers' councils and raising of wage rates; 5, a complete amnesty to all participants in the fighting.

Saturday, October 27, 1956: Formation of a new government is announced. The cabinet is headed by Nagy. Non-Communist personalities in the government include Zoltan Tildy and Bela Kovacs.

Sunday, October 28, 1956: Local negotiations with Soviet troops commanders reported and in some cases Soviet forces join the insurgents. The government announces a cease-fire and Nagy states that Soviet troops will withdraw from Budapest immediately, and that the security police will be dissolved. He also promises that no participant in the fighting is to be punished.

An emergency committee, composed of Janos Kadar, Antal Apro, Karoly Kiss, Ferenc Munnich, Imre Nagy and Zoltan Szanto, assumes temporary leadership of the Party.

Spontaneous rise to power of revolutionary workers' councils and local national committees. A series of political and economic demands accompany this rise. The major ones include: withdrawal of Soviet troops, political and economic equality of relations between the USSR and Hungary, revision of the economy, greater democratization of life, changes in government organization and personnel, dissolution of the security police, protection of all those taking part in the revolution, withdrawal from the Warsaw Pact, Hungarian neutrality, a call for free elections, free speech, press, assembly and worship.

The Patriotic People's Front announces that a country-wide Committee has been created to coordinate the activi-

246] THE PLAY WITHIN THE PLAY

ties of these various local national committees. The Budapest Chief of Police announces formation of Hungarian
National Guard units.

Monday, October 29, 1956: Szabad Nep answers the
Soviet Pravda attack on the revolution and defends the
Hungarian uprising.

Radio Free Miskolc calls for immediate withdrawal
of Soviet troops from Hungarian soil, not merely their
return to bases outside of Budapest; Hungarian Army units
are replacing them.

Heavy fighting continues in Budapest, particularly at
Kilian (Maria Theresia) Barracks.

Tuesday, October 30, 1956: Nagy announces abolition
of the one-party system, a return to the political conditions
prevailing after 1945, and negotiations for immediate withdrawal of all Soviet forces from Hungary. A new coalition
government is formed with Imre Nagy as Premier. Three
non-Communists—Bela Kovacs, Zoltan Tildy and Ferenc
Erdei—are included.

The recall of the Hungarian representative to the
UN, Peter Kos, is announced.

Tildy calls for reconstituting the Smallholders' Party;
Ferenc Erdei makes a similar appeal for the Peasant Party;
and Kadar implies to Communist Party members that he
agrees with both reconstitutions.

Cardinal Mindszenty is freed.

Hungarian Air Force threeatens to bomb Soviet tanks
unless they leave Budapest. Insurgents storm security
police headquarters in Pest, and burn down Party headquarters in Buda. The security police appeals to the
Writers' Union to intervene for its 10,000 members; they
will surrender if guaranteed amnesty.

Wednesday, October 31, 1956: Radio Free Kossuth
broadcasts Soviet declaration concerning changes in relations between USSR and Satellite States.

Ministry of Agriculture announces suspension of com-
pulsory deliveries of farm produce.

Cardinal Mindszenty arrives in Budapest.

Independent Smallholders' Party announces formation
of a new executive committee and resumes control of its
former newspaper, Kis Ujsag. Hungarian Social Demo-

cratic Party is reorganized in Budapest, with Anna Kethly as president, and Nepszava as its official publication.

Pal Maleter replaces Lajos Toth as First Deputy Defense Minister and Istvan Kovacs takes Toth's former job as Army Chief of Staff.

Nagy announces that the Hungarian government is prepared to leave the Warsaw Pact and has asked for negotiations on withdrawal of Soviet forces from Hungary.

A Trans-Danubian National Council is organized out of various area councils. It requests immediate evacuation of Soviet forces, repudiation of the Warsaw Pact, free elections, a declaration of Hungary's neutrality, and freedom of speech, press, assembly and worship.

Thursday, November 1, 1956: Imre Nagy announces Hungary's withdrawal from the Warsaw Pact, proclaims Hungarian neutrality, and asks the United Nations to put the Hungarian question on its agenda. Nepakarat, newspaper of the Free Hungarian Trade Unions, is published for the first time. The National Peasant Party, now called the Petofi Party, is reorganized. Kadar attacks past leaders and policies of the Hungarian Communist Party and announces the reorganization of the Party under the name of the Hungarian Socialist Workers' Party.

Soviet units surround Hungarian airfields, allegedly to protect evacuation of Soviet dependents from Budapest. Budapest ringed by Soviet tanks. The Hungarian Army asks all personnel to maintain discipline and avoid clashes with Soviet troops.

Friday, November 2, 1956: Hungarian government protests to the Soviet Embassy the re-entry of Soviet troops on Hungarian soil. The United Nations is notified of Soviet activities in the second official note within two days, and is requested to appeal to the great powers to recognize Hungarian neutrality.

Soviet troops take rail line from Zahony to Nyiregyhaza; hold Budapest International Airport, and Kalocsa Airfield.

United Hungarian Youth Federation is organized in Budapest.

Saturday, November 3, 1956: Considerable Soviet reinforcements and troop movements to the Austro-Hungarian border are reported. Russian tanks surround uranium mines at Pecs.

The Hungarian government is reorganized after resignation of most of its ministers. The new ministers, many of them non-Communists, take over the administration. New cabinet includes: Imre Nagy, Premier and Minister of Foreign Affairs, Zoltan Tildy, Istvan Bibo, Anna Kethly, Ferenc Farkas, Geza Losonczy, and Janos Kadar as Minister of State, and Pal Maleter, Minister of Defense.

Negotiations for withdrawal of Soviet troops continue, and further Soviet troops movements are reported.

Cardinal Mindszenty addresses the people.

The National Council of Dunapentele appeals to all free radio stations to broadcast to Soviet troops in Russian to counteract Soviet propaganda.

Sunday, November 4, 1956: Imre Nagy announces Soviet attack on Budapest. Russian forces take over most of the country: airfields, highway junctions, bridges, railway yards. Heavy fighting reported in Csepel and Kobanya. Soviet paratroops in action near Gyor. Fighting at Pecs as Hungarian troops resist Soviet efforts to take uranium mines and airfields. Heavy fighting in Budapest. Gyor and Sopron fall to the Russians. Fighting continues in all parts of the country and the situation remains confused.

New government changes announced: Janos Kadar, Premier; Ferenc Munnich, Deputy Premier and Minister of Security; Imre Horvath, Minister of Foreign Affairs; Istvan Kossa, Minister of Finance; and Antal Apro, Minister of Industry; Imre Dogei, Minister of Agriculture; Sandor Ronai, Minister of Internal Trade.

Repeated free radio broadcasts call for Western help.

The Hungarian Writers' Union appeals for Western aid.

Soviet-held radio stations order surrender of arms, and resumption of work. Many free radio stations fall; Radio Free Kossuth goes off the air after broadcasting repeated SOS calls.

Monday, November 5, 1956: Fighting continues throughout the country. Soviet-controlled radio stations repeat ceasefire and return-to-work appeals. Free radio stations broadcast military instructions to the remaining resistance groups and repeated appeals for Western help. Fighting continues in the 8th District of Budapest, on Csepel Island, in the Lake Balaton region and in Kecskemet. Russians claim to have taken Szombathely, Miskolc, Debrecen, Szolnok, and Pecs.

Tuesday, November 6, 1956: The Kadar government appeals to friendly nations and the Soviet Military Command for food and medicine. Fighting continues in Pecs, Budapest, Dunapentele, Szombathely, Hegyeshalom, and other areas. Soviet-controlled stations broadcast an ultimatum to the patriots. Reports of continued fighting and local successes are broadcast by the free radio stations, as well as appeals to Soviet troops and requests for Western help.

Wednesday, November 7, 1956: Fighting continues. Government stations claim restoration of order. Soviets fight in Szeged, Szolnok, Hodmezocasarhely, Pecs and Dunapentele. Individual free amateur and military shortwave stations continue to broadcast at intervals from unknown locations.

Thursday, November 8, 1956: Continued resistance urged by free radios. Fighting continues in Pecs, Dunapentele, Budapest and its suburbs, and in the Bakony region. Budafok and Negyteteny bombed by Soviet aircraft.

Istvan Dobi, Chairman of the Presidential Council, appeals for order to the Hungarian peasantry, promising a "Socialist democracy" and guarantees of legality. State Minister Gyorgy Marosan addresses a similar appeal to workers and peasants. The government orders surrender of all weapons to Soviet troops by the evening of November 9. Those surrendering their arms before the deadline are promised immunity.

Budapest Radio announces that order has been restored in Gyor, Szeged, Komarom and Szekesfehervar, but admits fighting still going on in Budapest.

The government issues repeated appeals for order; ministers plead with the people to return to work, citing food and fuel shortages which endanger the health of the population.

Friday, November 9, 1956: Fighting continues, particularly heavily in Csepel and Kulsokobanya, as well as in the 3rd, 6th and 20th districts of Budapest and in the suburbs. Fighting also reported in Dunapentele, Kalocsa, Gyor and Komlo.

A selection of a few broadcasts during those fateful days completes the picture.

Tuesday, October 30, 1956—Radio Free Miskolc. 1000—The Hungarian people ask the UN to refuse to receive Peter Kos, who is a traitor to his country, and not to listen to the declarations he delivers in the name of the former and present Hungarian governments. The Hungarian people ask the UN to intervene immediately in the interest of Hungary. . . . The Hungarian people also ask the UN to entrust Hungarian representation to a neutral State. For the time being, the Hungarian people cannot send a delegate to the UN because they cannot elect the government they want.

Tuesday, October 30, 1956—Radio Budapest, Home Service. 1328—Premier Imre Nagy and members of the government will now address the Hungarian nation. Here is Premier Nagy:

"Hungarian workers, peasants, intellectuals. As a result of the revolution . . . and the mighty movement of democratic forces our nation has reached the crossroads. The national government, acting in complete agreement with the Presidium of the Hungarian Workers' Party, has arrived at a decision vital to the nation's life.

"In the interests of further democratization . . . the Cabinet has abolished the one-party system and has decided that we should return to a system of government based on the democratic cooperation of the coalition parties as they existed in 1945. In accordance with this decision, a new Cabinet has been set up within the national government. Its members are Imre Nagy, Zoltan Tildy, Bela Kovacs, Ferenc Erdei, Janos Kadar, Geza Losonczy and persons to be nominated by the Social Democratic Party. The government will submit a proposal to the Presidential Council . . . to appoint Janos Kadar and Geza Losonczy Ministers of State.

"The national government appeals to the headquarters of the Soviet Command to begin the immediate withdrawal of Soviet troops from Budapest. At the same time we wish to inform the people of Hungary that we are going to request the Soviet Union to withdraw all Soviet troops from Hungary.

"In the name of the national government I wish to declare that we recognize all the autonomous democratic local authorities which were formed during the revolution, that we rely on them and want their support.

"Fellow Hungarians! To safeguard the achievements of the revolution we must first of all establish order. Fratricidal war must stop immediately. Avoid all further disturbances!"

Minister of State Zoltan Tildy:

"The nation's will has been fulfilled and the national revolution has triumphed. . . . I stand before the microphone deeply moved. I have not written down my speech and therefore it may be disjointed. But I want to congratulate Hungarian youth from the bottom of my heart. I declare before the Hungarian nation—before the whole world—that these young people and the soldiers and workers who fought with them are not only worthy of the youth of March 1848 but have surpassed March 15, 1848, by their heroic struggle and . . . their achievements. The least the Hungarian nation can do is to declare the day on which this struggle began a national holiday in memory of their heroic battles. . . . The national government will bury the heroes of the revolution with military honors and it will take generous care of the wounded and the families of those heroes who fell in battle.

"In this connection, I want to ask the representatives of fighting university youth to send their delegates to me at the parliament building. Premier Nagy will also await them. We shall charge them with an official mission: the formation of a National Guard Battalion to help restore order.

"I want to announce a few other measures. I inform the country that Peter Kos, former representative of Hungary at the UN, has been recalled and that a new UN delegation will be appointed which will represent the views of this government."

Tuesday, October 30, 1956—Radio Free Kossuth, to

Diplomatic Missions. 1709—The Revolutionary Committee of the Ministry of Foreign Affairs issues a declaration in support of the revolution. It condemns the "unwarranted interference of Soviet troops," and demands that those responsible for the bloodshed be brought to account. It repudiates the declaration made by UN representative Peter Kos, and demands his immediate recall as well as the recall of members of the Foreign Ministry abroad who opposed the peoples' interests. In conclusion, the Committee calls on Foreign Ministry employees to participate in the restoration of order and to report to their offices on Wednesday.

Wednesday, October 31, 1956—Radio Free Kossuth. 1100—Tass reports from Moscow that the Soviet government has instructed its military command to withdraw military formations from Budapest as soon as the Hungarian government considers it appropriate. At the same time, the Soviet government is ready to enter into negotiations with the government of the Hungarian People's Republic and with other governments which are party to the Warsaw Pact on the withdrawal of Soviet troops from Hungary as well.

Thursday, November 1, 1956—Radio Free Kossuth. 1713—Premier Imre Nagy . . . today asked to see Mr. Andropov, USSR Ambassador Extraordinary and Plenipotentiary. Nagy told him that the Hungarian government had received authoritative information on the entry of new Soviet military units into Hungary. He demanded their immediate withdrawal. He informed the Soviet Ambassador that the Hungarian government is giving immediate notice of the termination of the Warsaw Pact and is declaring Hungary's neutrality. He added that the Hungarian government is appealing to the United Nations and . . . the four Great Powers to safeguard the nation's neutrality.

The Soviet Ambassador acknowledged the protest . . . and promised to ask his government for an immediate reply.

The Premier informed . . . all heads of diplomatic missions accredited in Budapest of the contents of his talk with the Soviet Ambassador. He also sent a telegram to the UN Secretary-General . . . informing him of the Hungarian government's decision and asking that the matter be placed on the agenda of the next General Assembly session.

Friday, November 2, 1956—Radio Free Kossuth. To Mr. Dag Hammarskjold, Secretary-General of the United Nations, New York:

Your Excellency, the Chairman of the Council of Ministers of the Hungarian People's Republic wishes . . . to bring the following supplementary information to the knowledge of Your Excellency:

I have already mentioned in my message of November 1 that new Soviet military formations have entered Hungary, that the Hungarian government had informed the Soviet Ambassador about this, that it had repudiated the Warsaw Pact, that it had declared Hungary's neutrality and had turned to the United Nations to guarantee the neutrality of the country. On November 2 the government of the Hungarian People's Republic received new important information, Army reports, according to which considerable Soviet military formations have crossed the country's frontier. They are advancing toward Budapest, occupying railway lines, railway stations, railway traffic installations and so forth on their way. Reports have also been received about Soviet troop movements, in an East-West direction, in western Hungary.

In view of the above-mentioned facts the Hungarian government deems it necessary to inform the Soviet Embassy in Budapest and the other diplomatic missions accredited to Budapest about the steps directed against our People's Republic. The Hungarian government has at the same time made concrete proposals to the Soviet government concerning the withdrawal of Soviet troops stationed in Hungary, and the place for negotiations concerning implementation of the repudiation of the Warsaw Pact, and has also communicated the names of the Hungarian governmental delegation. In addition to this, the Hungarian government has proposed to the Soviet Embassy in Budapest the setting up of a mixed committee to prepare for the withdrawal of Soviet troops.

I ask Your Excellency to call on the Great Powers to recognize Hungary's neutrality. The Security Council should instruct the Soviet and the Hungarian governments to begin negotiations immediately. I ask Your Excellency to inform the members of the Security Council about the above facts, and to accept the expression of my sincere esteem.

Signed: Imre Nagy, Chairman of the Council of Ministers and Acting Foreign Minister of the Hungarian People's Republic.

Saturday, November 3, 1956—Radio Free Gyor. 1105—The newspaper Igazsag (Truth) yesterday asked the Revolutionary Committee of the Ministry of Foreign Affairs three questions. The questions were: 1. Is it true that the Hungarian delegate at the UN, who played such an ignominious role, was actually Leo Konduktorov, Soviet oil engineer? 2. Is it true that Konduktorov was given the new name of Dr. Peter Kos by the Hungarian Ministry of Foreign Affairs? 3. Why is it that the Ministry of Foreign Affairs did not inform the nation of these facts when Konduktorov's assignment had become known?

This morning the Revolutionary Committee of the Ministry of Foreign Affairs gave the following answers: It is true that Peter Kos is in reality a Soviet citizen and his name is Leo Konduktorov. The Revolutionary Committee of the Ministry of Foreign Affairs further stated that before Imre Nagy's declaration it had demanded the immediate cancellation of Peter Kos' appointment. Meanwhile, the Revolutionary Committee of the Ministry of Foreign Affairs has prepared a proposal for the immediate removal of the Rakosiist and Stalinist diplomats. Necessary steps have already been taken for the recall of certain officials in the diplomatic service.

Saturday, November 3, 1956—Radio Free Kossuth, in French to Europe. 1900—The majority of the Soviet units now in Hungary were on the move all Saturday. According to reports received from the northeast frontier, new Soviet formations entered Hungarian territory Saturday morning. According to observers a great number of (Soviet) armored vehicles are held in readiness near the Soviet frontier. The most important movements were affected near Szolnok, Nyiregyhaza and Debrecen in Eastern Hungary. Soviet troops have appeared in the regions of Bekescsaba and Szarvas, Eastern Hungary.

According to reports from Nyirbator (near Soviet border) Soviet armored vehicles and motorized infantry crossed the frontier near Beregsurany between 0700 and 1200 (GMT). A convoy of trucks carrying Soviet families moved from Debrecen toward Vasarosnameny. Following the occupation of the railroad stations in Zahony and Nyiregyhaza, Soviet troops took over the station of Debrecen early this morning. According to information from Miskolc . . . Soviet troops are building railroad lines between Nyiregyhaza and Zahony.

Soviet troops have occupied highway No. 4 running between Szolnok and Abony and stopped all vehicles moving toward Budapest. This morning Soviet trucks carried infantry from this region toward Budapest. The airport at Kunmadaras is under the control of Soviet troops.

In several districts the population is in contact with Soviet troops . . . through Revolutionary Committee delegates. . . . The (Soviet) officers and soldiers say that they have come to fight against the Facists, against those who wish to restore the Facist regime in Hungary. The people explain to them that there is no Fascism in Hungary, that the Hungarian people are fighting for freedom, for an independent Hungary, and for the well-being of the workers. Soviet officers, without exception, reply that they will not fire on the Hungarians and they also ask for the understanding of the people, for they have come as soldiers, under orders.

The soldiers who arrived in Gyor said that they had travelled 600 kilometers to get there. They had been told that the Americans wanted to attack Hungary and that they must defend the Hungarian workers. It is obvious that the Soviet soldiers are unaware of the true situation and that, on seeing the enthusiasm of the people, they are more and more convinced that the Hungarian people are fighting for the independence of their Fatherland and for the well-being of the workers.

Sunday, November 4, 1956—Radio Free Kossuth. 0420—Attention! Attention! Premier Imre Nagy will address the Hungarian people:

"This is Premier Imre Nagy speaking. Today at daybreak Soviet troops attacked our capital with the obvious

intent of overthrowing the legal democratic Hungarian
government. Our troops are in combat. The government is
at its post. I notify the people of our country and the entire
world of this fact." [Announcement repeated in English,
Russian, Hungarian and French.]

0458—Imre Nagy, Premier of the national government, appeals to Pal Maleter, Defense Minister, Istvan
Kovacs, Chief of the General Staff, and the other members
who went to the Soviet Army Headquarters at ten o'clock
(2100 GMT) last night and have not yet returned, to
return at once and take charge of their respective offices.

0508—Announcement that Imre Nagy has sent the
text of his notice of the Soviet attack to UN Secretary-
General Dag Hammarskjold.

0544—Announcement of an Associated Press report
that the UN Security Council has received Hungary's
appeal.

0612—Attention, attention, important announcement:
The Hungarian government appeals to the officers and men
of the Soviet Army not to shoot. Let us avoid bloodshed.
The Russians are our friends and will remain our friends.

0655—Report from New York. The Associated Press
reported at 0624 that the United States early this morning
asked the Security Council of the United Nations to hold
an emergency meeting on Sunday to discuss the Soviet
offensive in Hungary. The request was submitted by American Ambassador Lodge less than an hour after news agencies reported large-scale Soviet attacks in all of Hungary.

The Security Council had discussed the Hungarian
question Saturday night and adjourned the debate until
Monday morning. Lodge, however, requested the Council's
chairman to hold the meeting earlier should the situation
deteriorate.

0656—Attention, attention. You will now hear the
manifesto of the Union of Hungarian Writers:

This is the Union of Hungarian Writers! To every
writer in the world, to all scientists, to all writers' federa-
tions, to all science academies and associations, to the
intelligentsia of the world! We ask all of you for help and
support; there is but little time! You know the facts, there
is no need to give you a special report! Help Hungary!

Help the Hungarian writers, scientists, workers, peasants, and our intelligentsia!

Help! Help! Help!

0724—SOS! SOS! SOS!

Sunday, November 4, 1956—Radio Free Dunapentele, to Europe. [In Hungarian, Italian, French, German.] 1200—Attention! Attention! This is the last free Hungarian station!

This morning at 0130 Russian forces launched a general attack on the Hungarian nation. We ask the United Nations to send immediate help! We ask for parachute troops to be dropped over Danantul (Western Hungary). It is possible that our broadcasts will soon stop and you will hear us no more. We will only by silent when they have killed us. This morning at 0130 the Soviet troops launched a general attack against Hungarian troops. We do not know when we shall be massacred. [Repeated several times.]

Attention! According to unconfirmed news Czechoslovak tanks are also involved in the fighting.

1300—Attention: Radio Free Europe, attention:

Continue to relay our news.

We give only important news.

1421—Attention, Radio Free Europe. We ask for immediate armed help! We shall report again if possible. We now interrupt our broadcast. We shall report again if possible.

[Dunapentele was not heard again.]

Radio (free) Csokonay. 1520—We request Radio Free Europe to relay immediately the following message to the Secretary-General of the UN:

Appeal to the Secretary-General of the UN!

We speak to you in the name of the entire Hungarian people. Soviet troops are attacking our country for the second time in two weeks. They have turned our country into a battleground without regard for our people and our national values. The first time they interfered in our domestic affairs at the request of a government alien to the people. The Hungarian people energetically and unmistakably repulsed this attempt with arms in their hands. By fighting we made it possible for Imre Nagy to become

Premier. He proclaimed the supreme wish of the Hungarian people for neutrality and independence.

After this the entire Hungarian people joined Imre Nagy and they are still behind him. Although we have only been in possession of neutrality for two days we expect the whole world to respect it! Our government has cancelled the Warsaw Pact and ordered negotiations for withdrawal of Soviet troops. We accuse the Soviet Union:

1. Of armed aggression from outside the country.

2. Of having arrested the Minister of Defense, Maleter, and his staff, who went to negotiate the withdrawal of troops.

Since the only legal Hungarian government, that of Imre Nagy, has been imprisoned, and since that was the only organ which represented the official attitude of the Hungarian nation, in the name of our country we ask that the UN, by every possible means, pass a final resolution for the restitution and the protection of the liberty which we had already once won.

We now address a message to the delegates of the UN member States:

In the coming hours you will decide the life or the death of this nation. While your sons are at peace and happy, we sons of the Hungarian nation are falling under the cruel fire of Soviet tanks and bombers. We turn to you for you are our last citadel of hope.

Exercise the opportunity which your nation has given to you and save our country from destruction and slavery! We are asking for immediate and effective help which will save us from further bloodshed and will restore our independence. Show that the UN can carry out its will, and by its resolution make it possible for our country again to be free! We appeal to your conscience and call on you to act immediately.

1615—Attention, Radio Free Europe. We heard your acknowledgement of receipt of our message to the Secretary-General of the UN.

We now interrupt our broadcast for an indefinite period.

Long live freedom, long live the free Hungarian people!"

Sunday, November 4, 1956—Radio Budapest, Home Service. 2248—To the UN Secretary-General, Dag Hammarskjold, New York [text of telegram]:

The Hungarian Revolutionary Worker-Peasant Government hereby confirms the mandate of Mr. Kos, or in his absence that of Mr. Szabo, in the United Nations as the permanent representative of the Hungarian People's Republic in the United Nations.

The Hungarian Revolutionary Worker-Peasant Government states that the appeal made by Imre Nagy to the UN organization requesting that the Hungarian question be discussed in the United Nations has no legal force and cannot be regarded as an appeal sent by Hungary as a State. The Revolutionary Worker-Peasant Government categorically opposes the discussion both by the Security Council and the General Assembly of the above-mentioned question since this question lies exclusively within the competence of the Hungarian People's Republic.

Signed: Premier of the Hungarian Revolutionary Worker-Peasant Government, Janos Kadar; Foreign Minister, Imre Horvath.

Wednesday, November 7, 1956—Radio (Free) Rakoczi. 0935—The Commander of Dunafoldvar [passage unintelligible] talk . . . For a moment the noise of battle ceased during the negotiations . . . but the town was ordered to surrender. An artillery attack followed the Military Command's announcement that it would defend the town to the last man.

In the name of all honest Hungarians we appeal to all honest men in the world.

Must we appeal once again?

Do you love liberty? So do we.

Do you have wives and children? So have we.

We have wounded . . . who have given their blood for the sacred cause of liberty, but we have no bandages . . . no medicine. . . . And what shall we give to our children who are asking for bread? The last piece of bread has been eaten.

In the name of all that is dear to you . . . we ask you to help. . . . Those who have died for liberty . . . accuse you who are able to help and who have not helped.

The UN is able to stop further bloodshed. . . . Or shall we lose faith in the (world's) conscience and decency . . . when we are fighting for world freedom?

This is our message today, when, according to our information, the UN will meet in an extraordinary session.

This is our message to President Eisenhower. . . . If, during his Presidency he stands by the oppressed and those who are fighting for freedom, he shall be blessed after his re-election. . . .

We have received no answer to our appeal . . . that Dunapentele be declared a Red Cross center in Hungary. . . .

Radio Rakoczi, Hungary . . . We have read an appeal to the UN and every honest man . . .

(Radio) Free Europe, Munich! Free Europe, Munich! Repeat whether you have received our message.

1012—Attention! Attention!

An appeal to the UN! An appeal to the UN!

In Egypt the UN resolution was carried out. . . . We ask for similar measures in Hungary. We emphasize that similar measures must be taken immediately in the Hungarian affair.

Free Europe, Munich. . . . Attention!

We ask you to repeat in Russian the following appeal to Soviet soldiers in Hungary:

Soldiers!

Your State was created at the cost of bloody fighting so that you could have freedom. Today is the thirty-ninth anniversary of that revolution.

Why do you want to crush our liberty? You can see that it is not factory proprietors, not landowners, and not the bourgeoisie who have taken up arms against you, but the Hungarian people, who are fighting desperately for the same rights you fought for in 1917.

Soviet Soldiers! In Stalingrad, you showed how you could defend your country against a foreign invader. Why are you surprised that (we are defending?) . . . our country? [passage unintelligible].

Soldiers! Do not take up arms against the Hungarian nation.

Radio Free Europe, attention! Attention! I expect

you to forward the above message in the Russian language.
We ask you to acknowledge the above message!

1055—Radio Rakoczi requests a definite answer from
Radio Free Europe regarding our appeal this morning.

1115—Radio Rakoczi, calling Munich, Munich!

Please tell us on . . . which wave lengths Hungarian
radio stations are broadcasting. We are isolated. We wish
to contact them . . .

Attention, attention, Munich!

Under all circumstances remain on this wave length.
We shall definitely report on this wave length again although there may be longer intervals between broadcasts.
But we shall make every effort to report. Remain on this
wave length. . . . Please tell us the wave lengths of the
other radio stations . . . still in the hands of the freedom
fighters.

Against this background of human tragedy, which the
wire agencies and broadcasting networks were relaying almost
hourly to New York, the Security Council met on request of
the United States, Britain, and France on October 27, 1956.
On November 1, Imre Nagy informed the Secretary-General
that Soviet troops were again entering Hungary and that the
Hungarian government was demanding their withdrawal. The
following day there was again an urgent appeal from Imre
Nagy in which he asked the Security Council to instruct the
Soviet and the Hungarian governments to start negotiating
the withdrawal of Soviet troops, Hungary's withdrawal from
the Warsaw Pact, and the recognition of Hungarian neutrality.
A draft resolution, originally submitted by the United States
on November 3, and calling on the USSR to withdraw without delay from Hungary was blocked by the Soviet veto as
could have been expected. Whereupon an emergency session
of the General Assembly met the following day and stayed in
session until November 10. It passed a number of resolutions
calling upon the Soviet Union to withdraw its troops, all of
which were ignored.

But the real drama had been played out even before the

Security Council met, on October 23 and the days immediately following. It became clear almost at once that the US government, in spite of Mr. Dulles' many truculent statements against Soviet imperialism in previous months and years, was not prepared to risk a confrontation with the USSR over Hungary. Possibly Washington was not aware that during a few crucial days Moscow wavered. If the United States had backed the UN with more than words it might have made the difference between the Russians honoring the agreement they had already reached with Nagy's government, or reneging on it and crushing the Hungarian revolution with tanks. There were indeed "hawks" and "doves" in the Kremlin during that decisive last week of October, the "doves" being led by Mikoyan and the "hawks" by Suslov and the military, with Khrushchev undecided during several days. These are not mere speculations; schizophrenia in the Kremlin was attested before the UN Special Committee on the Problem of Hungary and is described in the Committee's report.

Once the opportunity was missed, however, and the Soviet government became convinced that the United States would not actively provide leadership, nor would the revulsion of world opinion be translated into effective action by the UN, the repression of the Hungarian revolution was swift and ruthless. Nor did it end with the clamping of Soviet military control over Hungary. Nagy and other members of his government who had taken refuge in the Yugoslav embassy were arrested by Russian troops when they were boarding the bus that would take them to their residences, in accordance with a written promise by the puppet government of Janos Kadar. Nagy was executed almost two years later, in a cold-blooded act of political vengeance that gave world opinion a delayed shock of disgust. But the UN was unable to do anything to forestall Nagy's execution in June, 1958, just as it had been powerless to have any of its resolutions applied twenty months earlier.

On the humanitarian side, however, the UN was able to

give succour to the Hungarian refugees. And the report of its Special Committee remains to this day perhaps the most significant, in political terms, of all the thousands of documents produced by the world body, just as in human terms it is undoubtedly the most telling. Just a few paragraphs in the final part of the report, embodying its conclusions, could witness to this double impact:

What took place in Hungary in October and November 1956 was a spontaneous national uprising, due to long-standing grievances which had caused resentment among the people. One of these grievances was the inferior status of Hungary with regard to the USSR; the system of government was in part maintained by the weapon of terror, wielded by the AVH or political police, whose influence was exercised at least until the end of 1955, through a complex network of agents and informers permeating the whole of Hungarian society. In other respects also, Soviet pressure was resented. From the stifling of free speech to the adoption of a Soviet-style uniform for the Hungarian army, an alien influence existed in all walks of life. Hungarians felt no personal animosity towards the individual Soviet soldiers on Hungarian soil, but these armed forces were symbols of something which annoyed a proud people and fed the desire to be free.

The thesis that the uprising was fomented by reactionary circles in Hungary and that it drew its strength from such circles and from Western "Imperialists" failed to survive the Committee's examination. From start to finish, the uprising was led by students, workers, soldiers and intellectuals, many of whom were Communists or former Communists. The majority of political demands put forward during the revolution included a stipulation that democratic socialism should be the basis of the Hungarian political structure and that such social achievements as the land reform should be safeguarded. At no time was any proposal made for the return to power, or to the Government, of any figure associated with pre-war days. "Fascists" and "saboteurs", heavily armed, could not have succeeded in landing on Hungarian airfields which were under Soviet supervision, or in crossing the Austrian frontier, where a closed zone was shown by the Austrian authorities to the military attaches of France, the United Kingdom, the United States of America and the USSR.

The uprising was not planned in advance. It was the universal testimony of witnesses examined by the Committee that events took participants by surprise. No single explanation can determine exactly why the outbreak occurred just when it did. Communist spokesmen, including Mr. Kadar and the members of his present Government, have recognized the bitter grievances of the Hungarian people before 23 October. They have spoken of a "broad, popular movement" caused by the "bitterness and indignation" of the masses. Two factors would seem to have brought this resentment to a head. The first of these was the news received on 19 October of a successful move by Poland for greater independence from the USSR. This news was largely instrumental in bringing the Hungarian students together in the meetings of 22 October. The second factor was the acute disappointment felt by the people when Erno Gero, First Secretary of the Central Committee of the Hungarian Workers' (Communist) Party, in his speech on the evening of 23 October failed to meet any of the popular demands and adopted what was considered a truculent tone towards his hearers.

Although no evidence exists of advance planning, and although the whole course of the uprising bears the hallmark of continuous improvisation, it would appear that the Soviet authorities had taken steps as early as 20 October to make armed intervention in Hungary possible. Evidence exists of troop movements, or projected troop movements, from that date on. It would appear that plans for action had therefore been laid some time before the students met to discuss their demands. The Committee is not in a position to say whether the Soviet authorities anticipated that the grievances of the Hungarian people, stimulated by events in Poland, could no longer be contained. Signs of opposition were evident before the 23rd; the Hungarian Government had reason to foresee that trouble was brewing. While the evidence shows that Soviet troops from outside Hungary were used even in the first intervention, no clause of the Warsaw Treaty provides for intervention by armed forces of the Soviet Union to dictate political developments within any signatory's frontiers.

The demonstrations on 23 October were at first entirely peaceable. None of the demonstrators appear to have carried arms, and no evidence has been discovered that any of those who voiced the political demands or joined the demonstrators had any intention to resort to force. While disappointment at Mr. Gero's speech may have angered the crowds, it would hardly of itself have sufficed to turn the demonstration into an armed uprising. That this happened was due to the action of the AVH in opening fire on the people outside the radio building. Within a few hours, Soviet tanks were in action against the Hungarians. This appearance of Russian soldiers in their midst not as friendly allies, but as enemies in combat, had the effect of still further uniting the people.

There have been many speculations about what might have happened if the United States had taken a more forceful stand during the first few days of the Hungarian Revolution, if the UN had thus been in a position to do something more than proclaim its indignation—or if the Secretary-General had taken it upon himself to act, as he showed himself capable of doing on other occasions.

However that may be, looking back today, almost ten years later, it can be said that even though it failed the Hungarian Revolution did have a positive and beneficial effect on international developments. If it had not been for the bloody sacrifice of the people of Budapest and all Hungary it is doubtful whether the relative liberalization within the Soviet bloc would have come to pass. The Kremlin learned its lesson and it is difficult to imagine nowadays the Soviet government acting in such a brutal and pitiless manner against any state within its orbit of influence.

In a curiously illogical way which could never have been predicted at the time, the Hungarian Revolution paved the way for coexistence and for the relaxation of tension between East and West, and in this sense contributed to the search for disarmament and international security.

Last but not least, what happened in Budapest and what happened later on the Austrian-Hungarian border as thousands of escaping refugees were hunted down and shot did more for the promotion and support of human rights than the United Nations had ever been able to accomplish. At the same time it weakened irrevocably the appeal of communism to intellectuals, artists, and common people not only in the West but also within the confines of the Soviet bloc.

30

CONGO: THE COSTLY LESSON

Over the years, considerable consternation and almost equal indignation at the Soviet Union's abuse of her veto power in the Security Council has been recorded in the Western press and pronouncements of statesmen and diplomats. These pronouncements, many of them uttered in the chamber of the Council on occasions when the Russians once more wield their veto, came usually from American representatives. But not exclusively; British and other Western delegates have also gone on record with similar remarks, pointing out the harm done by the Soviets to the organization and to the cause of peace.

Actually, a great power can also do serious damage to the UN by failing to veto a resolution to which she is viscerally opposed. By not using her veto privilege in these circumstances, she commits the United Nations to a dangerous course of action: that of trying to execute a task which will be obstructed by one of the big powers. That is, if the Secretary-General, as the executive branch of the UN, insists on carrying out the Security Council resolution.

This other peril inherent in the veto privilege of the big powers had not often been discussed or denounced in public. At least, not until the summer of 1960, when the United Nations plunged into the Congo operation, a venture that did serious damage to the prestige, the effectiveness, and the

THE PLAY WITHIN THE PLAY

finances of the organization, and whose scars will not fade for
a long time. In retrospect it now appears clear that the damage
suffered by the organization was in good part due to the fact
that not one but three of the big powers had serious misgivings about UN intervention, the USSR, United Kingdom,
and France, but all three refrained from using their veto power.
Of these three powers, the first two strenuously endeavored at
different times to obstruct UN efforts; the Soviet government
was undoubtedly harsher and more blatant in its opposition,
but the British government was more effective—in point of
fact, painfully so.

The United Nations became involved in the Congo primarily because Dag Hammarskjold decided it should. The
Secretary-General invoked Article 99 to call a meeting of the
Security Council, and together with Mongi Slim of Tunisia
prepared the resolution of July 14, 1960, that was to set in
motion the Congo operation. Britain and France were against
it but, instead of vetoing the resolution, simply abstained. The
Soviet Union was hesitant but the Africans insisted on a vote
that same night. The resolution passed with the vote of only
two of the big powers, USA and USSR. (Taipeh instructed
its delegate, who represents China, to abstain.)

As at the time of Suez, there was again the incongruous
alliance of Washington and Moscow against London and
Paris. This time, however, Moscow would come to regret it.

But that was the future. During this opening stage of
the Congo affair, sweeping away the remains of imperialism
and colonialism in Africa was almost as popular with the
Secretary-General and with the Americans as it was with the
Russians. The word "neo-colonialism" had not yet begun to
circulate in UN halls and corridors; nor was the new white
man-versus-black man relationship in Africa, which the term
defined with some accuracy, yet understood at Turtle Bay.
When the Security Council met again less than a week later,
on 20 July, it unanimously commended the Secretary-General,
who had told the members that "the UN has embarked on its

single biggest effort under UN colours, organized and directed by the UN itself." He added that although the Belgian withdrawal was under way "we have in no way passed the corner." He would be asking member states for much more, and they should bear in mind their responsibilities "because we are at a turn of the road where our attitudes will be of decisive significance, I believe, not only for the future of the Organization but also for the future of Africa. And Africa may well in the present circumstances mean the world."

Today it is somehow hard to evoke with any credibility the reception given to these last words, delivered with that restrained, almost metallic tone that Hammarskjold reserved for his more dramatic pronouncements and which was a refined form of theatricality. His words were received in the galleries by a reverent, awed silence more appropriate for a cathedral than for the Council chamber.

In the United States, at the time the honeymoon with Africa had reached its dizziest, most romantic heights; going to the succor of an African nation evoked in the American public all the fervor of the crusading spirit. That the objectives of American foreign policy in the Congo coincided with the lofty purposes of the Secretary-General was welcomed as a happy but undoubtedly well-deserved coincidence.

Was it wise for the organization to get itself so frustratingly entangled in the heart of Africa? The answer should be sought, not in the framework of what is known today about independent African states, but rather in terms of the erratic knowledge and unrealistic mood prevailing in 1960. Africa was taken much more seriously than it is now. It was held to have a real economic future; but above all the continent as a whole, and especially the twenty-odd black nations about to emerge as independent states, was actually considered capable of playing a significant role in world politics.

Today, after having observed the economic and political performance of the African states, those delusions seem incredibly naive. But until a very few years ago they were held not only by Dag Hammarskjold and the group he had collected around him, but also by the chanceries of both superpowers. It is easy to recall that Washington's feeling about Africa was at the time quite divorced from reality; what is not so readily remembered is that Moscow shared many of the delusions current in the State Department and in the White House.

On two points in particular the political minds in Moscow and Washington reasoned along parallel lines. Both capitals were convinced that the African leaders and their peoples were capable and eager to make a choice between Soviet communism and western democracy, and having made the choice to back it with some sort of economic and political sinews. Consequently, the United States felt that a serious effort should be made to keep the USSR out of Africa; conversely the Soviets believed that it was worth their while to attempt to gain a foothold on the black continent.

The two smaller big powers, unlike the two superpowers, know what Africa was about, and never shared for a moment the delusions of Russians and Americans. Both Britain and France conducted themselves with cold realism throughout the whole Congo operation, the difference being that the British got considerably more involved than the French; but this was because they had more at stake in the Congolese economy—or rather in that of Katanga. During the whole affair Belgium was denounced for its "economic imperialism" through Union Minière du Haut-Katanga, and yet the Belgian state was only one of the major stockholders; another one was Tanganyika Concessions Ltd., incongruously named since its interests were in copper-rich Rhodesia and Katanga, but chummily known in the City as "Tanks."

Three of Union Minière's directors were British, one was present chairman of "Tanks," the other, ex-chairman, while all three happened to be Privy Councillors to the Crown during the Congo episode. As to "Tanks," apart from its substantial ownership of Union Minière, it also owns all the debentures and 90 percent of the stock of the Benguela Railway Company, which offers the only economically sound outlet for the Katanga Mines, at the port of Lobito in Portuguese Angola.

In 1961, which saw the high mark of chaos in the Congo, Union Minière stoutly upheld its money-making tradition, reporting net profits of 1,526,580,449 Belgian francs, or roughly 30 million dollars; while profits after taxes reported by "Tanks" were 3,296,325 pounds, somewhat over 9 million dollars.

Thus the Congo depended for its survival as a political entity on the mineral wealth of Katanga, which was controlled by outside Western groups operating primarily from Brussels and London. These financial groups were not in favor of Katanga's secession *per se*; however, Moise Tshombe, who had led Katanga into secession, was not solely a venal Congolese politician like the others; he also possessed enough political astuteness to see to it that the maintenance of order as well as of secession was desirable.

Consequently, viewed by financiers from Brussels and London, Tshombe looked like a sensible man who deserved to be backed since he was assuring the flow of profits from Katanga while the rest of the Congo wallowed in anarchy and civil strife. Only with the greatest difficulty were UN troops preventing wholesale slaughter through the vast territory; now they insisted on stamping out secession in Katanga. Tshombe's white mercenaries were prepared to resist the blue berets and for a time it looked as if they could beat the international battalions; but whether the mercenaries won or lost, the smooth flow of copper from Katanga to world markets would certainly be disturbed. Therefore the United Nations was a bad influence. In Europe the governments and the press should be made to understand this.

In the end the UN did stamp out secession in Katanga. But the cost for the world organization was almost unbearable, for not only was the UN pushed to the brink of insolvency but also all future operations similar to the Congo endeavor became unthinkable.

In any case, preventing secession in a member state was never conceived to be one of the UN's central responsibilities. As a matter of fact, in recent years secession has successfully overtaken several "nations" in Africa and in Asia without the United Nations bestirring itself.

So the Congo episode might turn out, after all, to have been a useful lesson. Still, at ten million dollars a week (the sum the UN was spending on its military and civilian operations), Congo College charged the UN a stiff tuition for its education.

31

OUR MEN IN HAVANA

In UN circles crisis is not as overworked a word as in newspaper headlines. East River diplomats are conditioned to refer instead to a "situation" or at most a "problem" and skirt the ominous word. But during a week in October, 1962, the word was used without compunction, for the crisis stared everyone in the face; and when it was over UN delegates agreed that it had been by far the worst they had ever known.

As the week began, President Kennedy announced on television to the American people and to the world at large that he was blockading Cuba. The President called it a "quarantine" but it was a blockade and thus, the diplomats reminded each other, an act of war according to all textbooks on international law.

An act of war against Cuba was in itself sufficiently disquieting; memories came to mind of the abortive Bay of Pigs invasion. But what really concerned the delegates was that the blockade could also become an act of war against the USSR. A dozen Soviet ships were on the high seas, bound for Cuba, and unless they veered from their course they would run afoul of the blockading line of US destroyers. The Russian freighters would be boarded and searched for missiles; if they refused to heave to and submit to the search they would be attacked and if necessary sunk.

It was also known in the UN corridors that both super-

powers had gone on nuclear alert. The knowledge had been
gleaned from a few bits of information mingled with speculation that was not only chilling but also plausible. All leaves
for the Soviet armed forces had been canceled—that was a
piece of "hard" news released by Tass and immediately picked
up by all other international news agencies. That American
armed forces had gone on "condition red" was an "unconfirmed
report," but it sounded plausible, even probable, as it circulated in the delegates lounge on Tuesday morning. A few of the
diplomats did not know what "condition red" meant; others
who did would attempt to joke about it. For instance, a small
group of influential delegates spent most of the morning in
the lounge, sitting in the highbacked chairs by one of the vast
windows overlooking the river. Around eleven a senior European correspondent came over to speak to them, seeking "reactions from diplomatic sources," for Europe was five hours
ahead in time and his deadline was getting close. One of the
delegates said to him, with an attempt at joviality:

"We won't even ask you to sit down, unless you answer
first at least one of two questions."

The correspondent grinned and asked: "If I guess right
do I get a free drink?" The ambassador nodded and the news-
man immediately went on: "First question, are the Russian
ships in the Atlantic turning back; second question, have the
Americans gone on condition red?"

The laughter that followed had a shrill edge to it. It
spread through the group in ripples and took a long time to
subside. When it finally did the correspondent added:

"My guess would be to say yes to both questions."

The group was now quite businesslike all of a sudden.
"May we ask you who is your source?" said another delegate.

The correspondent shook his head. "It's a guess, just as
I said. A hunch. Nothing to go on except what we all know
already."

The group relapsed into its dismal mood, and the ambassador who had first spoken to him said: "Sit down and I
will get you a drink, but I wish you knew a little more."

The journalist was annoyed. He was on the point of telling the assembled delegates that they were the source of news, not he. But on a day like this he could not afford to be the least bit uncivil to a group like this one, so instead he sat down, saying:

"I do have a piece of hard news out of London. Ian Fleming's publishers have asked him to authorize another zero for 007, since they expect the sales of James Bond books to go up by the hour."

This time the laughter was much more relaxed.

ও   ও   ও

By the time the Security Council met in the afternoon of that same Tuesday, delegates in tense and terse consultations were groping for a way to wedge the UN in between the two superpowers, and by the following day, Wednesday, the formula had been found. Through their UN delegates an impressive total of forty-five countries had called on the Secretary-General to move into the crisis.

It was on Wednesday, October 24, that Thant sent to both President Kennedy and Premier Khrushchev an urgent appeal proposing "the voluntary suspension of all arms shipments to Cuba and also the voluntary suspension of the quarantine measures involving the searching of ships bound for Cuba."

Kennedy's answer to the Secretary-General was that the blockade could not be suspended, since "the existing threat was created by the secret introduction of offensive weapons into Cuba, and the answer lies in the removal of such weapons." But within a matter of hours reports began to arrive at the UN indicating that the Soviet ships en route to Cuba were altering course and that Khrushchev was accepting the Secretary-General's proposals. It was the beginning of the end of the Cuban missile crisis.

It should not be assumed that the UN had played a central role in avoiding a confrontation at sea between the

United States and the Soviet Union, an event that threatened war. American power and Kennedy's determination to use it, since the very security of the United States was at stake, had forced the Russians to retreat. The chilling "eyeball-to-eyeball" confrontation between Kennedy and Khrushchev had been going on since Monday.

Of the dangers inherent in the situation, the most immediately ominous was the impending clash on the high seas, for every hour that passed brought the Soviet freighters closer to the blockading line of US warships. On Wednesday the Secretary-General offered the Kremlin a face-saving formula for averting the immediate peril and ordering its Cuba-bound vessels to change course, and in the "eyeball-to-eyeball" confrontation Khrushchev had blinked. By the end of the week, however, the Soviet Union formally agreed to withdraw from Cuba its missiles and other offensive weapons.

The first blink had been the hardest for the Russians, even though it made sense, since no vital interests of the Soviet Union, much less its security, were at stake in the Caribbean. Still, it was apparent to the whole world that they were submitting to American power; at that juncture the UN gave Moscow a way to save face. The ships were diverted because the Secretary-General of the United Nations had asked comrade Premier Khrushchev to consider the interest of world peace—not the threat of US destroyers.

Of course the UN provided only a face-saving device, but this should not be lightly dismissed. In a political-military crisis of the first magnitude a great power may find itself forced to court even the danger of nuclear war if the alternative is an intolerable and widely publicized loss of prestige.

And thus it happened that during the Cuban missile crisis the United Nations truly came of age in its central and primordial task of trying to avoid the third and doubtless the last world war. True, the UN played a modest role and its effectiveness was strictly circumscribed. But the fact remains that during those days of October, 1962, nuclear war had been a stark possibility; if a United Nations had not existed the world would have been even closer to the brink.

꿔 꿔 꿔

Many observers believe it would have been better if UN participation in the Cuban missile crisis had been held to this limited but crucial and indispensable role. Unfortunately history does not always conform to the rules of drama, and there was for the UN an epilogue with comic overtones supplied by, of all people, Fidel Castro.

Fidel had of course been involved in the crisis from the very beginning. After all, the two superpowers were acting the way they did because one of them liked him very much while the other disliked him intensely. At least that is what they had been saying and Fidel had come to believe it. He was not, however, as well versed as he thought himself to be in the pitiless realities of power politics. When the going got rough both the Soviet Union and the United States acted as though they had altogether forgotten about his existence— which in a way they had.

Fidel was annoyed, for while he enjoys being hated he resents being ignored. When Thant arrived in Havana, Fidel had been driven into a foul mood both by his friends the Russians and his enemies the Americans. Besides, the Secretary-General brought along with him fourteen boxes and crates loaded with office equipment, together with a clerical staff. This did nothing to improve Fidel's temper; it looked as though the United Nations was prepared to settle down and set up housekeeping—although no one in Havana had asked the UN to do so.

True, Fidel had invited Thant to visit him right at the beginning of the crisis, when things looked grim and Fidel as yet had no indication that Khrushchev would slip out of the island with his missiles under his arm, so to speak. The invitation was in answer to a special message the Secretary-General

had sent him on that fateful Wednesday, October 24. While
Kennedy and Khrushchev had received identical appeals from
Thant, Fidel got a specially drafted message telling him that
"it would also contribute greatly to the same end if the construction and development of major military facilities be suspended during the period of negotiations." Whereupon Fidel
had asked Thant to come to Havana and talk things over.

Thant flew to Havana the following Tuesday, October 30.
By then not only had the crisis been solved, but also Washington and Moscow, both relieved beyond words at having extri-
cated themselves from such a dangerous situation, were now
in a mood to be as considerate to each other as the situation
would permit. Fidel was in quite a different state of mind.
When Kennedy first demanded that the missiles be brought
out of Cuba, he proposed that actual removal of the weapons
be subject to UN inspection. Khrushchev agreed to this, and
everyone was pleased with the tactful solution.

Everyone, that is, except Fidel Castro. Moscow had forgotten to ask his opinion on the matter and did so only later,
as an afterthought. This seems to be a trait common to superpowers whenever a truly sticky situation develops. Similarly,
Washington forgot to consult the other nations of the hemisphere or the OAS when it decided to send the marines into
the Dominican Republic in 1965. While it pleased the Russians immensely to point this oversight to the world at large,
their own failure to consult Castro did not help the situation
in Havana in the fall of 1962.

From the moment of his arrival Thant's mission was
played as a comedy of errors. To begin with his first political
contact on Cuban soil was, oddly enough, with a representative of Brazil rather than of Cuba. Thant and his party had
flown into Havana on a Brazilian plane, one of Varig's Boeing
707s chartered for the occasion. As the Boeing rolled to a stop
on the runway of Havana airport one of Thant's aides pointed
to a Caravelle jet poised on the cement apron not far from the
control tower. "That's the Brazilian flag on the fuselage. It

must be the plane that brought President Goulart's representative from Brasilia."

There had been some vague news about Brazil's left-leaning president sending a special representative to offer his good offices to Thant and Fidel. Brazil was one of the very few countries of Latin America that had not yet broken relations with Cuba, and the Brazilian embassy in Havana was one of Fidel's favorite haunts.

Even so, Thant was not prepared to plunge into the intricacies of Latin American politics the very moment he put his foot on Cuban soil. But that was precisely what happened. As the Secretary-General descended from the Boeing, Raul Roa, Cuba's foreign minister stepped forward to greet him and then at once introduced him to General Albino Silva, chief military aide to the president of Brazil.

It was a strange opening scene for Thant, but his interview with the Soviet ambassador later the same day was even more odd. For one thing, it was apparent that the Cubans were not overly pleased that the Soviet ambassador came to see the Secretary-General. In fact, at that juncture they didn't seem to be pleased with anything the Russians did. The night before Thant's arrival Fidel had driven back into Havana from the countryside, where he had been inspecting troops. Upon his arrival in town he had gone directly to the Brazilian embassy, although it was already past midnight. All the "barbudos" that had gone with him on the military inspection trip—some forty-five of them—drove in his wake into the embassy, a palatial mansion that had belonged to one of Batista's henchmen, who had ended up a very rich senator. Most of the bearded ones dispersed themselves happily on the grounds, fortified by embassy scotch, while Fidel and a few of his inner circle remained in the high-ceilinged "organ room," for Batista's senator had installed in the immense living-room what he claimed was the world's largest organ outside a cathedral.

The organ room was probably the proper environment for Fidel's mood, since he spent a good part of the night complaining in a thundering voice at the way his allies had let him down. "I'm almost as angry at the Russians as at the Americans," he said at one point. "We are a small country but I was quite prepared to keep the missiles in Cuba. We were the only ones who were not afraid at all during last week."

ᔋ   ᔋ   ᔋ

If Fidel had been buoyant during the preceding week, the Soviet ambassador in Cuba had obviously taken a view of the situation. He was a tense if obsequious young man, surprisingly young to be the ambassador of the USSR in as sensitive a post as Havana. He was wearing a serge blue suit and had light brown shoes that were scuffed and worn at the heels. His clothes would go quite unnoticed in the disheveled and unwashed atmosphere of Havana at that time, but what did rivet everyone's attention was a small and dazzlingly white comb that stuck out of the ambassador's breast pocket. He had long blond hair that kept falling over his eyes, but he would brush it back with his hand instead of reaching for the white comb.

Just as everybody was getting used to the ambassador he startled the Secretary-General's aides by saying he would like to bring in his friend, the Soviet general commanding the missile installations, who was waiting outside, and introduce him to Thant and to the assembled company. (The Secretary-General also saw the ambassador alone.)

This announcement took everyone by surprise. Only a week before Valerian Zorin, presiding over the Security Council, had hotly denied Adlai Stevenson's accusations about missiles. The Americans had proved that there were indeed missiles installed, and there were Soviet military personnel to man the installations, but had never referred specifically to a Soviet general in command of the whole show. A "general of the Soviet rocket forces," as the interpreter punctiliously translated.

The ambassador's white comb was immediately forgotten and everyone awaited with interest the entry of the general of

Our Men in Havana

the rocket forces. If the ambassador did not look ambassadorial, neither did the general look martial. He was young and stocky and dressed in tweeds in spite of the climate; he kept adjusting his tie and he smiled with his teeth and his eyes looked worried just like his ambassador.

The delegates at UN Headquarters deduced that the crisis had been a close thing; these two were among the very few people outside the Kremlin, the White House, and the Pentagon who knew how close it had been. Obviously neither of the two men with their gaunt faces and restless hands wanted to look back at the week that was.

❧   ❧   ❧

Fidel Castro gave quite a different impression—that he had actually enjoyed the week that was, and that deep inside he missed the touch-and-go situation. There was nothing gaunt about him; rather he looked flabby and just a little potbellied. He is a handsome athletic six-footer who now neglected the outdoors and gave too much thought to food and drink. He smoked a cigar most of the time.

He was not mad at the United Nations; he even had some civil words for the world organization. But no, he would not permit any kind of inspection on Cuban territory, even under UN auspices. Yes, he was aware that both the Soviet Union and the United States had agreed on UN inspection. But everyone seemed to forget that it was for Cuba to decide and Cuba of course would be delighted to have UN inspection if the UN would inspect the American bases ringing Cuba and preparing aggression. Florida was full of such bases; other countries, such as Guatemala and Nicaragua, should also be inspected. Since he imagined the Americans would not let the UN inspect their own territory, there was no point in discussing the matter. Missiles? The missiles were of course for defense and the Russians had installed them and now they wanted to take them away and he would not oppose it, since they had never given the missiles to Cuba. But he would be the one to inspect how they were taken out, not the UN.

All this was spelled out at considerable length, in a calm voice, speaking a cultured, deliberate Spanish. But his eyes darting around all the time, resting for long moments on one of the Secretary-General's aides who was jotting down, for Thant's benefit, a condensation of what the Cuban was saying, to gain time before the official interpreter, sitting at the end of the long table, would intone the consecutive translation. The aide jotted down a tight, edited form, a few words for a whole cluster of meandering phrases, and Fidel was obviously annoyed, but at the same time fascinated, by the editing technique.

After the meeting with Fidel Castro and the other members of the Cuban government, Thant and his aides were taken back to the two plush houses in Havana's embassy district that had been assigned to them for their stay. The drive took them first along the scenic avenue that skirts the seashore beginning at Morro Castle and leading to the city's better residential sections. There were sandbagged antiaircraft emplacements along the avenue and beyond them stretched a calm Caribbean. At one point the young attaché who was sitting by the driver in the Secretary-General's car twisted himself around and pointing out to sea with an outstretched hand and finger informed Thant:

"There is one of the patrolling American destroyers." All those sitting in the back of the car dutifully craned their necks. There was haze out at sea and they could see nothing. The young Cuban insisted: "Just beyond the three-mile limit. All the time they stay there." He sounded proud and almost gay about it. It was agreed that the silhouette of a destroyer could be seen through the haze.

The silhouettes of the militiawomen, on the other hand, were clearly visible on the streets of the city. They were as typical of the period as the antiaircraft guns. The American-tourist Havana of bygone days was but a memory. The Coca-

Cola signs had been replaced on the billboards by patriotic exhortations and the slinky whores in their bright dresses were no longer to be seen. In their stead militiawomen stood guard at public buildings, rifles slung over their shoulders. Their tight blue-denim uniforms revealed generous curves.

ఇ   ఇ   ఇ

When Thant's party arrived at the elegant residence assigned to him, a group of militiamen had just finished unloading fourteen boxes and crates from a truck. Thant and his senior aides had not been aware that such an amount and variety of equipment had been loaded on the plane. Even typewriters had been crated and put aboard. Anyone who had seen the stuff being unloaded at Havana airport and piled into a truck would not have been surprised at the reaction of the Cubans. The story spread around Havana that the Secretary-General of the United Nations had come to try to convince Cuba to allow the UN to inspect the missile sites, and brought a whole mission to do the job, complete with all the necessary equipment.

If Thant had known about the boxes and crates he would probably have stopped it there and then in New York, but after all the Secretary-General of the UN should not be expected to check the freight accompanying him on a difficult and delicate political mission. When he was told in Havana what had occurred, he was angry and upset, but it was too late. The boxes and crates were piled inside the garage, to be reloaded on the plane when the Secretary-General and his party left Havana the following day.

What had happened was typical of the UN administration and no one at Headquatrers was surprised. The general services department of the UN had decided it would be quite a savings to sneak all the equipment needed aboard the Secretary-General's plane. It had never occurred to them that it might be politically unwise; although "general services" has cornered a sizable proportion of the UN's high-echelon jobs

and is one department bristling with P-5s and D-1s, the level
of intelligence and the educational background is what would
be expected in the sanitation department of a provincial town.

A closing commentary was made by one of the political
aides to the Secretary-General, on the flight back from Havana:

"I hate to think that general services loused up our whole
expedition. I prefer to think that Fidel is such an intractable
character that he would not have made any concessions even
if we had brought along no more office equipment than one
ballpoint pen for the whole group."

℘   ℘   ℘

Actually Fidel might have been led to make concessions, typewriters notwithstanding, if Thant had pressed more vigorously
the UN case. It was a unique opportunity to place the UN in
a position of authority and influence in one of the world's most
sensitive spots. The establishment of a "UN presence" might
not, in the long run, have pleased Washington, but that was
precisely the argument that the Secretary-General could have
used with Fidel Castro who would have understood and appreciated it had it been forcefully and cogently presented. Instead,
Thant was thrown off balance by Fidel's particular mixture
of exuberance and cunning. From the beginning he was *pris de
vitesse* by the Cuban caudillo, and never regained the initiative.

The failure to establish a "UN presence" in Cuba gave
the United States a justification to continue its reconnaissance
U-2 overflights on a regular basis, a permanent source of fric-
tion and one of the main obstacles to establishing peaceful
coexistence in the Caribbean.

32

FAILURE IN ASIA: VIETNAM

When U Thant took office as Secretary-General of the United Nations in November, 1961, Asia had already contributed to the world's troubled areas. A nagging, smoldering conflict over Kashmir still dragged on between India and Pakistan. And Vietnam was beginning to emerge as a potential battleground between the US and the communist powers, principally China.

But all in all Asia took a low priority in comparison with Africa as a threat to world peace and security. Nothing in the Far East could be compared in gravity with African developments. For in the Congo one crisis followed hard on the heels of another, and the death of Dag Hammarskjold, only six weeks earlier, had brought to the surface conflicts between the parallel UN and US policies on the one hand, and those of Britain, Belgium, and France on the other. The Soviets, still smarting from having been outmaneuvered by the United Nations and the United States, had not yet decided to cut their losses in Africa (that decision would not become definitive until after the ouster of Khrushchev).

In Algeria the war was in its sixth year and its more crucial stage; the revolt of the generals was only a few months old and De Gaulle was now fully engaged in the delicate operation of negotiating with the rebels for Algerian independence while at the same time keeping control over the professional army and the one million French *colons* in Algeria, while breaking the ruthless OAS elements in metropolitan France.

Africa also held the headlines as a wave of black nationalism swept the continent. And there was bitter fighting in Angola and in a few other areas. Asia by comparison looked like a peaceful continent.

But this began to change after Thant came in, slowly at first but then swiftly. With each passing year Africa lost prominence on the world scene, while Asia began to command almost undivided attention from the two superpowers. Not that African problems had been solved, but rather Washington and Moscow had learned at long last that what happened in Africa did not greatly matter one way or the other.

Not so in Asia, for the Chinese colossus stood there, and whether its feet were made of clay or of missiles only time could tell. India, once regarded by the Americans as Asia's stabilizing power, turned out to be unsteady. The Indians took a sound licking from the Chinese in the Himalayas, fought a pointless campaign against Pakistan, and finally lapsed into chronic famine relieved solely by American donations of wheat.

Against this background of a menacing China and an eroding India, Vietnam grew into a major threat to world peace as the sixties unfolded. The thaw in American-Soviet relations, which had been hailed as the end of the cold war in 1963, again reached the freezing point by the end of 1965, when increases in military spending in the US were matched by a reversal in the downward trend in the defense expenditures that the Soviet Union had begun three years earlier. Early in December, 1965, Moscow announced a five percent increase in its military budget.

ဢ   ဢ   ဢ

Before Thant had served the first half of his five-year term Asia had become the continent containing the more serious threats to world peace. The demand for UN action, muted at first, grew perceptibly almost from month to month, while statesmen and diplomats congratulated themselves on having chosen for Secretary-General an Asian, highly respected by all factions in his continent and yet committed to none of them, a man who was deeply knowledgeable and deeply concerned about the dangerous developments in his part of the world. With Thant as its spokesman the UN should be in the best possible position to do something effective in Asia.

ᶘ   ᶘ   ᶘ

Three key episodes marked Thant's startling transformation from an eminent Asian statesman in a position to act positively into a Secretary-General whose motives, methods, and foibles were questioned by some powers and denounced by others.

First there was the refusal by the United States in August, 1964, to meet with representatives of Hanoi in Rangoon, the capital of Thant's Burmese homeland. The meeting had been arranged by Thant and Washington's refusal angered and distressed the Secretary-General. Then about a year later it was Hanoi's turn; while Washington was now willing and eager, the North Vietnamese government did not even bother to answer Thant's messages.

The third episode occurred in December, 1965, only a few months later, when a number of prominent members of Asian delegations to the United Nations told *The New York Times* that the Asian Secretary-General was no longer useful in promoting peace in Asia. Hanoi actually refused to accept two letters written by Thant regarding a peaceful settlement. The Hanoi authorities, who a year before had welcomed Thant's intervention and agreed to send representatives to Rangoon, now considered the Secretary-General of the United Nations a mere spokesman for the United States, and said so in public.

Both of Thant's letters to Hanoi were written after Adlai Stevenson's death in July, 1965. On the eve of his death Ambassador Stevenson had, in a conversation with Eric Sevareid, included some acutely embarrassing remarks about Thant's role in the Vietnamese conflict. It is probable that the essence of this conversation, which had leaked out in London and Washington during the summer, reached Hanoi and other communist capitals almost immediately. The November 30 issue of a major American magazine put the whole episode before seven and a half million readers in the United States and as many more abroad as would care to read Sevareid's article, entitled "The Final Troubled Hours of Adlai Stevenson." The paragraph that did much to make a number of Asian envoys lose confidence in their fellow Asian read: "Time was passing, the war was expanding. The pressures on U Thant, supposedly the Number One peacemaker of the globe, were mounting from all sides within the UN. So he proposed an outright cease-fire with a truce line to be drawn across not only Vietnam but neighbouring Laos. U Thant then made a remarkable suggestion: United States officials could write the terms of the cease-fire offer, exactly as they saw fit, and he, U Thant, would announce it exactly in those words. Again, so Stevenson said to me, McNamara turned this down, and from Secretary Rusk there was no response, to Stevenson's knowledge."

PART VII

THE REVIEWS

⋙ 33 ⋘

PUBLICTY ON THE EAST RIVER

It used to be said of Henri Poincaré and Aristide Briand, two of France's leading political figures in the period between the two world wars, that "Poincaré knows everything and understands nothing, while Briand knows nothing but understands everything." It could be said that world public opinion, like Poincaré, knows everything about the United Nations and understands nothing; while those responsible for this curious situation understand virtually everything about the world organization without really knowing much about it. The result is a public image of the UN which has little to do with the facts of life on the East River.

This public image is molded to a large degree by the news about the UN filtered from the senior officials of the organization's various departments, members of delegations, and the governments themselves. It reaches the public mainly through the press corps accredited to the UN, but also through a few other channels, and some not inconsequential finishing touches are added.

What emerges as the "UN image" is moreover inexorably conditioned by the peculiar conditions under which the organization functions, the first and foremost being an emotional climate of either irresponsible criticism or unalloyed praise. Before it ever reaches the public, news about the United Na-

tions is submitted to critical or gushing treatment; the results
tend to be distorting and confusing.

The critical approach although not so recurrent as the
gushing approach, is the most upsetting for everyone concerned. Informed, probing, and constructive scrutiny, which
the UN direly needs, is unfortunately seldom forthcoming. The
world body is often enough subject to searing criticism, but
usually of an uninformed, and even vicious, kind. Some of it
does harm, because of the influence wielded by the information media bent on systematically criticizing the United Nations. One of the best examples is the *London Daily Express*,
which carries weight with British public opinion with its circulation of around four million in the United Kingdom. Within
UN circles there is a tendency to dismiss the *Daily Express*
by pointing out that it reaches the lowest denominator among
the British public, and that in any case its judgments on world
events are not taken too seriously by its readers.

It becomes more difficult to view with detachment the
anti-UN attitude of another British newspaper, the *London
Daily Telegraph*, with a much smaller circulation than the
Daily Express but wielding considerable influence in important
circles; particularly since the *Telegraph* is held in much higher
respect than the *Express* for judgments on international developments and its articles and editorials are often quoted in many
capitals.

This became cruelly apparent to the UN during the Congo
operation, when the *Telegraph* was staunchly upholding
Tshombe's secession movement in Katanga, at a time when
Union Minière du Haut Katanga and Tanganyika Concessions
Ltd., two financial groups where British private capital participated generously, were viewing with unmistakable sympathy
Tshombe's efforts to wrest Katanga's mineral riches from any
control by the central Congolese government. This attitude of
one of the most respected European newspapers was unpleasant for the UN through the painful unfolding of the
Congo operation, and it became gravely disturbing when UN
troops had to engage in military operations against Tshombe

in order to rid Katanga of the foreign mercenaries, as enjoined by the Security Council. The blossoming of headlines about the "UN war," and of irresponsible, shrill criticism in the world press, which undeniably had an effect on UN conduct and on the actions of Secretary-General Dag Hammarskjold during the weeks preceding his death, was undoubtedly sparked by important and respected newspapers such as the *Daily Telegraph*. It was not confined to the British press. In the United States an important sector of the press took up with gusto the dramatization of what was happening in the Congo. New York's two leading newspapers, *The New York Times* and the New York *Herald Tribune*, stuck to a line of fairly subdued and sympathetic reporting in regard to the UN, but many of the leading newspapers in other important cities, particularly Chicago and Los Angeles, were highly critical of the UN.

The *Daily Telegraph* and the *Daily Express* found their counterpart on the continent. In France *Le Figaro*, with its wide readership and its close connections with high government sources, led most of the metropolitan Paris press (with the significant exception of *Le Monde*) in what resembled at one point a crusade against the UN.

Disingenuous attitudes of UN officials in the Congo, particularly in their dealings with the large group of foreign correspondents in Leopoldville and in Elisabethville, did little to improve the temper of the world press in reporting and interpreting what was happening in the Congo.

There was a specific incident with *Le Figaro* which in a way reflects the UN attitude toward the press. At one of the most tense moments of the clashes between the "blue berets" and Tshombe's white mercenaries and black Gendarmerie, a special correspondent of *Le Figaro* reported in a dispatch to the newspaper that a colonel of the Indian brigade had said the Ghurkas would take no prisoners. Shortly afterwards an indignant cable from a UN official in the Congo was received by the UN representative in Paris excoriating the report, and was communicated by him to *Le Figaro* with a request that a clarification be published. The editors did so, asking him for a formal UN denial, since they were cabling their correspondent that if the UN could prove that the Indian colonel had not spoken as reported, he would be dismissed. Then arrived in rapid succession two cables from the Congo. The first one was from the same UN official, drafted with consummate skill in Secretariat bureaucratese; a minor masterpiece in ambiguity, hinting strongly that *Le Figaro*'s correspondent was lying, but without ever saying so unequivocally. The other cable was from the French journalist, confirming his first dispatch and stating that besides himself two other foreign correspondents were present when the Indian colonel had announced his ominous intentions, and that both were prepared to bear witness to it. The editors of *Le Figaro* mercifully did not press the matter further.

The incident described does not mean that the UN is always caught in the crossfire of well-grounded criticism. On the contrary; quite often it is treated as fair game for unjustified attacks and displays in sensationalism. But the tendency at UN headquarters and in the field is to overreact, to assume the stance of a victim of persecution and to attribute the worst motives to any information organ taking the organization to task. No effort is made to distinguish between irresponsible or malicious press reports and those which may be unsympathetic but factual.

ᔕ   ᔕ   ᔕ

At the other extreme stands the gushing brigade, represented at its caricatural level by droves of ladies equipped with flowery hats and a grim determination to love the United Nations and to be "internationally minded." They swarm about the Headquarters building, collecting printed "material" and demanding to be lectured at. They are usually referred to as the "NGO's," and in effect they all belong to one or another of the non-governmental organizations accredited to the UN.

The ladies with the flamboyant hats are the easy butt of

jokes and anecdotes; yet the gushing about the world organization that actually has distorted its image beyond recognition over the years does not come from them, but from groups, mostly in the United States, that are taken much more seriously. Groups of self-styled liberal "intellectuals" in the universities and "progressives" in government bureaus, sharing the incorrigible American penchant for introducing morals and preaching into completely alien fields, have contributed to forge a ladylike, if not a saintly, image of the UN that the harsh light of reality has done much to dissipate lately.

⋙ 34 ⋘

DO THE PEOPLE HAVE A RIGHT
TO KNOW?

In a speech prepared for the 1965 annual dinner of the Zionist Organization of America, Harry Truman expressed deep concern over "the agonizing slowness of the United Nations in developing an effective voice and sufficient moral force to keep the peace." The former president of the United States added that the UN "has yet to prove its capacity to discourage aggression."

An organization whose role is to discourage aggression and to develop an effective voice and sufficient moral force to keep the peace—this comes close to being an ideal definition of the United Nations. However, Harry Truman, who was himself a main protagonist in that major UN effort to "discourage aggression," the Korean intervention, knows only too well that it was not through moral force but because of the military strength that the United States foiled North Korean aggression against South Korea.

In complaining of the "agonizing slowness," President Truman reflected the mixture of stubborn idealism and self-centered pragmatism with which the average American regards the UN. But when it came to having recourse to the world organization, he did not look to its capacity to keep the peace or discourage aggression, but rather to other quite distinct but equally important functions which the United Nations has

developed. For in the sixties, as in the fifties, the UN's usefulness lies less in being an effective voice for mankind, than in
serving as useful machinery for the West. It is not through
its moral force but through its functional and logistic assets
that the organization has most effectively been serving the
United States, the West, and the world community of nations,
roughly in that order.

A realistic appraisal of the United Nations shows that it
possesses far stronger and more useful capabilities. In the first
place it is a meeting ground, then a training ground, and last
but not least a dumping ground. Moreover, it has developed a
reasonable amount of flexibility in the face of fast-changing
world conditions.

Mark Twain said about the weather in Missouri that if
you didn't like it all you had to do was wait a few minutes. The
same suggestion could well be made to those who hold strong
views against the United Nations. If they will only show a little
patience a quite different institution, perhaps more to their
liking, will emerge from the one of which they disapproved.

To label the UN as a stagnating or a dying institution
is one nonsensical criticism that is leveled at the world body.
The best proof of its vitality lies in the bubbling, unceasing
process of change and evolution that makes the organization so
modern, so metropolitan. Indeed it could be said that the UN
and New York belong intimately together; the United Nations
is in a sense a big-city creation, which enables it to change,
keeping pace with the times, with remarkable alacrity and
aplomb.

The most obvious current change (it may be more obvious
to Westerners than to others) is the loss of its outwardly
Western personality. This does not mean that the organization
is at long last becoming truly international, nor does it mean
an abdication by the West of its former hegemony. What is
happening is that the United States nowadays has to share its
influence over the UN with Afro-Asians. But this is a strictly
limited trend, and will presumably remain restricted to Afro-

Asian members. It is improbable that the trend will eventually embrace other regions. It would be hard to conceive of the communist world ever having any noticeable influence within the United Nations. As to Latin America, it missed the chance to establish its claim in the early years of the organization, and its voice will become ever more negligible.

Thus, US–Afro-Asian contacts and bargaining should increasingly dominate all deals at UN bodies. The Americans will be speaking for the West, with the rueful concurrence of the British and French. This is not necessarily disadvantageous for Western interests, for when it comes to issues that of first importance the West should stand united, and it can be as strong as ever in the UN, if it chooses to be. Also, Afro-Asian influence is bound to decline in the years ahead, unless and until China takes its place in the organization.

Another even more important current change is the introduction of a measurable dose of realism in UN activities. While the past favored the United States against its British and French allies, the new realistic approach is distinctly to the disadvantage of the Americans and tends to give a subtle authority to the other two western powers who not once in these twenty years indulged in the smug romanticism which was the essence of the American approach to the UN. For gradually but inexorably the UN has lost the aura Hammarskjold had woven for it. The melancholy epilogue of the Congo adventure symbolizes in a way the organization's incapacity to change the course of history in a key country where it would affect the evolution of an entire continent.

On the other hand a place like Cyprus, where no continental or ideological overtones are present, has profited from UN intervention. These two examples have driven home the fact that while the UN is never the solution for an international tangle of major dimensions, in smaller trouble spots it carries enough weight to sit on the lid of the simmering pot, provided the big powers do not bestir themselves unduly. As a Middle Eastern delegate puts it: "Now we have become realists at last.

We get the UN involved only in small things and preferably
only in a small way. It looks like it might work over these next
few years, and then we can make another try at being big and
ambitious. By then we might again have an SG like Dag."

ᔕ ᔕ ᔕ

It may be an attractive intellectual exercise to probe for
the realities behind the UN façade, but to world opinion only
the façade matters. That is probably one reason why it is no
easy matter to make the UN more productive, to allot it tasks
for which it was originally conceived. There is no doubt that
the organization could be immensely improved but to do so it
would be necessary to raise the level of the Secretariat, where
real power rests. This would run against powerful vested
interests, for obviously the contented bureaucrats in control are
not going to let themselves be jostled out of their sinecures.
Nor could they envisage the introduction of exacting standards
for future recruitment, even if the security of their present jobs
were guaranteed. It would create for them intolerable com-
parisons. For instance at the highest echelon, that of the under-
secretaries who surround the Secretary-General the central
figure, a former provincial government employee from the
south of India with boundless ambition could ill afford colleagues of high caliber and still retain his rank of "eminence
grise."

There are other under-secretaries and senior officials of
a quite different caliber, a few of them outstanding, but they
are all confined to jobs in the economic and technical fields, and
would not be allowed to offer their talents in the two spheres
that count, the political and the administrative.

The mediocrity of many key UN officials is no secret to
any of the member governments. They could do something
about it, or at least those governments which support the UN
financially could. Unfortunately, there is a disturbing unanimity
of thought among the chanceries of Washington, London,

Moscow, Paris, that the UN Secretariat should continue to be
staffed mostly by mediocrities in the political and administrative sectors.

This is not difficult to understand, since a certain independence of thought and action usually goes together with
above-average talent. Dag Hammarskjold was the best example
and no Western power—to say nothing of the Soviet bloc—is
willing to run the risk of that deadly combination of ability
and character either in the office of the Secretary-General or
of any of his key aides.

Therefore, since the reality of the United Nations is
marked by a great deal of discouraging mediocrity and petty
intrigue, and since the governments who could change this
state of things feel they should not, the question of the "image"
of the United Nations becomes of paramount importance. The
pervading desire for self-promotion of the Secretary-General
and his court is tolerated by the governments, since it con-
tributes to the false image of the UN. The alternative, telling
the public what the institution really is like inside, would in
the long run breed a disenchantment with the United Nations
that no responsible government is willing to accept. Consequently, building the "image," which is the central task to
which the Secretariat bends its efforts, is tacitly allowed by the
chanceries.

Of course this image of the UN could hardly have been
conceived if the organization were not located in the United
States. Only that peculiarly American yearning for unrelenting
over-simplification would have allowed the building of a UN
image which defies postulates of power politics and common
sense.

᷍   ᷍   ᷍

Once it is understood that the UN is not an international body
but rather a dependency of the United States that has been in
recent years infiltrated by Afro-Asians, the amused skepticism
of Europeans toward the United Nations becomes understand-

able. Furthermore, it then becomes possible to evaluate the saintly "UN image" built over the years by the self-promotion machinery operating out of the 38th floor.

Not surprisingly, these basic facts are understood only by the professionals: delegates and their foreign offices. The general public accepts quite docilely the image propounded by the US press and by the 38th floor. Does the public have a right to know?

The answer is different for geographical areas. For the United States it does not much matter what the American public is told about the world organization as long as the UN continues to serve basic US policies. In western Europe, on the other hand, public opinion, being politically mature, has long ago shed whatever illusions it might have had about the United Nations in the early years. The Suez crisis admirably completed this educational process and nowadays UN activities are presented with more lucidity and a greater sense of balance in the European press than anywhere else. In Latin America there still is a tendency to accept the rosy propaganda about the UN, particularly since the Latin American press relies heavily on US sources of information; nevertheless, the fact that the UN is of very little use to these countries is beginning to permeate public opinion. As a matter of fact, the growing indifference toward the United Nations has become a major factor in insuring the survival of the regional body, the Organization of American States, which in the eyes of many a Latin American leader has at least the negative merit of having so far kept the UN out of hemisphere affairs.

In a broader sense, however, in knowledgeable circles in both Europe and Latin America it is realized that even if the UN essentially serves American interests, since the United States is the leader and defender of the Western world, the organization at least vicariously is useful to all the West. Many European and Latin American political observers are persuaded that, from a purely pragmatic standpoint, there is no great harm in accepting the "UN image" that radiates from Turtle Bay to an unsuspecting public.

EPILOGUE

It can be argued that the United Nations has finally outgrown its infancy and adolescence. If a specific date for this change were to be selected, it should be Wednesday the 24th of October, 1962. On that day, at the height of the Cuban missile crisis, the Secretary-General at the request of forty-five member states sent his urgent appeal to President Kennedy and Premier Khrushchev; on the same day the organization had its seventeenth birthday.

Until that time, in spite of idealistic pronouncements, many of the UN's political activities had been similar to an adolescent's clamor for attention from the adults—who were in this case the power-conscious members of the Western alliance and the Soviet bloc. For instance, the organization's major peacekeeping endeavor to date, the Congo operation, had adolescent overtones in its fervent but futile pursuit of absolute, unrealistic goals.

Ever since the missile crisis, when the UN played a strictly secondary but undoubtedly useful role, there have been unmistakable signs of a slowly emerging political maturity. The years ahead will doubtless hold in store many setbacks and frustrations, but the world body may well be on its way to give genuine substance to the first paragraph of the Charter's Article 1, which reads:

The Purposes of the United Nations are:

1. To maintain international peace and security, and to that end: to take effective collective measures for the prevention and removal of threats to the peace, and for the suppression of acts of aggression or other breaches of the peace, and to bring about by peaceful means, and in conformity with the principles of justice and international law, adjustment or settlement of international disputes or situations which might lead to a breach of the peace. . . .

If such a hopeful trend affirms itself, it will result primarily from the unheralded but increasingly visible pattern of tentative cooperation within the UN by the two superpowers, the United States and the Soviet Union. This new factor has already dramatically reversed the situation prevailing from 1946 to 1962, which was one of a stubborn and sterile "confrontation" between the American and the Soviet delegations in the Security Council and also in the General Assembly; it may conceivably establish the climate necessary for a lasting solution to some of the towering problems of contemporary international life, such as Germany and Southeast Asia.

Most people find it difficult to understand why the United Nations has never been brought into such major areas of political or military conflict. "Why did the UN not become involved in Berlin, in Germany, and now in Vietnam?" This was the first question asked by a member of the audience during the discussion period that followed a recent lecture on the role of the world organization; in a way the question sums up a feeling prevailing among the public that the UN is not always present where it really counts.

Of course there are formal, legalistic explanations, with which only professional diplomats and foreign policy students are truly acquainted. UN participation in the solution of the "German question," many experts maintain, was ruled out of the organization's jurisdiction by the Charter's Article 107: "Nothing in the present Charter shall invalidate or preclude action, in relation to any state which during the Second World War has been an enemy of any signatory to the present Charter, taken or authorized as a result of that war by the Governments having responsibility for such action."

But not even the specialists can agree among themselves. There are those who maintain that Article 106 can be interpreted as allowing for UN efforts, through the Security Council, to help determine the future of Germany and Berlin. Article 106 reads:

> Pending the coming into force of such special agreements referred to in Article 43 as in the opinion of the Security Council enable it to begin the exercise of its responsibilities under Article 42, the parties to the Four-Nation Declaration, signed at Moscow, October 30, 1943, and France, shall, in accordance with the provisions of paragraph 5 of the Declaration, consult with one another and as occasion requires with other Members of the United Nations with a view to such joint action on behalf of the Organization as may be necessary for the purpose of maintaining international peace and security.

On the other hand, all experts are unanimous that no UN participation in a solution of the "German question" could be even remotely envisaged unless Moscow—as well as Washington, London, and Paris—were to agree to it. Until quite recently the entire Soviet bloc was adamant in its refusal to countenance any UN involvement. But early in 1966 the Soviet bloc, acting through the Polish UN delegation, proposed full membership in the United Nations for East Germany (who unlike the German Federal Republic does not have even observer status in the world body). The move was swiftly blocked by the Western powers, who agreed with the Bonn government that this aimed at paving the way for the eventual acceptance of the "two-Germanies" formula by UN members. However, the Polish proposal was also interpreted by some thoughtful diplomats as a jockeying for position on the part of the communist countries, whose attitude toward Bonn has been noticeably less intransigent in recent times. Similarly, in the German Federal Republic public opinion since 1965, spearheaded not only by intellectuals but also by religious and political personalities, has sought an acceptable solution for the reunification of the country, even if it involved formally renouncing former German territories incorporated by Poland when the Oder-Neisse frontier was imposed. In conclusion, it is no longer out of the question to foresee a UN role, presumably through the Security Council, in a German settlement.

ల౨ ల౨ ల౨

As regards the conflict in Southeast Asia, three of the four governments directly involved do not have a seat at the UN: South Vietnam, North Vietnam, and the People's Republic of China. This would not be an insuperable obstacle were the two superpowers willing to allow the UN to play a role—the kind of consensus by Washington and Moscow which was the very premise of the organization's conception in 1946. But consensus froze in 1946 when the cold war began, and over almost two succeeding decades the Soviet Union cast a hundred-odd vetoes in the Security Council.

The missile crisis, however, signaled the beginning of the end of the cold war. During these last four years a new era in international relations seems to be emerging, marked by a growing sense of joint responsibility on the part of Washington and Moscow as much as by a tacit understanding regarding their respective zones of influence all over the globe. Were it not for the Vietnam war, this thawing of tensions between the United States and the Soviet Union would be much more advanced. What is amazing, in the circumstances, is that the ideological content of the Vietnam conflict has not wiped out the trend. This is not only a reflection of the bitter antagonism that has developed between Russia and China, but also an indication of the non-militant posture that the Soviet Union is assuming in world affairs as it edges closer to the Western standards of an affluent society.

From a purely UN point of view the most remarkable

instance of the new US-USSR relationship was their close and
efficient cooperation in the Security Council on the 1965 resolution demanding a cease-fire from India and from Pakistan.
The subsequent mediation conducted by Soviet Premier Kosygin in his Tashkent meeting with India's prime minister and
Pakistan's president tended to focus world attention on this
successful and novel instance of Soviet diplomacy prevailing
on two Asian countries to settle their differences, at least for
the time being. But it should be borne in mind that Kosygin
would never have been able to carry the negotiations to a successful conclusion (for that matter, he would not have persuaded Prime Minister Shastri and President Ayub Khan to
come to Tashkent) if it had not been for the smooth behind-
the-scenes teamwork of Americans and Russians throughout
the Security Council debate, at a time when Indian and
Pakistani forces were still locked in combat.

ᔈ ᔈ ᔈ

If this new and revolutionary phase of Soviet-American relations survives the anguishing stresses and strains of the Vietnam war—and there are definite indications that it will—a new
era will begin for the United Nations. After twenty years,
which after all is not too long an adolescence in the field of
international affairs, the world body will finally begin to live
up to the designs and purposes of its founders, who predicated
the effectiveness of the UN on a basic willingness of the great
powers to use the organization, on the one hand, to avoid
head-on clashes and, on the other, to help resolve, or at least
hold in abeyance, differences among themselves.

Like most UN developments of any import, this one has
an ironic twist. The Soviet-American détente may evolve into
an entente, giving increasing significance and usefulness to
the UN; but this is not really that harmonious cooperation
among all the big powers of which so much was hopefully said
at San Francisco in 1945. For while it is true that the two other

Western powers, Britain and France, have been only too happy to witness the thaw in the cold war, the fifth big power, China, is violently opposed to it. None of the budding instances of East-West cooperation in the Security Council and other organs of the UN would have been even remotely conceivable had Peking's representatives, instead of Taipeh's, been occupying China's seat in the UN. But the People's Republic of China will not gain its legitimate seat in the organization in the immediate future. What seemed in the opinion of many inevitable for the 1966 session of the General Assembly, has now been pushed toward an unforeseeable future. The explanation offered by many students of UN affairs was the succession of military coups which took place in 1966 in half a dozen African countries, bringing into power rightist regimes who may be expected to instruct their delegates to vote against Peking in the UN. It probably goes deeper than this, however. The bankruptcy of Peking's militant foreign policy, under the twin opposition of Washington and Moscow, became visible not only in Africa, but also in Indonesia, where the military drowned in blood the most powerful communist party that ever existed in a country with a non-communist regime. The net result of these events in Asia and in Africa is that the Peking government will continue to be kept out of the United Nations, thus allowing the necessary climate for forging a Russian-American working partnership inside the UN. This may well prove to be the most significant event for the organization during the years ahead.

᪣   ᪣   ᪣

But the world body is not merely a political institution. The "United Nations system," as it is sometimes called, has set itself goals of economic and social assistance to its backward members which absorbs most of the resources of the UN proper and its family of specialized agencies, both in terms of budget and of personnel. It is not commonly realized that of some twenty-two to twenty-three thousand persons who are at any one time on the payroll of the UN and its agencies, less than two thousand work in the political field. The others, representing over ninety percent of the total manpower, are engaged in economic and social activities. In a broader sense, of course, they are partaking in a political enterprise, since the poverty and backwardness that afflicts the vast majority of the member states breeds despair and international strife. And, unfortunately, there are no indications that either the UN or its member states are winning the battle against poverty. Robert S. McNamara said in his Montreal speech of May 18, 1966:

> There can, then, be no question but that there is an irrefutable relationship between violence and economic backwardness. And the trend of such violence is up, not down.
>
> Now, it would perhaps be reassuring if the gap between the rich nations and the poor nations were closing; and economic backwardness were significantly receding.
>
> But it is not. The economic gap is widening.
>
> By the year 1970, over one-half of the world's total population will live in the independent nations sweeping across the southern half of the planet. But this hungering half of the human race will by then command only one-sixth of the world's total of goods and services.
>
> By the year 1975, the dependent children of these nations alone—children under 15 years of age—will equal the total population of the developed nations to the north.

ঙ   ঙ   ঙ

The Charter established an imposing machinery to help underdeveloped members; but the Economic and Social Council, to which twelve Charter articles are dedicated, has never been able to live up to the hopes that led to its creation. Perhaps what is needed is men rather than machinery.

I remember what an abiding, sincere interest Adlai Stevenson had in the economic and social problems of the underdeveloped countries, particularly those of Latin America. I was a witness to it, for when he visited Brazil a few years ago I had the privilege of being with him on three different occasions, in Brasilia, in São Paulo, and in Rio. To the best of my knowledge, no one knew then that he was to become his country's chief delegate to the United Nations, but I remember hearing, more than once, the observation that "a man like him belongs in the UN."

Men of Stevenson's intellectual and human stature are not found easily in any nation. But if somehow standards such as those by which he lived could come to prevail inside the UN, the organization would attract to its service men of high caliber. With such men present, in numbers, UN realities might bear a closer resemblance to the words of the Charter.

INDEX

Accra, 52
Addis Ababa, 52, 148
Afghanistan, 51
Africa, 5, 12, 82, 101, 106, 121–6,
  148, 268–9, 285–6, 307
Afro-Asian bloc, 6, 7, 11, 12, 87,
  88, 106, 109, 123, 139–40, 201,
  297–8
Albania, 23–6, 28–30, 32, 34–6,
  39, 42, 71, 108, 109 n., 153
Algeria, 115, 139, 285–6
Andropov, 252
Angola, 210, 271
Apro, Antal, 245, 248
Arab delegations, 109, 115
Argentina, 55, 82, 107
Arkadiev, Georgey, 186–7
Australia, 55
Austria, 55, 109 n., 243

balkanization, 12–13
Ball, George, 40

Bangkok, 201
Baroody, Jamil, 24, 27–9
Batista y Zaldívar, Fulgencio, 279
Bay of Pigs invasion, 273
Beaton, Leonard, 57
Beirut, 201
Belgium, 10, 55, 269–70, 285
Benguela Railway Company, 270
Berlin, 194, 204, 303
Bibo, Istvan, 248
Bizerte episode, 134 and n.
Black, Eugene, 215
"blue berets," 293
Brasilia, 309
Brazil, 36, 45, 55, 74, 82, 107,
  278–9, 309
Briand, Aristide, 291
Brookings Institution, 89
Brussels, 201, 271
Budgetary and Administrative
  Questions, Advisory Committee
  on, 50

Budo, Halim, 23–33, 38, 153
Bulgaria, 10 *n.*, 72, 74
Burguiba, Habib, 134 *n.*
Burma, 139
Burundi, 36, 37, 71, 210
Byelorussia, 73, 95
Byrnes, James, 94

Camara, José Sette, 34
Cambodia, 32, 71, 109 *n.*
Canada, 36, 49, 55, 74, 110
Canton, China, 209
Caradon, Lord, 35–6, 50
Carnegie Endowment for International Peace, *Issues Before the 20th General Assembly* 56 *n.*, 59, 60
Castro, Fidel, 72, 277–9, 281–2, 284
Ceylon, 82, 109 *n.*
Chambers, Whittaker, 95
Chiang Kai-shek, 63–5, 73–4
Chicago, 293
Chile, 82
China: *see* People's Republic of, *and* Formosa
Cleveland, Harlan, 17
"collective financial responsibility," 44, 48, 50
Colombia, 36
Common Market, the European, 109
Communists, American, 94–7
confrontation, 20, 107, 262, 275–6, 303
Congo, the, 10, 12, 19, 48, 125, 131, 136, 138, 140, 142, 201, 210, 243, 267–72, 285, 293–4, 302
Congo Civilian Fund, 100
Cook Islands, 24
Correspondents Association, UN, 135
Coulibaly, Sori, 34
Csepel Iron Works, 244
Cuba, 7, 14, 72, 105–6, 273–84, 302
Cyprus, 47–8, 161–6, 298
Czechoslovakia, 55, 72, 74

Daily News, New York, 15
Dakar, 121

Damascus, 201
"decalogue," the, 177–80
De Gaulle, Charles, 17, 33, 46, 92, 123, 136–7, 144, 204, 216
Denmark, 55, 108
"developed," "developing," 214
Development program, 101; Decade, 213; Board, 223
disarmament, 6, 58, 67, 74–5, 204–5
Djkarta, 140–1
Dobi, Istvan, 249
Dogei, Imre, 248
Dominican Republic, 278
Dutch colonialism, 140
Dulles, John Foster, 43
Dumbarton Oaks, 95

East Germany: *see* German Democratic Republic
Economic Commission for Africa, 121
Economic Commission for Europe, 202–3
Economic and Social Council, 18, 23, 25, 308
Ecuador, 65
Educational, Scientific and Cultural Organization, UN (UNESCO), 11, 225–6
Eisenhower, Dwight D., 260
Eisenhower, Milton S., 94
Elisabethville, Congo, 131, 293
Emergency Force, UN (UNEF), 91, 201
Encounter, 217
Egypt, 11, 48, 57, 65, 68, 201, 260
Erdei, Ferenc, 246, 250
Ethiopia, 28–9, 33, 51, 74, 147

"faire les deux kilomètres," 200
Fanfani, Amintore, 241
FAO: *see* Food and Agriculture Organization
Farkas, Ferenc, 248
Federal Republic of Germany (West Germany), 100, 102, 303
Fedorenko, Nikolai, 36, 40, 47, 52
Fifth Amendment (U.S. Constitution), 97
Figaro, Le, 293–4

Finland, 55, 109 *n.*, 243
Fleming, Ian, 275
Florida, 281
Food and Agriculture Organization (FAO), 225, 227-8
Ford Foundation, 222
Formosa, 63-4, 73, 80, 102, 307
Four-Nation Declaration, 304
France, 7, 10, 13, 16-17, 19, 33, 41-2, 44, 46, 51, 56, 60, 65, 68, 74, 111, 130, 134, 138, 226, 268, 270, 285, 298, 307
France Presse, 163
Frankfurter, Felix, 96
Fuchs, Klaus, 54

Gambia, 11-12
Ganz Machine Works, 244
Gardner, Richard, 17
Gardiner, Robert, 121
Gaza Strip, 233
Gebre-Egzy, Tesfaye, 28-9, 33
General Assembly, the 20th (1965), 11, 70-8, 241; the 19th (1964-5), 15-22, 25-7, 38-9, 45, 46-7, 52-3, 86, 99, 123, 133, 145, 209; the 13th (1958), 58; the 15th (1960), 58, 90; the 16th (1961), 59
Geneva, 54, 141, 149, 230; Trade Conference, 107, 109, 199-210
German Democratic Republic (East Germany), 55, 100-2, 226, 304
German Observer, the, 101-2
Germany: *see* German Democratic Republic *and* Federal Republic of Germany
Gero, Erno, 244, 265
Ghana, 20, 23-24, 51, 107
Goldberg, Arthur J., 43-4
Goulart, João, 279
Greece, 48
Gromyko, Andrei, 128, 130
Gross, Ernest A., 65
"group of 75": see *tiers monde*
Guatemala, 281

Hague, The, 44, 51, 140
Hammarskjold, Dag, ix, xi, 6, 10, 63, 94, 128; *Markings*, ix, 135; 131-9, 144-5, 186, 193, 243, 253, 259, 268-70, 285, 293, 298-300

Hanoi, 287
Harvard Law School, 96
Hegedus, Andras, 244
Herald Tribune, New York, 293
Hiss, Alger, 95-6
Hoffman, Paul, 149, 223-4
Holland, 55, 141
Holmes, Oliver Wendell, 96
Hong Kong, 209
Horvath, Imre, 248, 259
Human Rights Day, 117
Hungarian uprising (October 1956), press dispatches, 244-61; UN Special Committee Report on, 263-5
Hungary, 20, 36, 55, 72, 109 *n.*, 145, 242-3
Hutson, John B., 95
IAEA: *see* International Atomic Energy Agency
Iceland, 108
ICY: *see* International Co-operation, Year of
ILO: *see* International Labour Organization
IMO: *see* International Meteorological Organization
India, 12, 14, 55, 57, 65, 68, 74, 82, 221-2, 228, 285-6, 299, 306
Indonesia, 11-12, 55, 61, 140, 142, 307
International Atomic Energy Agency (IAEA), 55
International Bank for Reconstruction and Development, 91
International Co-operation, Year of (ICY), 70, 141
"international compound," 205
International Criminal Police Organization (Interpol), 236-7
International Development Association, 218
International Labour Organization (ILO), 131, 205, 225, 230, 242
International Meteorological Organization (IMO), 205, 208, 230

International Monetary Fund, 91, 215, 225–6
International Refugee Organization, 209
International School, UN, 25
Internal Security Subcommittee, 96
International Telecommunications Union (ITU), 200–1, 205, 207, 230
Interpol: see International Criminal Police Organization
Iran, 129, 237–8
Ireland, 58, 109 n.
"Irish Resolution," 59
Israel, 55, 57, 110
Italy, 55, 74, 109 n.
ITU: see International Telecommunications Union
Izvestia, 152

Jamaica, 106
Japan, 55, 74, 109
Jebb, Sir Gladwyn, 69
Jerusalem, 201
Jessup, Philip K., 194
Johnson, Lyndon Baines, 144; Administration, 41–2
"Jolly Jack": see Hutson, John B.
Jordan, 109 n.

Kabul, 52
Kadar, Janos, 244–5, 247–9, 259, 262, 264
Karachi, 201
Kashmir, 14, 57, 285
Katanga, 131, 270–1, 292–3
Kennan, George, 217
Kennedy, John F., 7, 123, 273, 275–6, 278, 302
Kennedy, Jacqueline, 117
Kethly, Anna, 247–8
Khan, Aga, 149, 210
Khan, Ayub, 306
Khrushchev, Nikita, 6–7, 123, 133, 144, 262, 275–8, 285, 302
Kiselev, Evgeny D., 187
Kiss, Karoly, 245
Kissinger, Henry: Necessity for Choice, The, 57
Konduktorov, Leo, 254

Korea, 7, 10, 19, 47, 64–6, 68–9, 296
Korean Reconstruction Agency, UN, 201
Kos, Peter, 246, 250–2, 254, 259
Kossa, Istvan, 248
Kosygin, Aleksei, 306
Kovacs, Bela, 245–6, 250
Kovacs, Istvan, 247, 256
Krock, Arthur, 41
Kuwait, 99–100

Lake Leman, 200
Laos, 109 n., 288
Latin America, 51, 82, 88, 97, 101, 105–6, 108, 110, 139, 301, 309
League of Nations, 199, 205–6, 208
Lebanese crisis, 86
Leopoldville, 135, 140, 201, 293
Lie, Trygve, 7, 10, 65, 93–7, 128, 130, 132, 134, 145; In the Cause of Peace, 64, 68, 129
Libya, 109 n.
Lodge, Henry Cabot, 67, 256
London, 201, 271
London Daily Express, 152, 292
London Daily Telegraph, 292
Los Angeles, 293
Losonczy, Geza, 248, 250
Lumumba, Patrice, 131

Macao, 209
McCarthyism, 96–7, 145
MacArthur, Douglas, 66
McNamara, Robert S., 288, 308
Maddox, John, 57
Malaysia, 11, 61, 141
Maldive Islands, 11–13
Malecela, John W. S., 35
Maleter, Pal, 248, 256
Mali-Senegalese federation, 11, 12, 34
Malik, Jacob A., 64, 194
Mao Tse-tung, 73
Marof, Achkar, 34
Marosan, Gyorgy, 249
Marshall Plan, 149
Mauritania, 33, 35
"mechanical majority," 8
membership, UN, 11, 12, 13, 53, 75, 100–2, 108 n., 111

Mexico, 55, 74
Mikoyan, Anastas I., 262
Mindszenty, Cardinal Joseph, 246, 248
"mirror of the world," 62
Miske, Ahmed Baba, 33
missile crisis, Cuban, 105, 123, 305
Monde, Le, 293
Mongi Slim, 139, 268
Morocco, 209
Munnich, Ferenc, 245, 248
Murville, Couve de, 134 *n.*
Mwesi Highlands, 210

Nablus, 201
Nagy, Imre, 244–50, 254–7, 261, 262
Nansen, Fridtjof, 208–9; Passport, 209
Naples, 201
narcotics, 232–8; UN Narcotics Division, 236
Nasser, Gamal, 48, 110
NATO: *see* North Atlantic Treaty Organization
Nehru, Jawaharlal, 12–13
"neocolonialism," 216, 268
Nep, Szabad, 246
Nepal, 109 *n.*, 210
Netherlands: *see* Holland
New Deal, 96
New Delhi, 201
New England, 89
New Guinea, 140–2
New York, 5, 82–4, 89–91, 201, 297
New York Times, The, 41, 81, 287, 293
Nicaragua, 281
Nigeria, 74
"nonaligned" countries, 6, 72, 109 *n.*
North Atlantic Treaty Organization (NATO), 109, 241
North Delegates Lounge, 194–5
Northeast Frontier Agency, 170
Norway, 65, 108
"Nth country," 55–61
"nuclear club," 54–6, 59
nuclear proliferation, 54–61

Oder-Neisse territories, 305
Olympio, Sylvanus, 123
onusiens, les, 79
Organization of American States (OAS), 278, 301
Organization for Economic Co-operation and Development, (OECD), 216

Pakistan, 46, 55, 57, 82, 285–6, 306
Palais des Nations, 199–210
Palestine, 201
Paris, 10, 134, 201
Paul VI, Pope, 70–1, 75, 226, 227, 241
Peacekeeping, 14, 16, 45–6, 48, 52–3, 145, 242, 276
People's Republic of China, 14, 18, 23, 33, 42, 56, 60, 63–5, 70–5, 80, 102, 201, 209, 221, 285, 305, 307
Perse, St. John, 136
Phelen, E. G.: *Yes and Albert Thomas*, 130–1
Poincaré, Henri, 291
Poland, 36, 55, 72, 74, 92, 130, 264, 304, 305
"population explosion," 227
Portugal, 109 *n.*, 209, 271
Pravda, 152
Princeton University, 163
"procedural resolution," 71, 73

Quaison-Sackey, Alex, 20, 23–4, 107, 143
"quarantine," 273
"quiet diplomacy," 131
Quo-Tai-Chi, 129

Rangoon, 287
Red Cross, 208, 260
"Red Poland," "Red China," "Red Russia," 66
Refugees, Office of the UN High Commissioner for, 208
Reporter, The, 144
"residual power," 7
Retreat from the UN Showdown, The, 41
Reuters' News Agency, 163
Rhodesia, 270

Rio de Janeiro, ix, 309
Roa, Raul, 279
Roman Catholic Church, 70
Ronai, Sandor, 248
Roosevelt, Franklin Delano, 95, 96, 127
"rotation," 241
Rome, 201
Rumania, 10 n., 274
Rules of Procedure, 26; rule 73 of, 29–30, 33
Rusk, Dean, 17, 288
Rwanda, 210

San Francisco Conference, 95
São Paulo, 309
Saudi Arabia, 24, 27–9, 32, 33, 48, 110
Scandinavia, 49, 73, 101, 108, 109
Schumann, Maurice, 68
Schwebel, Stephen, 131
Science and Technology, Conference on, 204
Secretariat, 12, 96, 97, 124, 167, 193
Seoul, 201
secession, 271–2
Secretary-General, office of, 6, 10, 18, 129–32
Security Council, 7–14, 17, 19, 33, 46, 47, 52, 53, 64, 65, 68, 99, 195, 267, 275, 293, 304
Selassie, Haile, 147–8
Senegal, 11, 12
Sevareid, Eric: "The Final Troubled Hours of Adlai Stevenson," 288
Shastri, Lal Bahadur, 306
Shonfield, Andrew: Attack on World Poverty, The, 219–23
Silva, Gen. Albino, 279
Singapore, 11, 12
"snowing under," 187
South Africa, 23, 109
South Lounge, 196
Soviet bloc, 42, 86, 92, 108, 200, 242, 265, 302
Soviet Union: see USSR
Spain, 109 n.
Special Fund: see UN Development Program
Stanleyville, 125

Stettinius, Edward L., 94
Stevenson, Adlai, 16, 30, 31, 36, 40–2, 94, 186, 280, 288, 308, 309
Stoessinger, John G.: Financing the UN System, 89
Subandrio, Mrs. 141
"substantive resolution," 71
Sudan, 12
Suez crisis, the, 48, 60, 86, 243, 268, 301
Sukarno, Achmed, 140–2
Suslov, 262
Sweden, 55, 74, 108
Syria, 11
Szabo, Mr., 259
Szanto, Zoltan, 245

Taiwan Straits, 60
Tanganyika, 210
Tanganyika Concessions, Ltd., 270, 292
"Tanks," 270
Tashkent meeting, 306
technical assistance, 40, 101, 219–24
Tel Aviv, 201
test-ban treaty (1963), 6, 7
Thant, U, 11, 15, 21, 63, 81, 128, 132–44, 187, 277–88
Thomas, Albert, 131
Tiberias, 201
Tibet, 210
tiers monde, 106–11, 118, 219, 226, 229
Tildy, Zoltan, 245–6, 248, 250, 251
Time, 95
Tito, Marshal (Josip Broz), 149
Toth, Lajos, 47
Trade and Development, UN Conference on, 25, 39, 124 n., 204
Trans-Danubian National Council, 247
Trinidad and Tobago, 106
"troika," 6, 7, 139
Truman, Harry S., 95, 296
Tshombe, Moise, 138, 271, 292
Tsiang, Dr., 65
Tunisia, 110, 134 n., 136, 139, 209, 268
Turkey, 48

Ujsag, Kis, 246
Ukraine, the, 73, 95
Ulbricht, Walter, 102
underdeveloped countries, 213–17
Union Minière du Haut-Katanga, 270, 271, 292
United Arab Republic, 11, 51, 55, 74
United Kingdom, 10, 35, 36, 49, 51, 56, 60, 65, 74, 110, 111, 134, 138, 167, 194, 226, 268, 270, 285, 292, 298, 307
United Nations, information services, ix; treasury, 5; lottery proposal, 15; deficit, 16; Pension Fund, 22, 25; budget, 50; Organization, 79–84; official languages, 80; staff, 80, 93, 94, 299–300; wives, 83, 117–19; U.S. financial support of, 85–91; U.S. influence on, 93–98; communications coverage, 105; fellowships, 121; fringe benefits, 149; salaries, 149; vacations, 150; bureaucratic functioning of, 105; working hours, 150; executive power, 168; specialized agencies, 225–29
United Nations Charter, Article 1, 302, 303; Article 4, 13, 304; Article 19, 15, 16, 18, 19, 31, 33, 40–3, 46, 48, 51, 52, 88, 99, 107, 141, 142, 145, 242; Article 27, 9; Article 2, 304; Article 97, 127; Article 99, 127–9, 268; Article 100, 172; Article 101, 181; Article 106, 304; Article 107, 303
"United Nations and Decolonialization, The," 122
"United Nations image," 291, 301
"United Nations Universal Declaration of Human Rights," 141, 206

United States, 14, 19, 28, 30, 33, 40–4, 46, 48, 51, 52, 63, 66, 74, 96, 98, 110, 111, 194, 226, 268–70, 285, 296, 298, 301, 303
"Uniting for Peace" resolution, 7, 8, 47
USSR, 7, 10, 16–19, 33, 40–4, 46, 57, 60, 64–8, 74, 79, 86, 95, 100, 111, 128, 130, 134, 138, 182–9, 226, 243, 267–70, 273, 280, 303

Vatican Council II, 227
Vatican State, 70, 71
veto, the, 9, 18, 19, 46, 53, 65, 86, 243, 261, 267, 268, 305
Vieille Cité, 203
Vienna, 201
Vietnam, 14, 34, 135, 136, 142, 285–8, 303, 305
Vishinsky, Andrei, 67
voluntary contributions, 49, 50

Warsaw Pact, 247, 252, 253, 258, 261, 265
West Germany: *see* Federal Republic of Germany
WHO: *see* World Health Organization
Wilson, Harold, 123
Wilson, Woodrow, 43
Woods, George, 215–16
World Bank, 214–16, 218, 226
World Court, 44, 50, 51
World Health Organization (WHO), 141, 205, 206, 225, 230
World Refugee Year, 209

Yalta, 95, 96
Yalu River, 66
Yemen, 47, 48, 183
Yugoslavia, 55, 65, 108, 149, 242

Zionist Organization of America, 296
Zorin, Valerian, 186, 280

A NOTE ABOUT THE AUTHOR

HERNANE TAVARES DE SÁ was born in Natal, Brazil, in 1911 and received his doctorate, with distinction, from the University of Louvain in 1935. He has been a professor of journalism at the Catholic University of Rio de Janeiro, editor-in-chief of *Visão*, Brazil's weekly news magazine, and until recently (1960–5) Under-secretary for Public Information at the United Nations. He now heads a new Brazilian publishing group. In 1959 he was awarded Columbia University's distin-guished Maria Moors Cabot Award for promoting friendship and understanding in the western hemi-sphere in the field of journalism. His book *The Bra-zilians: People of Tomorrow* was published in New York in 1947, and he has contributed articles and stories to *The Saturday Evening Post*, *National Geo-graphic*, and other periodicals.

A NOTE ON THE TYPE

The text of this book is set in Monticello, a Linotype revival of the original Binny & Ronaldson Roman No. 1, cut by Archibald Binny and cast in 1796 by that Philadelphia type foundry. The face was named Monticello in honor of its use in the monumental fifty-volume *Papers of Thomas Jefferson*, published by Princeton University Press. Monticello is a transitional type design, embodying certain features of Bulmer and Baskerville, but it is a distinguished face in its own right.

Composed, printed, and bound by
The Haddon Craftsmen, Inc., Scranton, Pa.

Typography and binding design by *Kenneth Miyamoto*